CULTURAL THEORY
AND CULTURAL CHANGE

edited by
MIKE FEATHERSTONE

SAGE Publications
London • Newbury Park • New Delhi

First published 1992

SAGE Publications Ltd
6 Bonhill Street
London EC2A 4PU

SAGE Publications Inc
2455 Teller Road
Newbury Park, California 91320

SAGE Publications India Pvt Ltd
32, M-Block Market
Greater Kailash — I
New Delhi 110 048

in association with *Theory, Culture & Society*
School of Health, Social & Policy Studies
Teesside Polytechnic, UK

British Library Cataloguing in Publication data
A Catalogue record for this book is available from the British Library

ISBN 0-8039-8743-9
ISBN 0-8039-8744-7 pbk

Typeset by Colset Private Ltd, Singapore
Printed in Great Britain by Page Brothers (Norwich) Ltd

CULTURAL THEORY
AND CULTURAL CHANGE

CONTENTS

Preface
Cultural Theory and Cultural Change: An Introduction

Mike Featherstone

The last decade has seen a marked increase in interest in culture in the social sciences. For many social scientists, culture has been seen as something on the periphery of the field as, for example, we find in conceptualizations which wish to restrict it to the study of the arts. Even when this view became extended to incorporate the study of popular culture and everday life, culture was still regarded by many as esoteric and epiphenomenal. It was often associated with the secondary and weaker term in a loose set of binary oppositions: economy/culture, production/consumption, work/leisure, practice/representation, rational/emotional, masculine/feminine. Culture was too often regarded as readily circumscribed, something derivative which was there to be explained. It was rarely conceived of as opening up a set of problems which, once tackled, could question and overturn such hierarchically constituted oppositions and separations. A set of problems which, when constituted in its most radical form, could challenge the viability of our existing modes of conceptualization.

Over the last decade there has also developed a heightened sense that the role of culture in social life cannot be restricted to a set of norms and values, unproblematically acquired by individuals through socialization and, once internalized, retained throughout the life course. Such notions, which were often linked to variants of the common culture thesis, become much more problematic when it is acknowledged that many contemporary societies are now having to develop a more differentiated image of themselves, one which has to take into account internal cultural complexity and multiculturalism. In addition, contemporary state-societies have had to start to learn to develop strategies to enable them to handle the increasing trans-societal flows of images, information, commodities and people which accompany the process of globalization. These and other processes of cultural change not only increase our sensitivity to cultural issues, they also raise the question of how culture is constituted, how we should theorize culture.

It is understandable that some should greet this rise in interest in culture with suspicion, for a good deal of the thrust of the current modes of theorizing culture has been to question the viability of one of the long established goals of the social sciences: to produce universal knowledge and develop theories which operate at a high level of generality. Yet, for others the sensitivity to particularity which accompanies a greater appreciation of cultural complexity, is perceived as a vital necessity. Hence we find this sensitivity to questions of difference and complexity has been sustained by a variety of theoretical frameworks, many of which increasingly intersect and cross over: feminist theory, anthropology, deconstructionism, critical theory, genealogy, postmodernism. This interest in moving the frame of reference from, for example, history to histor*ies*, from the study of the body to bod*ies*, leads to a descending spiral of deconceptualization as increasingly nuanced and differentiated modes of otherness, difference, diversity and particularity are discovered.

The challenge for contemporary cultural theory is to theorize the conditions of possibility for this shift in emphasis from conceptualizing universalism and unities to particularism and diversity, and to investigate the possibilities for reconceptualization and renewed syntheses. It is this question of how to theoretically conceptualize what are perceived to be new levels of cultural complexity, without doing an injustice to newly discovered particularities, which is perhaps behind a good deal of the recent rise of interest in culture in the social sciences. It is also one reason why the term postmodernism, under whose banner these questions are often debated, has attracted so much attention.

The papers gathered together in this collection address these issues in a variety of ways. There are, for example, a number of papers which seek to address themselves to the question of cultural change and how we are to depict the current phase. Meaghan Morris provides a sharp dissection of David Harvey's influential writings on the condition of postmodernity. Ulrich Beck discusses the question of whether we are entering the risk society. Alain Touraine asks if we have gone beyond social movements. Dennis Wrong discusses the idea of capitalism. Roland Robertson examines the global trajectories of the concepts of civilization and civilizing processes. It can be argued that cultural theory has necessarily to be sensitive to the role of those who form, produce, disseminate and police culture and we find analysis of the influence of cultural specialists and intellectuals in the papers by Pierre Bourdieu, Randall Collins, Mike Featherstone, Nancy Fraser and Bryan Turner. We have also included a paper which seeks to defend the recent rise of interest in the sociology of emotions, by Cas Wouters, as well as one on death and survival by Zygmunt Bauman. The latter paper points to the way in which, as we move through life, the very fact that we have survived, that we have outlived others, is a form of empowerment. The papers collected in this volume were initially brought together to mark the tenth anniversary of the journal *Theory, Culture & Society*. In this small sense we have survived. My appreciation and thanks go to all those who have helped to make this possible.

Survival as a Social Construct

Zygmunt Bauman

The prospect of life is death; the ultimate cause of death is birth —
only they who live can die; good health preserves life so that it
can meet its death when it comes; life is the only truly terminal
disease . . .

All these statements are both trivial and absurd. They are absurd
as they defy logic. And they are absurd as they spell out, in a form
still less dramatic and paradoxical than the existential incongruity
they attempt to grasp and report, the ultimate failure of rationality:
human inability to reconcile the transcending power of *time-binding*
mind and the transience of its *time-bound* fleshy casing. It is this
ultimate incongruity (not the one between animal instincts and
social norms, which made Durkheim's man a *homo duplex*, but
one between the freedom of a symbol-making and symbol-using
subject and its fatal dependence on natural body) that inspired
Pascal's comment: men are so necessarily mad that not to be mad
would amount to another form of madness. Death blatantly defies
the power of reason: reason's power is to be a guide to good choice,
but death is not a matter of choice. Death is the scandal of reason.
It saps trust in reason and the security reason promises. It loudly
declares reason's lie. It inspires fear that saps and ultimately defeats
reason's offer of confidence. Reason cannot exculpate itself of this
scandal. It can only try a cover-up.

And it does. Since the discovery of death (and the state of having
discovered death is the defining, and distinctive, feature of the
human) human societies have kept designing elaborate subterfuges,
hoping that they would allow them to forget about the scandal; failing to forget, to afford not to think about it; failing that, to forbid
speaking of it. In Ernest Becker's words,

> all culture, all man's creative life-ways, are in some basic part of them a fabricated
> protest against natural reality, a denial of the truth of human condition, and an

Theory, Culture & Society (SAGE, London, Newbury Park and New Delhi), Vol. 9
(1992), 1–36

attempt to forget the pathetic creature that man is . . . Society itself is a codified hero system, which means that the society everywhere is a living myth of the significance of human life, a defiant creation of meaning.[1] (1973: 33, 7)

Thanks to the elaborate effort of society, 'in normal times we move actually without ever believing in our own death, as if we fully believed in our own corporeal immortality' (Zilboorg, 1970).[2]

Social Deconstruction of Death

The most common expedient is to make the dead 'cease to exist'. Cemeteries, Baudrillard (1976: 195ff) suggests, were the first ghettos; indeed, the archetypal ghettos, the patterns for all ghettos to come. Funerals differ in their ritual, but they are always acts of exclusion. They proclaim the dead abnormal, dangerous, those to be shunned. And they expel the dead from the company of the normal, innocuous, these to be associated with. But they do more than that. Through applying to the dead the same technique of separation as they do to the carriers of infectious diseases or contagious malpractices, they cast the dead in the category of threats that lose their potency if kept at a distance. Better still, the dead, like the ill, insane or the criminal, are put in trust, into 'the care of licensed professionals' (Anderson, 1986: 16) and thus are supposed to disappear not only from sight, but from mind. The self-deceit is all too visible, though; the dead cannot be buried in the past, as their lot is the future of all those living in the present. As sites of confinement, cemeteries are not half as secure as leprosaria, lunatic asylums or prisons. Haunted houses and haunted lives testify to the porousness of cemetery walls.

Another common expedient is to deny the substance of death: its finality. One can do it in many ways. One can follow the Hindu pattern of privatizing death and compensating it with a collectivized immortality: accept the permanence of being — 'that which is can never cease to be' (*Bhagavad Gita*, quoted in Carse, 1980: 133) — and thus make life and death into exchangeable forms of eternal being, stages whose duration does not matter in view of the perpetuity of existence. One can go one better and try to bring that 'being' which is eternal closer home. This is what the Jewish faith has done, ascribing perpetuity to the special relationship — the covenant — between Jewish people and God. Personal death does not matter much as long as the conversation of God with His people — God's revelation to the Jews and the Jews' service to

God — goes on. One can think of the Socrates–Plato solution as of a secular version of the same, yet a version meant not for a popular consumption, but for the reassurance of the chosen few, able and willing to seek consolation in philosophy; one putting the eternal truth in place of the Jewish God, and replacing the conversation between God and His people by the conversations of philosophers with the Absolute. One can think as well of modern totalitarianisms, in their nationalistic, class or racist forms, as of other varieties of collectivized immortality; varieties particularly effective in devaluing the transient, expendable and mortal individual.

Or one can, with Christianity, insist on personal immortality. As the decay of the physical body of the dead was too evident and unexceptional to be refuted, the preservation of the body could not be entertained in any but a miraculous form (the idea is entertained again in our time, in the form of the miraculously potent science and technology — as an artificially induced hibernation 'until such time when the medicine for the now terminal disease will have been found'). But the preservation of the soul could be postulated without fear of empirical refutation; the care of the soul's unending future would then take precedence over the worry about the flesh destined for putrefaction. Hopefully, the experts attending to the soul's future would also take precedence over the specialists caring for the body's present.

This delicate construction, vulnerable at the best of times, has been delivered a shattering blow at the threshold of the modern era — once behaviour of bodies fell out of the rule of nature and moved into the area demanding human vigilance and reflective action (and thus also calling for the problem-defining and problem-solving experts). The ever more evident insufficiency of unreflexive custom as a guarantee of social existence was perceived as the withdrawal of God from the world; absent from the world of the living, God could no longer be addressed, conversed with or induced to intervene. Propelled into the world by the original act of creation, humankind was now left to its own resources — above all it had to build up its existence using the most perfect of God's gifts, reason. As David R. Hiley put it,

> the conceptual role human telos had played was filled by a philosophy of history as progress; that is, the transition from our untutored and discordant condition to the realization of our true end was cast in terms of a teleological conception of the human species. (1988: 46)

The transition was to be accomplished by human reason; that is, by making good choices, only good choices and ever better choices. Making good choices itself turned into the *telos*; there could be no other end to human existence, since any other end would put a limit to reason's power. The sole purpose of reason was its own application, its rule, its mastery. Reason's mastery over humans as persons was the only meaning of the emancipation of humanity as a species; the only sensible model for humanity reaching finally its destination, its *telos*. The species' eternal self-perfection, called *progress*, required now that everything else is temporal, transient and disposable; including the necessarily imperfect, non-final individual exemplars of humanity.

Harry Redner (1982: 13, 4–5) expressed the new, modern status of death as a paradox, as an irony of history: 'man is now mortal, precisely by having acted on the premise of Man's immortality'. This new, modern conception of individual mortality is not, to be sure, a whim of philosophy. It grows from the condition created by modern practice. 'Men have devised a way of systematically dominating, controlling, and disposing of all things . . . They can make themselves irrelevant, if not redundant, to their own solutions and so dispose of themselves'. For mankind to self-assert, each individual member had to be a *tabula rasa* to be written upon, an *empty cabinet* to be filled with contents. 'To achieve this immortality of Man, Progress has to exclude death by relegating it to the private sphere of the individual' (Redner, 1982: 34).

This was only superficially, however, a return to the Judaist expedient or opting for the Hinduist one. This privatization of death has a distinctly modern tinge. It does not play down the *significance of death*, by denying its finality and irredeemability. It does play down instead the *significance of life*, by denying its relevance to the progress of humanity, the only conceivable 'logic of history'. It proclaims the enhancement of individual life as the end point of progress and mission of history, but for the time being — before the end has been reached and mission fulfilled — it legitimizes the treating of life as a means to an end (be it a classless society, a race-pure society, a society fulfilling the destiny of a nation). Indeed, no purpose could be said to reside in the episode stretching from the birth to the death of the individual. This episode's meaning derives solely from the future, that is from being overcome and left behind.

Modern privatization of death comes together with the privatization of life. Both are to be filled with sense and purpose by those who live and die. There are many devices that help life to be lived with a purpose, or to be lived as a series or a succession of purposes. The most important of the devices are supplied by instrumental reason. There are no devices (there can be no specifically *modern* devices) to anticipate death as a meaningful event. Our own death cannot be thought of as instrumental. It invalidates the discourse of instrumentality as it spells the termination of purposeful action. This is where its horror resides in the modern world of instrumental rationality: the world where deeds are lived as means to ends and justify themselves by the ends which they serve as means. There is no way in which this horror could be argued away. It can be only barred from consciousness, tabooed as a topic, heaved out away from current concerns; or, in the typically modern way, split into small-scale worries, each one separately removable — so that the fearful finality and irremediability of the original worry can be never scanned in its totality.

The latter expedient strives to conceal the fact that death, as the ultimate end of life, cannot be resisted. The truth that death cannot be escaped is not denied — it cannot be denied; but it could be held out of the agenda, elbowed out by another truth: that each *particular* case of death (most importantly, death which threatens the particular person, me, at the particular moment, now) can be resisted, postponed or avoided altogether. Death as such is inevitable; but each concrete instance of death is contingent. Death is omnipotent and invincible; but none of the specific cases of death is.

All deaths have causes, each death has a cause, each particular death has its particular cause. Corpses are cut open, explored, scanned, tested. The cause is found: blood clot, kidney failure, haemorrhage, heart arrest, lung collapse. We do not hear of people dying of mortality. They die only of individual causes; *because* there was an individual cause. No postmortem stops before the individual causes have been revealed. There are so many causes of death; given enough time, one can name them all. If I defeat, escape or cheat twenty among them, twenty less will be left to defeat me. One does not die; one dies of a *disease* or of *murder*. I can do nothing to defy mortality. But I can do quite a lot to avoid a blood clot or a lung cancer. I can stop eating eggs, refrain from smoking, do physical exercises, keep my weight down; I can do so many other things. And while doing all these right things and forcing myself to abstain from the wrong ones, I have no time left to ruminate that the effectiveness of each thing I am doing, however foolproof it could be made, does not in the least detract from the uselessness of them all taken together. The cause of instrumental rationality celebrates more triumphant battles — and in the din of festivities the news of the lost war is inaudible.

This is how we are trained to think (or not to think). According to an American researcher, an average child who reached the age of fourteen by 1971 would have watched about 18,000 cases of death on TV (Hick, 1976: 86). Most of those people who died on the screen were killed. Some others (though not at all that many) failed in their fight against a disease, or did not fight it promptly or keenly enough. Each case of death ('as seen on TV') had a cause, and for the same reason was *avoidable*: contingent. That contingency, that avoidability, that encouraging and reassuring gratuity of death was the main topic of the TV drama in which people lost their lives: individual people, individual lives and in individual circumstances.

The doctors who stand between me and my death do not fight mortality either; but they do fight, gallantly and skilfully, each and any of its particular cases. They fight *mortal diseases*. Quite often they win. Each victory is an occasion for rejoicing: once more, *death has been avoided*. Sometimes they lose the battle. And then, in Helmut Thielicke's (1983: 44) words, the death of a patient — *this* patient, *here* and *now* — is 'felt to be a personal defeat. Doctors are like attorneys who lose cases and are thus forced to face up to the limit of their own powers. No wonder that they conceal their faces and turn aside.' A lost court case does not put in question the importance and the competence of lawyers; at worst, it may cast shadow on the skills of a particular barrister. A death that has not been prevented does not undermine the authority of the medical profession. At worst it may stain the reputation of an individual doctor. But the condemnation of the individual practitioner only reinforces the authority of the art: the doctor's fault was not to use the tools and the procedures he *could use*. He is guilty precisely because the profession as a whole is capable of doing what he did not do, though should have done. Or in case a learned council resolves that the suspicion of neglect has been ill founded, as the proper tools and procedures are not available *at the moment* — the cause of hiding the lost war against mortality behind loudly hailed victorious frays and skirmishes with cholesterols, infections and tumours receives another powerful boost. The means have not been invented *yet*; the equipment has not been developed, the vaccine has not been discovered, the technique has not been tested. But they will, given time and money. Conquest of no disease is *in principle* impossible. Did you say that another disease will threaten life once this one here and now has been conquered? Well, we will cross that bridge when we come to it. Let us concentrate on the task at hand, on this trouble here and now. This we *can* do; and this we will go on doing.

From a hangman, death has been turned into a prison guard. The horror of mortality has been sliced into thin rashers of fearful, yet curable (or potentially curable) afflictions; they can be now fit neatly into every nook and cranny of life. Death does not come now at the end of life: it is there from the start, in a position of constant surveillance, never relaxing its vigil. Death is watching when we work, when we eat, when we love, when we rest. Through its many deputies, death presides over life. Fighting death is meaningless. But fighting the *causes* of dying turns into the meaning of life.

This is a most radical reversal of Epicurus's reasoning, calculated to avert the terror of death: so long as we exist, death is not present, and when death is present, we do not exist: therefore, death affects neither the dead nor the living . . . Death is present, in the countless little daily prescriptions and prohibitions, that not for a moment allow one to forget. Commenting on Pascal's reminder that death that comes unexpected is less terrifying than the *thought of death* when one is not in danger, Thielicke (1983: 5) writes that the most terrible thing about death is 'death as *thought*: in the thought that lies like a shadow over the whole of life and impresses upon it the stamp of a being for death'.

Life as Survival

Norbert Elias (1985: 23) noted 'a peculiar embarrassment felt by the living in the presence of dying people. They often do not know what to say. The range of words available for use in this situation is relatively narrow.' Elias added a comment: 'Feelings of embarrassment hold words back.' Civilization lifted the threshold of shame; we do not discuss cruel and gory matters, we hide in closets things we once did in public, we abhor the flashes of realities the civilizing process proclaimed non-existent or at least unspeakable. Death is just one of these things that have been suppressed; hence the embarrassment that makes us numb.

Though Elias's description of our curious ineptitude in the face of death is unquestionably correct, his interpretation seems less so. In our times we do not lack words to talk about ostensibly the most intimate and private — bodily, physiological — functions. Two of them — one referring to sexual activity, another to an excretive function — have made a truly spectacular career in the languages of literature, film and their daily replicas, and came to serve the expression of the widest possible gamut of emotions, from the rudest to the most sublime. We use them profusely in speech, unhampered by embarrassment. We use them gladly and with relish. We actively seek the sights which those words evoke, and are prepared to pay a lot for the pleasure: *The Fly* has been a runaway box-office success, *The Texas Chain-Saw Massacre* a best-selling video for family use, *The Living Dead* stay firmly among the most popular film characters, while Tom and Jerry keep smashing and maiming each other, to the delight of successive generations of children. And yet we do not know what to tell the dying. Here, our vocabulary (or is it our imagination? our thinking power?) fails us. There must be something special about death that is responsible.

It is not delicacy of manners that deprives us of speech, but the simple fact that, indeed, we have nothing to say to a person who has no use for the language of survival; a person who is about to leave the world of busy pretence that that language conjures up and sustains. Once death stopped being the *entry* it once was and was reduced to an *exit* pure and simple; once it stopped being a stage in the forward march of mankind and came to be a thoroughly private ending of that thoroughly private affair called life — it also lost all meaning that could be expressed in a vocabulary geared, after all, to its collective and public denial. True, death reduced to a series of cases each with an individual cause of its own is ubiquitously present in the business of life; it spurs life efforts, it saturates the struggle for survival. By the same token, however, it loses its identity; it exists only in its denial. We may offer to the dying only the language of survival; the one language for which they have no use. Fear of death is the mainspring of culture — but culture is an effort to make death invisible and unspeakable.

There would be probably no culture were humans unaware of their mortality; but culture is an elaborate counter-mnemotechnic device to forget what they are aware of. Culture would be useless if not for the devouring need to forget; there would be no transcending were there nothing to be transcended. In the City of the Immortals, Jorge Luis Borges tells us, a hundred or so irregular niches . . . furrowed the mountain and the valley. In the sand there were shallow pits; from these miserable holes (and from the niches) naked, grey-skinned, scraggly bearded men emerged. I thought I recognized them: they belonged to the bestial breed of the troglodytes . . . (1970: 138)

The troglodytes knew not the art of writing; neither would they speak. Only after prolonged (and vain) effort to usher a troglodyte into the mysteries of human language did the visitor discover that his reluctant disciple was Homer; Homer who has been admitted to the City of the Immortals and come to know that he would never die. Once he learned of his immortality, it became clear to him that 'if we postulate an infinite period of time, with infinite circumstances and changes, the impossible thing is not to compose the *Odyssey*, at least once' (1970: 145). Thus the composition of the *Odyssey* that *cannot not be* loses its lustre; the composition is no longer a unique event, and thus not an act of heroism; it is useless as a vehicle of self-assertion.

Everything among the mortals has the value of the irretrievable and the perilous. Among the Immortals, on the other hand, every act (and every thought) is the echo of others that preceded it in the past, with no visible beginning, or the faithful passage of others that in the future will repeat it to a vertiginous degree . . . Nothing can happen only once, nothing is preciously precarious. (1970: 146)[3]

Let us observe that the Immortals conjured up by Borges all had a mortal past; they came to disdain struggle for the unique because they *ceased* to be mortals who made such a struggle into the content of life. Borges's Immortals construed themselves out of the *negation* of mortality. Even their contempt for all act and thought that cannot be unique was a tribute to their mortal past. They would not grasp it on their own, were they unaware of the possibility of mortality, were they Immortals (and aware of being immortal) 'from the beginning' (would there be a beginning then?). Whatever content the visitor found in their existence, came from the forgetting, invalidating or rejection of the substance moulded of the past fear of mortality; they derived their substance from that other one which they had left behind (and which could be spoken about only negatively, in terms of 'no more', 'is not', 'does not have') . . . The understanding that circumstances and changes are infinite and therefore *worthless* could appear only in so far as one remembered that the circumstances and changes were once finite and thereby *precious*; if one knew the value that was once born of finitude.

The genuine immortals would not be aware that they are *not mortal*; for this very reason they elude our imagination; their experience (if there was an experience) could not be narrated in our language. As to the human mortals, they are aware that they are *not immortal*; this is what gives measure to time, makes every moment both fearful and precious, makes being into action and existence into a purpose and a task. Inescapably, as Elias Canetti wrote (1973: 290), man is a *survivor*: 'the most elementary and obvious form of success is to remain alive'. We are not just alive; at every moment we are *still* alive. Success is always until further notice; it is never final. It must be repeated over and over again, the effort can never grind to a halt. Survival is a life-long task. Its creative potential in never exhausted. It is just locked up, in one fell swoop, at the moment of death.

Canetti insists that survival is not identical with the old and trivial notion of 'self-preservation'. The idea of self-preservation, sometimes discussed as an instinct, sometimes as a rational choice, hides or beautifies the gruesome truth of survival. Survival is targeted on others, not on the self. We never live through our own death; but we do live through the deaths of the others, and their death gives meaning to our success: we are *still* alive. Thus 'the desire for a long life which plays such a large part in most cultures really means that most people want to survive their contemporaries. They know that many die early and they want a different fate for themselves' (1973: 291). I would not conceive of my own performance as a success if not for the fact that performances of others proved unsuccessful; I can only measure my own performance against those other performances. I want to know what should I do to *outlive* others. I eagerly refrain from smoking once I believe that others who smoke develop certain terminal diseases.

Because this is how I plan my survival and measure its success, I may forget that the ultimate meaning of my staving off the danger of dying of cause A is the increase in probability that my death, when it comes, will be described as caused by B, C . . . Z. 'I do not want to die' always translates, in its pragmatic conclusions, into 'I would rather die of that than this'. As the 'that' cannot be exhausted, the truth of the translation must not be admitted into consciousness, and this requires that survival effort scores ever new successes. Survival needs constant reassurance; and the only convincing reassurance is the death of others: *not me*. Hence, Canetti insists, the sinister potential of survival which is glossed over in the tamed and castrated notion of 'self-preservation'. What the latter notion belies is the fact that *personal* achievement of self-preservation can be perceived as such (and hence inspire human effort) only if grasped in terms of a *social* relation of survival.

At the radical extreme of survival, says Canetti, looms murder: 'He wants to kill so that he can survive others; he wants to stay alive so as not to have others surviving him.' This wish can be suppressed, but it cannot be conjured away: 'Only survival at a distance in time is wholly innocent' (Canetti, 1973: 293, 292)[4]. Survival is never wholly innocent when reforged into action; blatantly so when, adorned in lofty ideals of fighting evil empires or disarming the enemies of mankind, be they carriers of disease or spoilers of harmonious order, it shapes itself up as war, crusade or genocide. The survivor's 'most fantastic triumphs have taken place in our own time, among people who set great store by the idea of humanity . . . The survivor is mankind's worst evil, its curse and perhaps its doom' (Canetti, 1973: 544).[5]

This is a dramatic, tragic vision of the inner tendency of survival. One wonders to what extent this tendency is truly *inner* (or innate); one is entitled to suspect that the destructive edge of survival is sharpened (and even more probably directed) by the socially organized setting in which the activity of survival takes place. It is this setting that may (or may not) arrange survival as a zero-sum game, and then split the habitat into a part that is threatening and has to be subdued or better still annihilated, and another part whose well-being enhances the chance of my own survival; this is what most societies have been doing all along, and continue to do. Like other in-built qualities of the human predicament, the impulse to survival is the stuff of which societies are patched together. This impulse has been neither created by society nor fought against. It is, rather, manipulated; *socially managed* in a way that, for one reason or another, is deemed useful. It is deployed to build and preserve boundaries. It is invoked, explicitly or tacitly, whenever hostility is to be directed, but also whenever loyalty to the cause and group solidarity are called for. It is not just, and not necessarily, destructive in its application. Or, rather, it can be put effectively to non-destructive uses precisely because of its destructive potential.

One such use can be traced back to what Norman O. Brown

(1959: 118ff)[6] dubbed the *Oedipal Project*: 'The project of becoming God — in Spinoza's terms, *causa sui*'. The oedipal project is a flight from infantile dependency, a wish to become 'the father of himself'. This stage in development always arrives, and once it arrives is invariably directed against the parents, the true embodiment of dependency — and this whatever the parents do and however they behave. The oedipal project is a drive to emancipation that cannot be achieved unless the bond of dependency is broken. However, the deepest, the ultimate dependency is that on one's own mortal body and for this reason the battle cannot be won. The oedipal project is just the first trial skirmish in a long series of battles doomed to defeat. The *causa sui* project remains unfulfilled, and as long as it is unfulfilled it feeds the need for ever new battles. It also needs ever new battlefields and war strategies, so that the struggle may continue while each successive engagement is lost. The tragic paradox is that the undeclared purpose of the struggle is gaining exclusive mastery over one's own body (and thus, by proxy, surviving its unsurvivable mortality: the dream of survival constitutes the body as its most potent target, as the body is the mortal side of the self, and — with its procreative function — is also the instrument through which individual immortality is expropriated by the species), but it is always the socially set framework of dependence that injects meaning into the experience of 'lack of mastery'. The battlefields are socially determined: hence also the war strategies, like the battlefields, cannot but transcend individuality of the 'incipient God'. It is on this interface that the survival needs of the developing individual meet and merge with the self-perpetuating processes of sociality: the survival-inspired *causa sui* projects are bound to remain forever unfulfilled, and because of their endemic inconclusiveness the continuation of sociality is assured. The drive to individual survival paves the way to the survival of human collectivity.

Or at least it can, in principle. Harmony is not preordained. It is always a social achievement. Survival is, potentially, as anti-social as pro-social; left unattended it may break the chain of sociality which, under different circumstances, it holds together. It can be put to socially destructive as much as to socially creative uses. More often than not, it is put to uses that are both destructive and constructive. As it is doomed and cannot but be doomed from the start, none of the possible uses can be foolproof from either the collective or individual point of view.

Which way survival will turn, depends on the *policy* of survival. Individual survival is (if at all) tamed and manipulated socially through socially administered policies. Policies deemed useful to the perpetuation of structure-spawning sociality tend to be institutionalized; policies seen as harmful tend to be crusaded against, marginalized or − if possible − suppressed altogether. Any social setting favours the selection of some policies and renders other policies unattractive or unrealistic.

Policies of Survival

To be pursued for any length of time more than purely idiosyncratically and quixotically, each policy of survival must meet one condition: it has to channel the horror of death (and thus to organize the individual's concern with survival) in such a way as to dovetail the resulting practice with the mechanism of social reproduction. In other words, it needs to harmonize individual self-constitution with the constitution of society (or, more generally, with the continuing flow of sociality). Several policies that meet this condition will be named and briefly discussed below.

1. *God*. Endemic lack of control over one's own mortality is reflected as inscrutability of Divine providence. But the latter comes together with the possibility of survival through the transcendence of the limitations imposed by the body. This policy of survival tends to downgrade the body; through mortification and neglect of bodily needs, as well as through construing bodily functions as inferior, shameful or sinful, the concern with prolongation of bodily existence is partly defused. The point of gravity in survival shifts, realistically, to the areas over which individuals do have control (or at least can realistically hope to gain it): to thoughts and deeds. It is through thoughts and deeds that transcendence, true immortality, may be achieved. The positive outcome is guaranteed; but the guarantee is valid only in so far as the required deeds are performed and prescribed thoughts are thought. This could be what Dostoievsky had in mind when he wrote that 'making man responsible, Christianity *eo ipso* recognizes his freedom' (Dostoievsky, 1979: 13).[7] The energy generated by the thrust to survival is put to a socially harmless − even socially profitable − use, while the dread of mortality is alleviated; man can really 'do something about it'. It does matter what he does and how he thinks. The choice of mode of life is relevant to survival, but this relevance hangs on trust in God. Only apparently such trust (which

must be complete and unreserved) implies a complete abandonment of individuality to the will of the all-powerful Other, God. In fact it offers a sought after package deal: individualizing consequences of survival concerns (through the dependence of survival on how the individual acts), together with the supra-individual guarantees of the means the individual is advised to deploy for the purpose.

These guarantees have the additional advantage of being immune to test — their ultimate proof is securely located beyond human experience. However harsh may be the trials induced by the action on which the guarantees are conditional, the guarantees themselves are never tried: an abstract entity, God, is not accessible to censure. His performance is not subject to empirical test, and trust in God is not conditional on anything that may be gleaned from human experience. God's power need not justify itself through practical performance and is therefore totally obedient to human fantasy; as such, it is a secure place to invest the dream of survival; the wisdom of the investment stands little chance of disavowal. As no other supra-individual safeguard against mortality, the succour that God offers depends solely on the strength and intensity of trust; and solely when invested in God can the trust really afford to be unconditional. No other policies of survival can match this achievement.

2. *Common Cause*. With the appearance of powers bent on the substitution of a designed, artificial order for the natural one and thereby opening the extant reality to questioning, the 'trust in God' policy of survival cannot but lose the very advantage that made it so strikingly effective: its other-worldly anchorage. God is now called to legitimize himself in performance open to critical scrutiny and empirical test. It is now the well-being of the body that is at stake, which the secular powers promise to improve; on this battlefield God stands little chance. The wisdom of providence is sorely tested, and the very assumption of its immortal solidity that formed so reliable a foundation for the resilience of other-worldly fantasy becomes now its major handicap. Secular powers, on the contrary, dwell on the non-finality of the human predicament: the human plight can be improved, and thus the sufferings of today do not undermine, in principle, their ability to promote happiness — they only supply motive for further action, more hope and more trust. In a sense, the very unsafisfactoriness of the present supplies the proof that life may be made more gratifying.

Like all remaining policies of survival and unlike the religious one, this one appeals to reason: resourceful powers may implement a reason-dictated, rational order on earth that will make human fate more palatable. Trust has now a mundane, this-worldly anchorage. It is to be located in collective designs that offer in exchange a guarantee of the propriety of the individual solution to the problem of survival. If it cannot defy individual death, it may (or at least aims to) invest individual life with meaning which renders bodily death as irrelevant as it was when the divinely guaranteed spiritual immortality was trusted. This is a *common cause* policy of survival.

Nationalism, the cause of the classless society and the cause of the racially pure society are the most potent examples of common-cause survival policies. Their potency derives from the presence of resourceful powers able and willing to contemplate the introduction and management of a *total order*; truly effective policies of survival can be only totalistic ideologies, offering a radical, global and permanent solution to the contradiction between the transience of bodily existence and the limitlessness of spiritual transcendence. For this reason, other — mostly single-issue — common-cause policies are wan and ineffective by comparison, however hard they try to emulate their achievement.

Like the religious one, the common-cause policy of survival (the more so the more totalistic it is) is bound to play down the importance of bodily death; but unlike the religious policy, it embroils itself in an unresolvable and ultimately lethal contradiction, since its declared end (and its sole claim to trust) is this-worldly happiness. Like the religious one, the common-cause policy promises immortality; but this immortality is vested in causes and collectivities, not individuals. It therefore invites individual rebellion, which tends to grow with the realization that the promise of a paradise which one would never enter anyway is a poor compensation for the sufferings that are required on the road to paradise with relentless regularity.

Common-cause policies of survival are vulnerable also for another reason. Their carriers and embodiments, the leaders, are visible, or at least cannot be made completely invisible; so are their deeds and the effects of their deeds; so is their lifestyle. They may be judged by what they deliver. They may also be judged by the degree to which they live their ideology. And they are so judged — seldom passing the test in every respect and for the duration of time. They may try to escape judgement, emulating the lofty withdrawal of God from the world; they may surround themselves by heavily armed guards and a wall of secrecy. Thanks to such expedients, they may hide for a time the fact of being mortal, bodily creatures, and not matching the immortality of the cause they preach. As, however, the cause they preach is anchored in this-worldly order, their prolonged absence weakens the cause and in the long run is unthinkable. Unlike God, they must be practically engaged with earthly matters. Each drawback in the latter is therefore interpreted as the case of their misjudgement, each error rebounds as a proof of mismanagement and sediments as a record of unreliability. Trust is vulnerable and needs constant refuelling. Ideological leaders need ever new proofs of credibility and trustworthiness; their performance stands for the viability of the recipe for immortality which legitimizes their claim to obedience. The survival value of the recipe requires their own survival. This need prods them toward the posture of Canetti's *radical survivors*. Not only must they stay alive as leaders, they must *outlive* their rivals (in fact, everyone likely to outlive them is a rival). This is why ideological leaders tend to turn into despots or dictators. Or, rather, only such among them as turn into despots or dictators stand a chance of going down in history as effective ideological leaders.

3. *Love*. According to Otto Rank (1932: 232), the modern person's dependency on the love partner 'is the result of the loss of spiritual ideologies'. Bereaved by God and His secular emulators, the modern person 'needs *somebody*, some "individual ideology of justification", to replace the declining collective ideologies'. Love takes over at the point where God and the Despot-with-a-Mission left off. Not that love is born of modern bereavement. But it is the modern predicament, one which emerged in the wake of the bankruptcy of tested old policies of survival, that has burdened love with new load which it was never before called on to carry.

It is now the partner in love who is expected to offer the space for transcendence, *to be* transcendence. He or she must be a mirror in which my fantasy looks real; my fantasy is to become real by the very fact of being reflected. My own self, confined as it is by the mortality of its own bodily carapace, is to acquire a vicarious immortality by sundering its private bond and being set free. It has to gain a new, unbound and more credible existence within the trans-individual 'universe of two'. I may dream that in the process the mortality of the self is defeated by the sheer feat of abandoning the hopelessly mortal individual body. But the new anchorage of survival is another body and another self, entangled much as my own in the mutual conflict from which only subterfuges pretend to offer an exit. Itself afloat, it can hardly hold the anchor fast enough.

'We want an object that reflects a truly ideal image of ourselves. But no human object can do this . . . No human relationship can bear the burden of godhood', thus Ernest Becker (1973: 166) sums up the fate of modern love. Hence what only superficially may seem to be a paradox: just when the functional importance of love has risen to unprecedented heights, its carrying capacity seems to have drastically fallen. The heightened expectations have multiplied the likelihood of failure. Defeats do not necessarily expose the lie ensconced at the bottom of the love strategy. They only gestate — in the partners — impatience and restlessness, the breathless search for the 'true partner' who must, just must, be waiting round the corner; for the 'universes of two' they result in endemic brittleness — the couples break at the first hurdle, as the partners prefer a new, as yet unexplored track to the chores of negotiating the already revealed obstacles of the old one.

Terminal dangers surround the love relationship on both sides. My bid for the confirmation of the self may be rejected or accepted with reservations to which I am not prepared to consent. But even if my bid has been assented to in full, the acceptance may fail to bring the expected satisfaction. It may not carry the degree of reassurance I sought. After all, my stakes in immortality have been invested in another mortal creature, and this brute fact cannot be concealed for long by even the most passionate deification of the partner. Unlike God or an anointed despot, my partner in love has the distinct disadvantage of being constantly within the field of my vision, of being watched by me at close quarters also in situations which make salient the truth of his or her bodily mortality. The despot fails as an object of survival policy once he publicly reveals the absence of supra-human potency by losing a battle; for a partner in love, it is enough to be human in humanity's endemic, irreparable duality. And it is precisely the partner's humanity that makes him or her fit to be an object of love; it therefore cannot but be drawn into love relationship.

These inner contradictions of love as a policy of survival are nowhere as prominent as in the case of an erotic relationship, where spiritual and sexual intimacy feed and reinforce each other (or are presumed to do so). In its natural function, sexual procreation is a method through which the species preserves its immortality at the expense of the mortality of its individual members; for this very reason it is singularly unfit for the role the policy of survival of the individual would wish it to play once it picks on the sexual union as the vehicle in which to escape death. Sexual intimacy cannot bear such exaggerated hopes; in modern practice the disappointment leads to the discrediting of the spiritual aspect of sex in its totality and the pronounced tendency to divest sexual intercourse of the last vestiges of spiritual union. No longer are the absolute and the transcendent sought in the sexual partner; what is expected from the partner is, at best, a willingness and ability to arouse and stimulate the 'perfect performance' — and thus reconfirm the value of the self in a roundabout fashion, by allowing it to stretch to the 'genuine', or fantasized about, limits (which, in *fantasy*, always means transcending the *genuine* limits).

4. *Self-care.* The survival policies have been surveyed so far in such an order as to expose the gradual shrinking of the space in which the thrust to immortality is vested. A policy falling upon itself, aiming back at its point of emergence, is a logical next step. This possibility has been already revealed in the effects of dashed sexual hopes: the sexual prowess of the Ego moving into the centre of expectation, with sexual intimacy with the Alter reduced to the role of an occasion for its release and display.

But the weight ascribed to the display of sexual prowess can be seen also from another perspective: in its case, the centre of gravity moves from transcendence as an achieved (and once achieved, constant) state, to the transcendence as a momentary event, as a performance. When seen in such a way, our example appears to be a specimen of a new type of survival policy; one that differs sharply from the policies considered so far, and which (perhaps due to this difference) shows an amazing capacity for expansion. What is involved here is an attempt to belie the ultimate limits of the body by breaking, successively, its *currently* encountered, *specific* limitations (this could be done personally as well as vicariously; here lies the secret of the fascination with the record-breaking performance of sportspersons, experienced as acts committed on behalf of the species as a whole). By the same token, the impossible task of escaping the mortality of the body is never allowed to be encountered in its awesome totality, as it is split into a never-ending series of concrete challenges, reduced to a manageable, and hence realistic, size. The time dimension of transcendence is turning here into a spatial issue: stretching the *span of life* is turned into the effort to stretch the *capacity to live*. Time all but disappears: it has been reduced and flattened out of existence, subjected to a process that 'narrows the present down to a chaos of evanescent events' (Redner, 1982: 280). What matters amidst such chaos, is the only stable point of reference, *the body*, living permanently the current moment; not what the body is bent on accomplishing in the future, but 'bodily fitness', body as multi-purpose instrument, ready for all challenges yet indifferent to the nature of any task it may confront.

Eschatology is dissolved in technology. It is 'how to do it', not 'what to do', on which the survival concerns focus; not what is to be done, but 'how well' it has been done, is the measure of each episode into which the struggle for survival now splits. The transcendence of mortality has been replaced with the mind-and-energy consuming task of transcending the technical capacity for living. This is a triumph of life-size instrumentality over the metaphysical purpose inscribed in eternity; the triumph of event over time, the livable present over future death. The future has been abolished, evicted from the field of vision. It has been replaced by Benjamin's *Jetztzeit*, the non-flowing time, time without continuation or consequence, a continuous present.

The worry about immortality can now all but be forgotten in the daily bustle about *health*. Mortality generates *Angst*, disease is pregnant only with *anxiety*. Illness can be conquered, and so anxiety (unlike the *Angst*) does not paralyse, but spurs into action. If immortality cannot be made into a realistic goal, health can. There are so many things and deeds one should avoid to protect health. Avoiding them is a time-consuming labour: consumption of time that would otherwise be shot through with metaphysical dread is the most gratifying aspect of health anxiety. One does not need to stand idle; one can do something about death: not about death in general, true, but about this and that cause of death, here and now. We are mindful of the doctor's remonstrations: let us concentrate on this trouble here and now; we will cross that other bridge when we come to it. We hear and read that even 'the longest-living men' whose major title to fame was longevity (not to mention the 'ordinary' very old) die finally of kidney disease or liver trouble or pneumonia; no one seems to die because of human mortality. A paradoxical reflection of such thinking is a belief, promoted by the medical profession and ossified into 'objective fact' through statistics, that 'death from natural causes alone is diminishing. There is an even more telling trend because many deaths from disease often have human intentionality — conscious and unconscious — as part of the cause' (Vaux, 1978: 62–3). 'Natural death' seems today suspicious; 'unexplained death' is a challenge to a world-view that no longer recognizes — not publicly, not loudly — the universality and inescapability of death, and splits mortality into a multitude of individual occurrences, each with its own cause, each with a principally defeatable cause, each essentially 'preventable'.

However thorough and prolonged the succour this policy of survival may bring, it has its own drawbacks. One may forget that the most a victory may bring is a temporary lull in enemy action, not final victory. But one is not allowed to enjoy the respite for long. Death is a momentary event, but defence of health and vigilance against its enemies is a life-long labour. Death comes at the end of life, defence of health fills the whole of it. The price for exchanging immortality for health is life lived in the shadow of death; to postpone death, one needs to surrender life to fighting it.

The self-care policy of survival construes death as an individual event, as an occurrence brought about by a particular cause, a cause which could be absent or could be avoided — as *contingency*. Each death is different; each death is individual; each death is a private experience; each death is lonely.[8] And so is life, once colonized by this kind of death: individual, different, unshared, lonely. If my death is cause by something I have done, or something I could prevent from happening, or my inaction or neglect, survival is reconfirmed as my private matter and private responsibility. The more consistently I deploy my strategy of survival, the more I am left alone. Loneliness is frightening and unbearable, because of my uncertainty as to how adequate are the weapons I deploy to fight off the threats to my body. The know-how as to what weapons to select, and the weapons themselves, I can obtain only from others — from those who control the access to weapons and possess the knowledge of how to use them. Being alone makes me dependent on others. It opens me up to others, but in a particular way, leaving a profound imprint on the shape of ensuing sociality. I need the others as purveyors of guaranteed means of private survival; as people whose authority I can trust so as to cede the responsibility for my choice and allay suspicions as to its propriety. Failing that, I need the others as means to re-collectivize my privatized fears. I need the others to lose private uncertainty in a shared audacity and temerity of numbers. And so I need the *experts*. And I need the *tribes*.

The Habitat of Survival

None of the policies of survival has been found faultless; none can be foolproof. What is more, the search for a foolproof (pragmatically reasonable or logically rational) policy of survival is itself a ruse — a conspiracy of silence about the ultimate futility of effort, to bury the truth that the ostensible purpose of the search cannot be reached (to put this Pascal's way, madness may be only replaced with another madness; to express this in Freudian terms, a cure for neurosis is another neurosis). The search is bound to remain inconclusive, and it is precisely for this reason that it is bound to go on. Policies of survival are, after all, more or less ingenious subterfuges designed to permit a life with the awareness of death — and such subterfuges, to be even moderately effective, need to rest their authority on false pretences, to pretend not to be what they are. In order to make life in the shadow of mortality livable (which they can do), they must lie that they allow us to conquer mortality (a promise on which they cannot deliver). They are ultimately frustrating; yet the disappointment comes after their work has been done.

Thus the effectiveness of the policies of survival is never total. But it may be greater or smaller, depending on the availability of resources which the pursuit of a given policy demands; ultimately, on the degree of 'fit', on co-ordination between a given policy of survival and the habitat inside which is has to be pursued. Habitat does not 'determine' the choice of policies; but it does render some policies more *realistic* (and thus more credible, more trustworthy, more likely to be chosen) than others.

Our present, *postmodern* habitat seems to be particularly hospitable to the policy of self-care. It thoroughly privatizes responsibility for the business of life: it stoutly refuses all preordained assignment to life-models, and instead construes life as a process of self-constitution. It also purveys supra-individually based certainty (or supra-individual tranquillizers to subdue the pangs of uncertainty) in both sought-after varieties — of expertise and of tribal symbols — thus making it possible to live with the always haunting and potentially devastating consequences of privatization.

Between the survival policy of self-care and the way knowledge production and knowledge distribution have been institutionalized in modern society, there is a remarkable degree of correspondence and mutual adjustment. The production of knowledge follows the principle of partition: dissembly of issues into smaller particles — small enough to be conceived of as mechanical entities (that is, such entities that warrant linking together causal explanation, prediction and control). Thanks to such a principle of institutional-ization, knowledge in modern society is *practical* — understanding is subordinate to, and generative of, managerial capacity. For the same reason knowledge is intimately associated with power. Pro-duction of knowledge is conditional on the power to divide and separate. Once obtained, knowledge feeds into power to manage and control. For the same reason again, there can be no knowledge (that is, institutionalized and legitimized knowledge) of totality other than a collection of partial knowledges concerned with the 'constitutive parts' (read: products of dissembly) of the totality. There is no knowledge of life, but only of life processes; the more minute the processes, the fuller the knowledge.

The distribution of knowledge is predetermined by the conditions of its production. Knowledge is available not as illumination, but as issue-bound instruction. Partial knowledge belongs to partial specialists; it is always the property of experts, who administer its apportionment. *Collectively*, the experts articulate the experience of prospective knowledge-recipients as an aggregate of manageable (and manageable *singly*) problems, thereby assuring the homo-morphy of experience with the pattern of knowledge production and knowledge ownership.[9] Translation of experiential intuition into problems recognized as legitimate objects of knowledge and thus amenable to expert management is a two-way process. It invites active interpretation of knowledge by its prospective beneficiary; but it is conducted under the supervision of the experts, who retain the final say in the matter of the adequacy of translation.

The experts do not speak *sotto voce*, though. Faced with the need to establish the attraction of their products,[10] spokesmen and practitioners of various fields of expertise have willy-nilly to engage in a competitive struggle, even if their products satisfy ostensibly non-exclusive needs and serve the solution of non-related problems. What they compete for is public *attention*. Experts' authority is conditional on the public recognition of the relative importance of the field they operate for the practiced mode of survival. Experts must therefore *alert* the prospective clients to the fact that what their knowledge and knowledge-products service has prime survival value. This can be done by arousing heretofore non-experienced *fears*: an element of daily life (preferably an element widely used or affecting a large population) is brought into relief and *problematized* as an object fit for special attention: revealed as harmful, poisonous or otherwise deleterious to the purpose of individual well-being, unless scrupulously and expertly controlled or reprocessed according to expert advice. Often addressed is the already deeply entrenched fear of inadequacy: the prospective beneficiaries of expert services are told that by abstaining from using the given advice or product they do a disservice to themselves; when neglecting experts' suggestions, they are bound to perform incompetently and thus less efficiently. 'Fear campaigns' may promote specific products of expert knowledge; even greater is however their summary impact, the promotion and sedimentation of the 'cult of specialists' — the generalized, diffuse feelings of helplessness and incompetence which demand permanent assistance of 'people in the know'. The value of expert services is built on the clients' *trust*; yet the prospective clients must first be primed by a demonstration of their individual inability to define their problems and deal with them adequately. The authority of the experts has its counterpart in the self-deprecation and low self-esteem of the non-specialists, and by proxy of non-specialism (dilettantism, common sense) as such. The fear campaign attains victory through the humiliation of its targets: successive chunks of lay knowledge and know-how are redefined as instances of ignorance and obscurantism.

Though from the collective rule of the experts (dependence of all chosen modes of survival, and of the choice itself, on expert services) there is no escape (even a protest against experts' mismanagement ends up as a call for more expert services, having been first brought into being by expert-supplied redefinition of past services), the principle of privatization of survival is in no way undermined. Neither is the perception of it as a freedom of choice being sapped; after all, submission to expert rule is always mediated by the decision of individuals pursuing their respective policies of survival. The experts cannot promote and defend their authority otherwise as appealing to the clients' autonomy and right to choose. They have to justify their collective rule as service: in terms of clients' private concerns with individual survival. The subtle interaction between the expert management of the habitat of survival and the autonomy of the individual survivors has been enticingly described by Michel de Certeau (1984: xviii):

As unrecognized producers, poets of their own acts, silent discoverers of their own paths in the jungle of functionalist rationality, consumers produce through their signifying practices something that might be considered similar to the 'erratic lines' ('lignes d'erre') drawn by autistic children . . . 'indirect' or 'errant' trajectories obeying their own logic. In the technocratically constructed, written, and functionalized space in which the consumers move about, their trajectories form unforeseeable sentences, partly unreadable paths across a space. Although they are composed with the vocabularies of established languages (those of television, newspapers, supermarkets, or museum sequences) and although they remain subordinated to the prescribed syntanctical forms (temporal modes of schedules, paradigmatic orders of spaces, etc.), the trajectories trace out the ruses of other interests and desires that are neither determined nor captured by the systems in which they develop. (Translation slightly amended by Z.B.)

Indeed, de Certeau's choice of the metaphor is apt. The relationship of dependence and autonomy is not unlike that of the grammar and vocabulary of language and formed sentences of speech: the latter are in no way 'determined' by the former and move freely within the frame it provides. From the vantage point of the experts, habitat is a territory of intended colonization and regulation; when, however, the relevancies are motivated by survival concerns, the same habitat appears as a space filled with unattached signifiers, a space 'of endless replacement, supercession, drift and play' (Hebdige, 1988: 71),[11] a space awaiting attribution of meaning: the act through which the presence of the individual, and the validity of his or her survival plan, can be confirmed and re-asserted.

A similar dialectics of dependence and choice applies to another constitutive feature of the postmodern habitat: the *tribes*, Michel Maffesoli suggested the concept of *neo-tribalism* to distinguish the contemporary variant of tribal life from the 'classical' notion of tribalism as codified by ethnographers. Neo-tribes are marked by their fluidity: the 'tribes' are both locally assembled and scattered. They are *momentary condensations* in the ever flowing stream of seductive choices. Tribes are incurably fragile, yet at every moment command tremendous emotional investment. Their 'substance', their materiality, is but that investment. And more often than not donning a motley dress or bizarre and multi-coloured hair-style is all there is to the act of joining the tribe. Hence the 'tragic superficiality' of tribe-forming *sociality* as distinct from the 'dramatic authenticity' of the social. Even if this tribe or another happens to declare an objective, a purpose — 'this is not essential; what is important is the energy expended on the formation of the group as such'. An inner organization, centre of authority, platform, statutes are all superfluous, as are the declared aims of a neo-tribe. Tribes, Maffesoli (1988: 98–9, 123) suggests, are their own purposes. They are no more, yet no less either, than momentary condensations of the incessant urge of sociality.

Where I differ from Maffesoli is in his placement of neo-tribalism in the context of the alleged 'mass-society' tendency; in his all too frequent references to the Dionysian roots of the 'join the tribe' urge; and in the resulting message of the unambiguously anti-individualistic impact of the neo-tribal phenomenon. I propose instead that — much as in the case of technology and expertise — the variegated, chequered and fluctuating tribal scene is engaged with the privatized individual in a subtle dialectical game of dependence and freedom. Tribes are simultaneously refuges for those trying in vain to escape the loneliness of privatized survival, and the stuff from which private policies of survival, and thus the identity of the survivor, are self-assembled. The tribe-forming and dismantling sociality is not a symptom of declining individuality, but a most powerful factor in its perpetuation. Neo-tribes are fickle, ephemeral and elusive products of life under conditions of privatized survival; but neo-tribalism, as a feature of the habitat, is a necessary and stable condition of 'realism' of the survival policies that respond to such privatization.

Neo-tribalism is an indispensable complement of a habitat in which private survivals are serviced by the variegated and often contradictory advice of the experts. The sum total of problems spawned by the finely dissected and inherently fissiparous network of expertise exceeds the absorptive capacity of individual attention. The choice, however, is a daunting task, as the hierarchies of relevance suggested by the experts servicing different problem areas are hardly ever compatible. It is in this difficult yet indispensable matter of choice that tribes perform a crucial function, as they sanction global *lifestyles*, each offering its own structure of relevances. One can say that the role of neo-tribes consists in selecting a number of disparate and scattered, partial 'problems of survival', and assembling the samples into comprehensive and relatively cohesive life-models. For the individual, joining a tribe means adopting a peculiar lifestyle; or, rather, the road to a coherent lifestyle leads through the adoption of tribally sanctioned structure of relevances complete with a kit of totemic symbols.

Hence the reproduction of tribes and of individual survival formulae are intimately inter-related; they are, so to speak, two sides of the same social process. The non-obligatory, non-coercive character of tribal 'membership' (one can hardly speak of membership, as it were, considering the absence of tribal executive powers, the rudimentary nature of formalization and almost complete lack of control over the individual adherents' decisions to 'join' or to 'leave' and move to another tribe) squares well with the status of survival as a private task and responsibility.

Survival as a Stratifying Factor

Unlike self-preservation, survival — let us repeat — is a social relation (not only in its consequences, but in its very constitution as an urge and a task). What prompts survival concerns is not simply the vision of an imminent exit from the sensuous, future-binding life, saturated with hope and expectation, but the awareness that others will go on living. It is this awareness that makes one's own death humiliatingly inconsequential and, by proxy, threatens everything that precedes death, the life itself, with degradation or destruction of meaning. Survival concerns always include, therefore, the comparative aspect: immortality not being a viable option, survival means living *longer than others*. Though born of the ostensibly universal human condition, survival concerns *differentiate*: death is a descent into depersonalized nothingness, but the most horrible aspect of death as a *thought* is the fact that this nothingness is utterly private, depersonalization personal. Life in general will not grind to a halt — and it is from the imagined perspective of that continuing life that my own future nothingness (again as a social relation) can be, and is, grasped and conceived. Those about to survive me will be spectators of the impending revelation of my nothingness. It is their gaze that will constitute my nothingness. And it is in relation to them that the nothingness ought to be (if this is at all possible) denied. Were it denied, freedom of judgement of those who will live after me would be constrained; their announcement of my descent into nothingness would be prevented or at least made less credible or final — and all this because of what *I am* or what *I do*.

This makes the effort to deny descent into nothingness into a *policy of stratification*: into a stratagem aimed at making some people 'less mortal' than others. Some people would succeed in bending future judgements so that they would not deny their survival; the rest will sink into oblivion precisely because they lack or miss the survival entitlements of the first.

People are stratified by their respective degrees of *freedom*; the ultimate meaning of a relatively superior status is always a wider range of possible choices, and the lower down a status is in social hierarchy, the less freedom their incumbents possess and the less they can be seen as genuinely 'voluntary subjects'. To be 'higher' means more freedom; to be 'lower' means more dependence. The verticality of social hierarchy is construed of comparative 'unboundedness' or 'boundedness' of choices. The universal urge to survival generates its own stratification. It could be argued as well that it underlies *all* social stratification.

The colonization of the future is bound to remain forever unpleasantly provisional and revocable; the future is, after all, the site of that uncertainty which has prompted the colonizing thrust in the first place. The denial of nothingness lacks all solidity if anchored in the future; even if addressed to future survivors and prompted by the wish to bind *their* judgements, it could derive its substantiality only from the roots struck firmly in the 'site of certainty' — the past. Paradoxically, the hope of transcending the present can be rooted only in making the past last. That hope lies behind the constant temptation to retrieve the past, never to let it out of living memory — as if to demonstrate in such a roundabout way the non-transience of things; more precisely, the non-transience of *certain* things, relevant to *certain* people. The thrust toward differential survival rebounds as a partisan retrieval of history. The struggle against the inequality of survival chances (unequal hopes to bind the future) chooses history writing and rewriting as its major battlefield. The war to colonize the imagined future is fought on the territory of imagined past.

Survival, let us repeat once more, is a social relation. Binding history may be hoped to be effective as a warrant for the binding of future only because other people cannot demonstrate the lasting visibility of their own past (better still: have no past of their own). The differentiality of survival requires a differential deprivation of history. The importance of long and carefully recorded pedigrees lies in the fact that most people cannot trace their ancestors beyond a second or a third generation; aristocracies, with their long survival record, stand out in a world populated by people without past. The existence of people with long pedigrees is deeply rooted and solidly entrenched — a fact they find easy to argue in view of the shallow and evanescent presence of all others. For similar reasons, the splendour of old, inherited riches can be never matched by the glitter of brand new fortune; the latter exudes the pungent odour of mortality which the former can claim to have dissipated and lost during its long march through past ages.

But new fortunes may be used to rob the holders of inherited ones of the tokens of their immortality: their castles and their adornments. The adornments now carry immortality by proxy: their acquisition bestows vicarious immortality on the new owners. They are ascribed an *immortal* beauty (or is it the beauty of immortality?). And, unlike the pedigrees, they are movable — so that they can service a flexible stratification, a hierarchy with mobility: a game of musical chairs which gives everybody a chance to win a battle in which most must lose. Of the precious ore of time-defying ancestry, charms and mascots of immortality are minted — fit for marketing and available for private acquisition. Aristocracy may have lost the monopoly of immortality; but the scramble for the trappings of its past glory is a posthumous tribute to the astounding success of its formula of transcendence.

Next to the timelessness of continuous blood kinship, stands the extemporality of mind. Lifton and Olson call this the 'creative mode' of immortality:

> One may feel a sense of immortality in this mode through teaching, art-making, repairing, construction, writing, healing, inventing or through lasting influences of any kind on other human beings — influences that one feels can enter into a general human flow beyond the self. In professions like science or art that have a long heritage, one is frequently aware of the historical sources of one's work and the tradition that one's own contribution is maintaining. (Lifton and Olson, 1974: 77)

From Plato's immortal ideas to Husserl's de-historicized subjectivity, philosophers struggled to reforge the ongoing conversation of history-conscious creators into the timelessness of truth (it is not for nothing that men of intellect have been dubbed the 'aristocracy of spirit'). The discourse that spans distances impassable for the 'ordinary' men and women simultaneously separates its participants from the mortals; it sets testing conditions of entry which only the chosen (or self-chosen) few can hope to meet. It plays impeccably the role all viable survival policies are expected to play: it establishes survival as social relation, as a stratifying vehicle, as the principle of inclusion that draws its potency from its practice of exclusion.

The Postmodern Deconstruction of Immortality

None of the traditional ways of dabbling with timelessness (themselves timeless) have been abandoned under postmodern conditions. And yet they have been, so to speak, relegated to the second league of public attention, elbowed out by a new, specifically postmodern, strategy of survival. It differs from other strategies by being geared to a wide, nay universal, use. It also differs from other strategies in that it attempts to resolve the haunting issue of survival by doing its best to take it off the life agenda. Instead of trying (in vain) to colonize the future, it dissolves it in the present. It does not allow the finality of time to worry the living — by slicing time (all of it, exhaustively, without residue) into short-lived, evanescent episodes. It rehearses mortality, so to speak, by practicing it day by day. Daily life becomes a perpetual dress rehearsal for death.

What is being rehearsed in the first place, is the *ephemerality* and *evanescence* of things. As soon as they are acquired, the coveted and dreamed of possessions are discredited and devalued by 'new and improved', more prestigious versions; before they have time to enjoy their acquisitions, their owners are shamed into disliking and wishing to replace them. The urge to mobility prevents the development of strong affections for any of the places that serve as no more than temporary stations. Dramas do not outlive the pressing of a button; books last from one railway stop to another. Nothing is 'for life': skills, jobs, occupations, residences, marriage partners: they come and go, and they annoy or bore or embarrass when they stay too long. The main function of the news is to chase yesterday's news off and to be driven away by tomorrow's news. The centre of public vision is permanently overcrowded: those who make it to the centre appear from nowhere and fade into non-existence. Their short-lived, but each time intense, all-stops-pulled cults celebrate birth *ab nihilo*, the painlessness of disappearance, the wonder of evanescence, the beauty of the fleeting moment, the glory of transience. The cults proclaim longevity to be boredom and turn permanence into a word of ridicule. Today's cults make tomorrow's cults necessary: there is in operation, as Thielicke (1983:18) suggested, a 'centrifugal tendency of a continually enhanced dissipation'. Skin-deep fascinations and commitments, never given enough time or enough attention 'to stick', leave a vacuum beneath. This void must be filled 'with ever new imports from outside' (Lifton and Olson, 1974: 27). The game goes on. For all practical purposes it needs no more reinforcement from outside. It self-perpetuates.

Another rehearsed quality of things and events is their *inconsequentiality*. 'No strings attached' is the sought-after ideal and the measure of value. Events are kept strictly separate and their autonomy is closely guarded; they should not, they do not affect the events of tomorrow and the deeds committed next door. Episodes may be stopped in the middle of action, started again, watched once more in slow motion. They are what they are: episodes, occurrences with no history and no follow-up, one-off happenings. Skills acquired today are useful for today and do not secure the skills called for by tomorrow's challenges. Enjoyment does not lend itself to moral scrutiny and does not impeach moral conscience. Sex does not result in social duty; preferably, not in emotional attachment either. Life is not a novel with a plot and a denouement; it is instead a railway station bookstand filled to overflowing with the latest bestsellers.

With transience and ephemerality reforged into daily practice, glorified and ritualistically celebrated, the strategy of survival comes full circle. It is now immortality, not mortality, which is deconstructed; but deconstructed in such a way as to show that the permanent is nothing but the sequence of evanescences, that time is nothing but a succession of episodes without consequence and immortality is nothing but a simple aggregate of mortal beings. Deconstructed, immortality reveals mortality as its only secret. Mortality need not be deconstructed: it ought to be lived. Consumer bliss is the final, long solicited and expected, yet slow to come, stage of secularization. Now, truly, *everything* is in human hands. But the meaning of 'everything' has changed.

Like many other policies of survival, the postmodern strategy has a stratifying potency. The richness, volume and fast pace of the impressions in which it aims to dissolve mortality do not come to all in the same measure. They rather set apart those who can reasonably hope for free access from those who have little chance of passing the entry gate. Access and non-access are not separate conditions; they depend on each other in what is a zero sum game of freedom. 'The cruel irony of history', writes Kenneth L. Vaux, 'is that as man learns how to increase human well-being through science, the number of persons who profit from these gifts is fewer and fewer'. He also offers an insight into what may be the cause of this irony: 'Reducing deaths from sudden causes like accidents and infections necessitates endurance of more costly deaths. While sudden coronary or cerebral death may be a blessing in terms of expense, cancer and the other degenerative disorders often devastate one's personal finances' (Vaux, 1978: 48, 43). If the plausibility of the postmodern deconstruction of immortality has been grounded in the promise of a richer and longer enjoyment of mortal life, this plausibility is unevenly distributed. It polarizes rather than unites the proposed practitioners of the new survival strategy. 'There is a tendency', writes Nicholas Garnham (1982: 289), 'towards a two-tier market structure in which choice, being increasingly expensive, is offered to upper-income groups — while an increasingly impoverished, homogenized service is offered to the rest'.[12] The offer is extended to a fairly large chunk of the population; but in every case it remains an offer to *contract out* 'from the rest' (on freedom as a social relation and stratifying factor see Bauman, 1987: Ch. 3). The condition of survival postmodern-style is refusal of solidarity. When translated into life policy, deconstruction of immortality results in deconstruction of sociality.

From the point of view of the social construction of survival (as in so many other respects) postmodernity is a two-tier habitat: deconstruction of immortality is reserved for the top layer, with the old quandary of coping with the horrors of mortality remaining the fate of the bottom tier; but this is a fate they must now bear alone, on their own, with the resources 'contracted out' together with their owners.

Notes

1. According to Becker (1973), the essential incongruity of the human predicament makes human existence irreparably *heroic*: an incessant struggle to transcend what in principle cannot be transcended. 'The fact is that this is what society is and always has been: a symbolic action system, a structure of statuses and roles, customs and rules of behaviour, designed to serve as a vehicle for earthly heroism' (1973: 4). 'But the truth about the need for heroism is not easy for anyone to admit'; in most men heroics

is disguised as they humbly and complainingly follow out the roles that society provides for their heroics and try to earn their promotions within the system: wearing the standard uniforms — but allowing themselves to stick out, but ever so little and so safely, with a little ribbon or a red boutonnière, but not with head and shoulders. (1973: 6)

Within society,

man cuts out for himself a manageable world . . . He accepts the cultural programming that turns his nose where he is supposed to look . . . He learns not to expose himself, not to stand out; he learns to embed himself in other-power, both of concrete persons and of things and cultural commands; the result is that he comes to exist in the imagined infallibility of the world around him. He doesn't have to have fears when his feet are solidly mired and his life mapped out in a ready-made maze. (1973: 23)

The shared understanding of death which we owe to the string of modern philosophers and novelists from Kierkegaard through Tolstoy and Nietzsche to Sartre, has been usefully summarized by Peter Koestenbaum (1976: 7):

Death is not an experience but either a felt anticipation or a sorrowful loss. In any event, death is an influential self-concept. And it is this certainty about our eventual death and that of all other human beings that is the key to understanding our human nature . . . Death — our own and that of others — explains what it means to be human (searching for meaning, immortality, freedom, love, and individuality) far better than psychological principles of sex and aggression, the biological instincts of survival and procreation, the utilitarian theories of happiness and approbation, or the religious ukase of God's will. *The anticipation of our death reveals to us who we are.*

2. Zilboorg, like Becker or Norman O. Brown, belongs to the branch of the psychoanalytic movement bent on correcting Freud's simplistic 'sexual reductionism' and pointing to the work of Otto Rank as its major source of inspiration.
3. The immortality of Borges's Immortals was *received* (through drinking from the river of immortality) — and they knew it. James P. Carse (1980: 9), suggests that 'death, perceived as discontinuity, is not that which robs life of its meaning, but that which makes life's meaningfulness possible'. I propose that there is a conjunction (indeed, a causal link) where Carse sees an alternative and an opposition. The perception of death makes life's meaningfulness possible — nay, unavoidable — precisely because it makes life first empty of meaning, and thus leaves it to the humans to conjure up any meaning that could fill the void.
4. It is plausible that it is precisely the suppressed presence of the true meaning of survival that adds to the already considerable difficulty we experience when addressing the dying.
5. Canetti goes on to suggest that the danger of the survivor has been if anything increasing, and reaching a totally new scale: thanks to the new technology of action and the new means the action can use,

a single individual can easily destroy a good part of mankind. To bring this about he can use technical means he does not understand; he can himself remain completely hidden; and he does not even have to run any personal risk in the process . . . Seen in retrospect, history appears innocent and almost comfortable. (1973: 544–5)

Against the looming danger, Canetti can draw little hope from past experience: 'Hitherto the only answer to man's passionate desire for survival has been a creative solitude which earns immortality for itself; and this, by definition, can be the solution only for a few' (1973: 545). Mortality, and its obtrusive companion, survival, are the twin keys to Canetti's (1985: 280) historiosophy: 'The efforts of individuals to ward off death gave rise to the monstrous structure of power. Countless deaths were demanded for the survival of one individual. The resulting confusion is known as history'. Indeed, for most of the time history has been written as a chronicle of survivors; as a record of the battles won by princes so that they could outlive, even if only for a time, their rivals for the survival, the hard core of all fame.

6. Brown undertook to correct Freud's concept of Oedipal *complex*, purifying it of the narrowly sexual content; or, rather, reversing the order of interpretation and representing the sexual aspects of the Oedipal crisis as derivatives, or manifestations, of an actively embraced *project*, aimed in the first place at mastery and control.

7. Dostoievsky (1979: 13) juxtaposes the religious solution to the conflict between freedom and dependency to that of the secular one, supported by modern science:

> making man dependent on any error in the social organization, the environmental doctrine reduces man to absolute impersonality, to a total emancipation from all personal moral duty, from all independence; reduces him to a state of the most miserable slavery that can be conceived.

8. Norbert Elias's (1985) 'loneliness of the dying' seems to be predictable outcome of the 'episodization' of death brought about by the self-care strategy. Rather than being a manifestation of the delicacy of civilized emotions, the sight of the dying is repulsive to our contemporaries in so far as it demonstrates the ultimate futility of the effort to substitute the 'problem of health' for the 'problem of life'. The loneliness of the dying — keeping them out of sight (and preferably, through entrusting them to the professionals, also out of mind) — is a fitting corollary of the loneliness of irreparably individual concerns with health and fitness of the body. Similarly, one doubts whether Elias does not mistake the self-pretence of our age for the truth of history, when suggesting that in 'less developed societies' 'the magic practices' meant to deal with death are more widespread than in our own (1985: 46), or when he implies that our scientific knowledge representing death as a regular natural process is 'capable of giving a sense of security' (1985: 77) — in contrast to 'fantasy-explanations' of the pre-modern age. One may think of the countless survival, death-exorcizing practices that fill the whole life of modern men and women; they may be sanctioned by contemporary experts as sound, but the way they are performed does not differ greatly from the compulsion of magical rites. One may as well observe that the 'security' offered by modern science scores a poor second to that promised by the beliefs modern sciences discredited and tried to root out.

9. For a fuller discussion of the relationship between the organization of expertise and the structure of life-world, see the chapter 'Privatization of Ambivalence' in my *Modernity and Ambivalence*, (Bauman, 1990).

10. Harold Perkin (1989: 378) observed that 'most professional expertise does not enjoy a natural scarcity, and its value has to be protected and raised'. Vying for the only truly scarce resource — the share of *public attention* devoted to their products — experts create their own professional institutions, pursuing a twin purpose of 'educating' the public so that it rises to the comprehension of the importance of their services, and closing off the already won share of public attention to potential competitors. Experts find themselves obliged

> to justify the highest status and rewards they can attain by the social necessity and efficiency they claim for the services they perform. That on occasion the

service is neither essential nor efficient is no obstacle to the principle. It only needs to be thought so by those providing and receiving it. Justification by service to the clients and society lies at the root of the professional social ideal. (1989: 360)

The authors of studies collected in *Information Technology Impact on the Way of Life* (EEC Conference on the Information Society held in Dublin 18–20 November 1981, edited by Liam Bannon et al., 1982) propose that in the case of information, an expert product fast rising in volume and importance, the absence of demand (of perception of need) is a rule, and thus competition for public attention becomes fiercer than ever before:

> with the majority of these products, supply comes before demand and the technical discussion on the characteristics of the products takes the place of any analysis of social demand. These technical arguments are twofold. On the one hand, since these new technical capabilities have appeared, it is necessary to utilize them so as not to be behind the times; on the other hand, their use allows one to do more, better and with less effort then before, and thus can only lead to greater happiness. (Victor Scardigli, François Plassard, Pierre-Alain Mercier, 'Information Society and Daily Life', in Bannon et al., 1982: 41)

We can comment that the success of the propaganda campaign depends not so much on convincing the prospective clients that the possession of the new product will increase their happiness, but on creating an atmosphere in which the non-possession, 'normal' and hardly anxiety-arousing before, is experienced as a nuisance and a threat and becomes intolerable: by new standards, the non-possession is tantamount to inadequacy and instils fear of failure. Gordon B. Thompson coined a useful term to set apart the majority of information technology products: *ethereal goods*. None of them has a use (and thus an exchange) value guaranteed in advance by the extant pattern of needs; the ethereal good 'has to win its consensus of value . . . The value of an ethereal good is a function of the attention given to that good by the society' ('Ethereal Goods: The Economic Atom of the Information Society' in Bannon et al., 1982: 88–9).

11. The dialectic of dependence and autonomy is inescapable, as 'we are invited to live our whole lives inside someone else's borrowed frames' (Hebdige, 1988: 152); the opposition inscribed in the mechanism of survival rebounds intellectually as 'the opposition between vertigo and ground which leaves us with that alternating sense of placeness and rootedness which is the very rhythm of modernity. The dilemma opened up with modernity will never be resolved. The rhythm will not stop' (1988: 244).

12. A.E. Cawkwell (1987: 2–3) has quoted a poignant rendition of the same problem by Jo Grimond: 'The new technology has not been used to make services cheaper and better for ordinary people. Big business, the better professional firms and such like have been able to contract out of deteriorating services. When I complained of the postal services to a fellow sufferer she replied: "Of course my husband's firm send anything urgent by motor-bicycle or telex." This is not an option open to most of us.'

References

Anderson, Ray S. (1986) *Theology, Death and Dying*. Oxford: Blackwell.

Bannon, Liam et al. (eds) (1982) *Information Technology Impact on the Way of Life*. Dublin: Tywoly Inter. Publ.

Baudrillard, Jean (1976) *L'échange symbolique et la mort*. Paris: Gallimard.

Bauman, Zygmunt (1987) *Freedom*. Milton Keynes: Open University Press.

Bauman, Zygmunt (1990) 'Privatization of Ambivalence', in *Modernity and Ambivalence*. Cambridge: Polity Press.

Becker, Ernest (1973) *The Denial of Death*. New York: Free Press.

Borges, Jorge Luis (1970) 'The Immortal', in Donald Yates and James E. Erby (eds) *Labyrinths: Selected Stories and Other Writings*. Harmondsworth: Penguin.

Brown, Norman O. (1959) *Life against Death: The Psychoanalytical Meaning of History*. New York: Viking Books.

Canetti, Elias (1973) *Crowds and Power*. Trans. by Carol Stewart, Harmondsworth: Penguin.

Canetti, Elias (1985) *The Human Province*. Trans. by Joachim Neugroschel, London: Andre Deutsch.

Carse, James P. (1980) *Death and Existence: A Conceptual History of Human Mortality*. New York: John Wiley and Sons.

Cawkwell, A.E. (ed.) (1987) *Evolution of an Information Society*. London: Aslib.

de Certeau, Michel (1984) *The Practice of Everyday Life*. Trans. by Steven F. Rendall, Berkeley: University of California Press.

Dostoievsky, F.M. (1979) *The Diary of a Writer*. Trans. by Boris Brasol, Salt Lake City: Peregrine Smith.

Elias, Norbert (1985) *The Loneliness of the Dying*. Trans. by Edmond Jephcott, Oxford: Blackwell.

Garnham, Nicholas (1982) 'The Information Society is also a Class Structure', in Liam Bannon et al. (eds) *Information Technology Impact on the Way of Life*. Dublin: Tywoly Inter. Publ.

Hebdige, Dick (1988) *Hiding in the Light*. London: Routledge.

Hick, John (1976) *Death and Eternal Life*. San Francisco: Harper and Row.

Hiley, David R. (1988) *Philosophy in Question; Essays on a Pyrrhonian Theme*. Chicago: University of Chicago Press.

Koestenbaum, Peter (1976) *Is there an Answer to Death?* Englewood Cliffs: Prentice Hall.

Lifton, Robert Jay and Eric Olson, (1974) *Living and Dying*. New York: Praeger.

Maffesoli, Michel (1988) *Les Temps de Tribus: Le declin de l'individualisme dans les sociétés de masse*. Paris: Meridiens Klincksieck. (English translation forthcoming, Sage Publications.)

Perkin, Harold (1989) *The Rise of Professional Society: England since 1888*. London: Routledge.

Rank, Otto (1932) *Modern Education: A Critique of its Fundamental Ideas*. New York: Knop.

Redner, Harry (1982) *In the Beginning was the Deed; Reflections on the Passage of Faust*. Berkeley: University of California Press.

Scardigli, Victor, François Plassard and Pierre-Alain Mercier (1982) 'Information Society in Daily Life', in Liam Bannon et al. (eds), *Information Technology Impact on the Way of Life*. Dublin: Tywoly Inter. Publ.

Thielicke, Herbert (1983) *Living with Death*. Grand Rapids: Eydermans.

Thompson, Gordon B. (1982) 'Ethereal Goods: The Economic Atom of the Information Society', in Liam Bannon et al. (eds) *Information Technology Impact on the Way of Life*. Dublin: Tywoly Inter. Publ.

Vaux, Kenneth L. (1978) *Will to Live — Will to Die*. Minneapolis: Augsburg Publ. House.

Zilboorg, G. (1970) 'Fear of Death', *Psychoanalytic Quarterly* 12: 465–75.

Zygmunt Bauman is Emeritus Professor of Sociology at Leeds University.

Thinking About Limits

Pierre Bourdieu

I

As a sociologist interested particularly in the sociology of education and of communication, it is difficult for me to give a lecture, on whatever topic, without asking myself certain questions: should I arrive with a paper that I have prepared in advance, that I have already given in different surroundings? The lecture is essentially a repetitive product. I dislike giving omnibus lectures which will do for all countries, from Vladivostok to San Diego. But how can one respond to the elementary imperatives of successful communication, or at least ensure that it is less dismal than usual?

In antiquity, the Sophists, whose portrait Plato drew in unsparing fashion, were in a situation analogous to mine. They would arrive in a town where they were unknown yet familiar. They would have been preceded by a great uproar: there was publicity. There were impresarios who would say, 'Empedocles is going to be at my house. It is very important. He has some extraordinary things to say.' On these occasions, the great Sophists would make, what they called, an 'epideixis'. We can translate that as 'exhibition'. They put on a show. They would write ceremonial texts, spectacle-texts, extremely condensed and worked over, a sort of compendium in which they put all of their thinking.

A situation like that, where one is going to make an extraordinary communication, as Max Weber put it, absolutely outside the routine, is a situation of a prophetic type. The prophet, an extraordinary person who appears and then disappears, belongs to discontinuity, which is a part of what it is to be prophetic. The prophet will always leave. This is the difference between the prophet and the priest, or between the 'auctor' and the 'lector': the 'auctor' is extraordinary, intermittent, non-repetitive. How, then, are we

Theory, Culture & Society (SAGE, London, Newbury Park and New Delhi), Vol. 9 (1992), 37–49

to avoid the temptation to the extraordinary, to the *show*, to the intellectual *happening*?

It seems to me that what was justified in the 'epideixis', at least if one wants to locate it in the order of rationality and not of magic, was the intention to offer a global idea. It makes the lecture more compelling, and it allows for other reading. This kind of initiation is not simply a resumé, it gains from being made by the author him or herself.

So, one cannot be satisfied with the lecture pure and simple. The *lecture* is whatever one reads. So, what is the point? Very often I say to myself, 'I am asked to give a lecture at the University at San Diego, why couldn't I send a cassette? A cassette and an actor to make gestures during the delivery of the discourse . . .' So that the *lecture* should not be a *reading*, one must try to be something of an 'auctor' and treat the subject in a way that is particular to the situation.

II

When we think about communication, on what it is to read a text or listen to a speech, we are led to things which are so simple that everyone agrees about them: that the understanding of a text by Erasmus, one of Habermas's courses or the presentation that I am currently giving, has all the more chance of being adequate the more the categories which are used to structure the discourse are closer to the categories which are used to decipher it. The ground of a theory of decipherment adequate to a philosophical or literary text is a *double historicization*. In order to escape history, paradoxically, there is no other way than to historicize. Historicization, which apparently relativizes, is a way of avoiding relativity.

It is evident that the structures of thought that I am going to put to work in my discourse, the oppositions that I use, are historically constituted. The categories of thought through which you are going to listen to what I say to you are also situated and datable. One of the ways of mastering communication is to make conscious, for those who speak and those who receive, the categories of emission and reception. It is already an important contribution to all communication, especially to pedagogic communication, to say, 'Bear in mind that what you say involves categories and structures of thought, and that you should work to improve your comprehension of such categories, in whose name you are going to understand, or at least think that you do.' Against incomprehension, there are some simple defences. You can say, 'Please repeat that, will you put it another way.' But against false comprehension, illusory comprehension, there is nothing to be done.

I will try, following this, to make explicit a few principles of behaviour which I have followed in my research work, and which may not be obvious. I will try to emphasize those which seem to me to be of the kind that we do not share already, and so to pose some problems. What I say is closely related to the fact that I am saying it in an unfamiliar country. I think that we are all provincials, enclosed in particular intellectual traditions, and that we are all threatened by a form of intellectual ethnocentrism. Perhaps it is because the systems of concepts and rankings through which we organize reality are in part the product of scholastic traditions. If one wanted to advance a modern version of the theory of national character — which has gone completely out of fashion, although we encounter national differences in everyday life without knowing how to specify or analyse them — it would begin, for me, with a theory of the educational systems in as much as they are formative of the structures of understanding, and constructive of our taxonomies.

There is a celebrated article, one of the finest texts of the sociological literature, by Durkheim and Mauss, 'The Primitive Forms of Classification', where they anticipate the most modern developments of structuralism, and where they show that, in the thinking of archaic societies, one finds dualisms and oppositions — hot/cold, east/west, dry/wet — and that these oppositions, these basic dichotomies organize every thought and all practice. These oppositions are applied to everything, in order to consider the opposition between the sun and the moon, the toad and the frog and even, but already more difficult, between wheat and barley. Our own intellectual apparatus, believing itself free from all constraint, is full of oppositions of this type, neither more nor less deep. When you say 'quantitative sociology/qualitative sociology', you are not far from 'masculine/feminine'.

To put this another way, in each epoch there are oppositions of this type in the heads of both thinkers and listeners. They function as the most absolute system of censure, since they are, as with the Kantian categories, the things which structure what is thought, and therefore they are themselves extremely difficult to think. But, I think that one of the fundamental tasks of social science, if it is not to be stupidly positivist, is to think the structures of thought of the thinker. For example, if the state is so difficult to think, it is because we are the state's thinkers, and because the state is in the head of the thinkers. Put like that, this has the feel of a phrase that still floats too much in the air, but one can see for example in Durkheim's texts all that his thinking on the state owed to the fact that he was a functionary of the state.

Therefore, we are constantly threatened by this intellectual ethnocentrism which consists in allowing categories of historically constituted thought, which are often related to the education we have received, to think in our place. The educational system is a great producer of taxonomies. This is why I like to say, to irritate my colleagues, that the worst obstacle to the development of scientific thought is the teaching of the professors, who, when they should be teaching things openly, in a supple, elastic and multiple way, spend their time making dichotomies and classifications. There we have one of the antinomies of thought: if we are not educated, we cannot think much at all, yet if we are educated we risk being dominated by ready-made thoughts. The professor is simultaneously someone very dangerous and indispensable, someone we cannot do without, and someone of whom we must be extremely distrustful. This is my message to the young. I say it laughingly, but I think it is very serious.

The main thing that I want to get across is this: sociology, which is described — with just reason — as revealing to people the things which determine them, this sociology is a formidable instrument of freedom when it is applied to the sociologists' own thought. It is often said of *my* sociology that it is deterministic: perhaps because it is more precise than others, and because it is interested in the determinisms that are ordinarily forgotten, in the specific determinisms which weigh heavily on the thought of the thinkers. Because they regard themselves as especially free, they are especially irritated by a sociologist who discovers that they are especially determined. The famous relativist circle, that the sociologist produces with a particular force, reminding us that nothing can be thought unless through instruments of thought which are socially constituted, is, in relation to these instruments of constraint, an instrument of extraordinary freedom. First, it draws our attention to the very existence of these constraints, and that already provides for the possibility of freedom; and second, it provides the means to objectify these constraints, and in objectifying them, to control them to a certain extent.

III

What I now very quickly want to address is the epistemological tradition in which I have begun to work. This was for me like the air that we breathe, which is to say that it went unnoticed. It is a very local tradition tied to a number of French names: Koyré, Bachelard, Canguilhem and, if we go back a little, to Duhem. One should study the historical reasons for its existence, since it was not at all a national miracle, but no doubt related to favourable conditions within the structure of the education system. This historical tradition of epistemology very strongly linked reflection on science with the history of science. Differently from the neo-positivist Anglo-Saxon tradition, it was from the history of science that it isolated the principles of knowledge of scientific thought.

That thinking on science is very easily transferable from the sciences of nature, out of which it was constituted, to the human sciences. Additionally, that is easier to do within the French tradition than in the German tradition, where one of the main obstacles to that transfer was constituted by the opposition 'Erklären-Verstehen' (explanation–understanding) which is an ideological opposition. In Fritz Ringer's (1969) excellent book, *The German Mandarins*, which is a sort of psychoanalysis of the European intellectual unconscious, it is shown how the opposition between explanation and understanding had ideological functions in order to defend the identity of the humanities against the rise of the natural sciences. This was a defence of intuition against more rigorous forms, against mathematization and formalization. This is the example par excellence of a historical opposition which later becomes a category of unconscious thought, which organizes the commentaries that journalists write about books, or which transforms itself into the subject of dissertations. This particular opposition is a very great obstacle to the unification of epistemology, since it gives rise to the problem of 'unified science' and to the 'particularity' of the human sciences.

IV

The French tradition proposes, then, a reflection which is much more general, from which I have drawn an epistemological programme which can be summed up in one statement: 'The scientific fact is conquered, constructed, confirmed' (see Bourdieu and Chamboredon, 1991). The *conquest* of the given is a central concept in Bachelard's thought, and he sums it up in the term, 'epistemological break'. Why is this phase of scientific research important, and why does it separate, as seems to me to be the case, the tradition that I represent from the dominant Anglo-Saxon tradition? It is because to say that the scientific fact has to be fought for is radically to defy, in this regard, all of the 'givens' that social scientific researchers find before them. Researchers in the social sciences have, within arms' reach, just at their fingertips, preconstructed facts which are wholly fabricated: so many terms, so many subjects. At conferences, you can listen to these preconstructed concepts being exchanged, dressed up in theoretical tinsel, and having the air of scientific facts. This is currently how subjects and their limits are defined; the preconstructed appears to be everywhere. If we take the lists of thesis and dissertation subjects, I think that 80 per cent of their subjects are realities which lie ready-made in reality. So, I have devoted half of a course at the Collège de France to the notion of *profession*. This simple word, in my opinion, has thrown a good part of American sociology into complete disorder. It is a catastrophic notion, which presents an obstacle to the real construction of a great many subjects, a notion overloaded with ideological baggage. One of the functions of this notion has been to allow sociologists to think of themselves as 'professional' (with a concomitant concern for their own social identity, and their separate deontological demands, etc.). In a more general way, social problems have tended to be converted too quickly into sociological problems. A 'social problem' (juvenile delinquency, drugs, AIDS), constituted as such by the fact that it is hotly disputed and fought over, passes lock, stock and barrel into science. Social problems draw attention to critical sociological questions, but they must be approached with a redoubled epistemological vigilance, with a very sharp realization that they must be demolished in order to be reconstructed.

Let me take another example. Very often the positivist epistemological tradition attempts to escape from the problem I pose by means of the notorious *operational definition*. Imagine constructing a research programme into European intellectuals. How are you going to choose your sample? Everyone knows how to construct a sample. It's no big deal, and can be learnt in any course on methodology: drawing white balls or black balls, anyone can do the job. But how do you construct the box that the balls are in? Nobody asks that. Do I just say, 'I call "intellectual" all those who say that they are "intellectuals"?' How do we construct the limits?

The subjects, the concepts, the words themselves that we use to speak about the social are, then, socially preconstructed, socially constituted. It is an extremely trivial thing, quickly said but as quickly forgotten. The word *role* for example, a word which I have never used, is a terrible word. It is a condensation of an entire philosophy of the social world, which one should at least be conscious of when taking it on. Faced with such philosophically charged words, there are several solutions. Bachelard has an extremely fine expression: 'science is a pair of inverted commas'. When we come to the use of of learned terms, we should recognize that scholarly formulations are themselves often located within a tradition. When the term 'habitus' is used, one can be unaware and not know that one inscribes oneself within a whole philosophical tradition.

I said, 'Facts are conquered, constructed and confirmed'. In saying that, I designate three states of an epistemological approach to things which in the practice of research are clearly simultaneous. But to say that facts are 'conquered' is to say — and this is the only point on which I will be Cartesian in this *Maison Descartes* — that we should practice radical doubt. That sounds ridiculous, antiquated, scholastic . . .

Sociologists, especially positivists, who are so hard to please in matters of empirical proof, are negligent, uncaring and incredibly lax when it comes to questions of epistemology. When it comes to coding data, for example, they employ the most naïve systems of classification. In *Homo Academicus*, I fastened on certain celebrated taxonomies, used by sociologists of education to classify professors in various ways, which are disquieting. Afterwards, there are some very clever exercises on the computer. But what is put into the computer is the pre-thought, ready to think with just a few alterations. So I insist on this phase, perhaps especially in this country where I guess that the positivist tradition is very strong — I hope I am mistaken.

V

Next, the scientific fact is *constructed*. In my view, this is the decisive moment of scientific practice, the moment of maximum vigilance. It is the moment of the construction of the object. Ordinarily, we speak of 'choosing a subject'. There are all sorts of books, a whole Anglo-Saxon literature on 'How to do a thesis', 'How to choose a subject'. In actual fact, the construction of the object is the fundamental operation. For example, when I wanted to study the institutions of higher education, there existed a whole series of monographs, in French and other languages, which bore upon the Grands Écoles. I think that these objects had only been taken because they had offered themselves under the form of already prepared statistics and preselected documents.

My alternative hypothesis was that the truth of what happens in these little enclaves, which is what the Grands Écoles are, the truth of these small universes is in their relation with the other universes, in the structure of the relations between the universes. The truth of each of these small preconstructed objects, of this given which offers itself, is in the relation with a whole ensemble of preconstructed objects which does not give itself at all, which is hidden from indigenous perception, and even from learned enquiry. I could, then, have done a beautiful piece of traditional empirical research on the École Normale Supérieure or the École des Hautes Études Commerciales. But in this case I would, at bottom, have studied something cut out in such a way that, the lines having been inscribed, what was essential would have remained outside. So, at risk of conforming less to the positivist methodology, at the risk of having a heap of problems of comparability, I had to work more broadly.

When you are within the preconstructed, reality offers itself to you. The given gives itself, in the form of the notorious *data*.[1] This is one of the reasons that the given is so dangerous. Historians very often forget that data have been left by people who had an interest in letting them trail behind them. They forget that the people who constructed these givens invested them with their categories of unconscious construction. There are statistics from the sixteenth century, which are not interesting in themselves, but for the professional categories which are invested therein. Additionally, lots of things have been systematically destroyed, lots of things are secret. There is an advance in historical documentation every time that there is a revolution, because revolutions open the so-called personal archives, and let secrets jump out.

Thus the work of construction is difficult. Often, one has to be content with a small isolated subject; the logically valid construction of an object is not always attainable for a single researcher, or even for a group of them. Often, the very idea of construction is destroyed by the way in which information is offered. If you do research yourself, you will know that from your own experience. When someone says to you, at the end of an interview, 'Ah! I have a very interesting document for you', you should be on your guard. In general, important documents are very hard to get hold of. In contrast to that, *data* are things which are given to you.

VI

Now we come to the empirical phase: confirmation. In the linear process, 'conquering', 'constructing', 'confirming', I put this phase third as a sort of final term, but it is actually mixed with the others. Clearly, these constructed objects, and the system of hypotheses that allows their formation, must be constantly tested against reality and subjected to verification. This goes without saying. To construct an object is to construct a model, but not a formal model destined merely to turn in the void, rather a model intended to be matched against reality.

Here I would like quickly to bring something up about which none of us is clear. In his book on the Enlightenment, Cassirer clearly contrasts the Cartesian and Newtonian traditions. I think that this is still an opposition which can be seen in the division of scientific labour. According to Cassirer, the Cartesian tradition is a deductive tradition which always claims to move from the principles to the facts. The Newtonian tradition, however, is much more inductive, and sets out from the facts in order to construct models which are capable of providing a complete account of them. He recalls what the Cambridge School, at the time anti-Cartesian, called the 'morbus mathematicus'. That is exactly to the point: the mathematical malady. Kant said that mathematicians are dogmatic, that the model of mathematical thought was the ontological argument: you have a theoretical reality, and you think that it exists; since it is logically thinkable, it exists.

The approach I am proposing, where facts are 'conquered', 'constructed' and 'constated' is not at all of the deductive Cartesian type, which starts with a theoretical construction in order to move toward the facts. What is needed are means of constructing facts in such a way that models can be developed. This is systematically opposed to the kind of deductivism found in some forms of economics and, regrettably, some forms of sociology, in Chicago today for example. Sociological practice is more and more confounded with computer work, with exercises in game theory, which rest on the hypothesis that one can, by setting out from formal principles, deduce behaviours, groups of behaviours or the organizational forms of social reality. We do not, however, have to choose between these disastrous alternatives of theoretical formalism and a positivist hyper-empiricism drowned in data. What I have tried to propose is a sort of third way, which places the idea of construction, which is to say thinking about the ways in which the object is apprehended, at the very start. It is a construction which is self-validating, because it grasps reality. The antinomy between constructivism and realism does not exist.

VII

I have tried up to this point to bring out one of the basic principles of my way of doing research and of conceiving science. The sort of philosophy of science that I have tried to develop has, from the first, challenged the Germanic distinction between 'explanation' and 'understanding' which has been a kind of a priori Diktat according to which the human sciences are not the same kind of sciences as the rest. It is on the basis of that affirmation that I have been located within the positivist camp. I have tried to see how the particular can be treated scientifically, without assuming a priori limits, without instituting an extremely unscientific mode of questioning from the outset. This unscientific mode is a defensive system, established by certain philosophies of the person, which demands that there are things beyond science, in particular the 'person', 'creation', the 'creators', which is to say, in brief: the narcissistic ego of the intellectuals. My position is that everything is an object of science, and if there are particular difficulties, particular instruments must be found to overcome them. For me, there are no a priori frontiers.

This sort of nihilism which imposes a priori limits on science is always taking new forms, and the philosophers are there to say: 'Warning! Boundary line! Further passage is forbidden.' There is today, for example, a neo-nihilist current called postmodernism, which originated in France and which now also spreads in the United States. It is a sort of campus radicalism which depends on challenging the kinds of questions that I have formulated so as to deny the possibility of a social science. It is said, for example, 'All science is text, and what the anthropologists bring back with them from the field are texts; there are only ever texts on texts, metatexts: reality does not exist.' This means that young French ethnologists can produce 'brilliant' work without ever going through the considerable ordeal of actual field work. What is the point of field work if it is only going to result in a text? This is a French perversion.

Bachelard, who never developed the sociology implicit in his epistemology, emphasized that epistemology is not a matter of ahistorical reflection. One does not say the same thing in epistemology no matter what the time or place. One develops more or less this or that principle of epistemology according to the state of the epistemological unconscious in the given society. For example, in a society dominated by positivism, it is necessary to accentuate constructivism. To put this another way, epistemology is a politics of science. Gerschom Scholem, the great historian of Judaism, said to me one day, 'I never speak of Judaism in the same way when I am in New York, as when I am in Paris, or in Berlin, or in Jerusalem. Yet, I never lie.' This is also valid for epistemology.

The reflexivity which I recommend is not an end in itself. That is just a Parisian vice, or a form of radical chic. Inexperienced students will tend to postpone the moment of going into the field. They want first to 'develop their problematic'. So, we must push them a little to go into the field. This does not mean that they must not be reflective, but they have to go into the field *and* be reflective about it. Furthermore, there is a tendency to make epistemology, the critique of instruments of knowledge and criticism, an end in itself. For my part, I do not make use of it in order to cancel out science, but in order to make science still better. To put this another way, this sort of radical doubt is only a preamble to a more controlled science, a science more conscious of itself.

I would cite here one of Descartes' phrases: one of the tasks of philosophy is 'limites ingenii definire', to define the limits of the mind. Sociology has the particular characteristic that sociologists are apparently condemned to sociologism, to relativism. In fact, sociology has the extraordinary privilege of having an instrument of knowledge which can be applied to itself. But sociologists never do this, least of all the Marxists who continually use sociological knowledge to objectify and reduce their opponents, to look into their heads and say, 'You are only a . . .' Many people become sociologists in order to continue their politics by other means. We must draw attention to this; it is a sin of youth. Many technical errors in the construction of the object or of the sample are grounded in this desire, this 'libido dominandi' which disguises itself as 'libido sciendi'.

Many of the principles of positivist epistemology have no other function than to obstruct people who have ideas. They obey the logic of 'ressentiment', in the rigorous, Nietzschean sense of the term: not being capable of inventing ideas, I will make sure somehow that those that have them will be culpable for having them. Behind epistemological choices there are social forces. We all know that violence hides behind the most noble and pure *statements*. But with a more developed consciousness of the fact that the taking of epistemological positions always involves the position in the scientific field of those who take them, and the type of capital which it commands, we see that scientific strategies which are presented as absolute and universal choices are often little more than rationalizations of their own limits. This one is a mathematician and says that formalization is necessary; that one is a philosopher who says we must do phenomenology. All this amounts to saying, 'You must be like me', which means: mutilated. Many of the actual debates in social science are debates of this type. They are debates which are organized around people caught within their pre-established limits.

For example, the development of discourse analysis is related to the appearance of video. This is a technological development which heralds the possibility of recording discourse. And there are those, previously subordinated by others who demanded statistical data, who say, 'Now, we too have data, we have video'. There is now a heap of conferences where nothing but video is seen, and where every word pronounced is commented upon with a pointer. This is positivist positivity, where one kind of data is opposed to another. It becomes something like a war of religion. Many epistemological conflicts are wars of religion. What for me is disastrous, is that all these strategies are self-mutilating. People struggle against each other, but for their own satisfaction, to pander to their own limits. This is the epistemology of resentment.

So, when I say 'limites ingenii definire', I am saying that the limits of human understanding must be defined, not in universal terms, but in terms of their social constitution. At every moment, we are limited by social censorship. There are external censors, 'repressions', a term very much in vogue in the 1970s. Any scientific universe is full of instances of such censorship, which prevent certain things from being said. However, among the most rigorous censors, among those which are most difficult to get around, there are the internalized censors, the categories of thought which make a whole collection of things unthinkable, the categories of thought which determine that there is only black and white, and that grey areas do not exist. So, defining the limits of thought is not at all an exercise in pure speculation. There is nothing more practical. At every instant, enormous scientific errors, which are never exposed in the texts on methodology, are born out of this internal censorship. This thinking about limits is not in any way an end in itself, nor is it a 'spiritual supplement' as Bergson might have put it. Nor is it, to cite Marx, 'a spiritual point of honour', something extra just there to create a good impression. For me, it is something vital.

Translated by Roy Boyne

Notes

'Penser les limites' is the introduction to four Leçons de sociologie given in December 1989 at the Maison Descartes, Amsterdam. Edited from tape by Dick Pels and Rokus Hofstede.

1. Evidently, Bourdieu does not refer to the famous 'data' of American empiricism, but rather to those which appear in Durkheim's familiar phrase from the *Règles*: 'A thing is in effect all that is given, all that is offered, or rather forces itself upon our observation. To treat phenomena as things is to treat them as *data*, and this constitutes the starting point for science . . .' (cited in Bourdieu and Chamboredon (1991: 154)) (Editor's note).

References

Bourdieu, P. (1988) *Homo Academicus*. Stanford: Stanford University Press.
Bourdieu, P. and J.-C. Chamboredon (1991) *The Craft of Sociology: Epistemological Preliminaries*. Berlin and New York: de Gruyter.
Ringer, F.K. (1969) *The Decline of the German Mandarins: The German Academic Community 1890–1933*. Cambridge, MA: Harvard University Press.

Pierre Bourdieu is Professor of Sociology at the Collège de France, Paris.

THEORY CULTURE & SOCIETY

announces their

10th Anniversary Conference

'The Relationship Between Theory, Culture and Society'

16-19 August 1992

Seven Springs Mountain Resort, Pittsburgh,* USA

We would like to invite TCS readers and other interested parties to participate in the 10th Anniversary Conference of the journal's publication. The conference will feature a number of plenary sessions, panels, workshops and round tables focusing on the full range of interests covered in TCS.

For further information please contact:

Mike Featherstone, TCS, School of Health, Social & Policy Studies, Teesside Polytechnic, Middlesbrough, Cleveland, TS1 3BA, UK
Tel: 0642 342346/7   Fax: 0642 226822

Roland Robertson & Kate White, Department of Sociology, University Center for International Studies, University of Pittsburgh, Pittsburgh, PA 15260, USA
Tel: 412 648 7118   Fax: 412 648 2799

****

* The conference will take place just prior to the 1992 American Sociological Association Conference to be held in Pittsburgh. The venue is 1 hour from Pittsburgh.

The Uses and Abuses of French Discourse Theories for Feminist Politics

Nancy Fraser

This essay grows out of an experience of severe puzzlement. For several years now I have been watching with growing incomprehension as increasing numbers of feminist scholars have been trying to use or adapt the theory of Jacques Lacan for feminist purposes. I myself have felt a deep disaffinity with Lacan, a disaffinity as much intellectual as political. So while many of my fellow feminists have been using Lacanian ideas to theorize the discursive construction of subjectivity in film and literature, I have been relying on alternative models of language to develop a feminist social theory. Until now, I have avoided any explicit, metatheoretical discussion of these matters. I have explained neither to myself nor to my colleagues why it is that I have looked to the discourse models of writers like Foucault, Bourdieu, Bakhtin, Habermas and Gramsci instead of to those of Lacan, Kristeva, Saussure and Derrida.[1] In this essay, I want to begin to provide such an explanation. I will try to explain why I think feminists should have no truck with Lacan and why we should have only the most minimal truck with Julia Kristeva. I will also try to identify some places where I think we can find more satisfactory alternatives.

What Do Feminists Want in a Discourse Theory?

Let me begin by posing two questions: what might a theory of discourse contribute to feminism? And, what, therefore, do feminists want in a discourse theory? I suggest that a theory of discourse can help us understand at least four things, all of which are interrelated. First, it can help us understand how people's social identities are fashioned and altered over time. Second, it can help us understand how, under conditions of inequality, social groups in the sense of collective agents are formed and unformed. Third, a theory

Theory, Culture & Society (SAGE, London, Newbury Park and New Delhi), Vol. 9 (1992), 51–71

of discourse can illuminate how the cultural hegemony of dominant groups in society is secured and contested. Fourth and finally, it can shed light on the prospects for emancipatory social change and political practice. Let me elaborate.

First, consider the uses of a theory of discourse for understanding social identities. The basic idea here is that people's social identities are complexes of meanings, networks of interpretation. To have a social identity, to be a woman or a man, for example, just *is* to live and to act under a set of descriptions. These descriptions, of course, are not simply secreted by people's bodies; still less are they exuded by people's psyches. Rather, they are drawn from the fund of interpretive possibilities available to agents in specific societies. It follows that in order to understand anyone's feminine or masculine gender identity, it does not suffice to study biology or psychology. Instead, one must study the historically specific social practices through which cultural descriptions of gender are produced and circulated.[2]

Moreover, social identities are exceedingly complex. They are knit from a plurality of different descriptions arising from a plurality of different signifying practices. Thus, no one is simply a woman; one is rather, for example, a white, Jewish, middle-class woman, a philosopher, a lesbian, a socialist and a mother (see Spelman, 1988). Moreover, since everyone acts in a plurality of social contexts, the different descriptions comprising any individual's social identity fade in and out of focus. Thus, one is not always a woman in the same degree; in some contexts, one's womanhood figures centrally in the set of descriptions under which one acts; in others, it is peripheral or latent (see Riley, 1988). Finally, it is not the case that people's social identities are constructed once and for all and definitively fixed. Rather, they alter over time, shifting with shifts in agents' practices and affiliations. Thus, even the *way* in which one is a woman will shift, as it does, to take a dramatic example, when one becomes a feminist. In short, social identities are discursively constructed in historically specific social contexts; they are complex and plural; and they shift over time. One use of a theory of discourse for feminist politics, then, is in understanding social identities in their full socio-cultural complexity, thus demystifying static, single variable, essentialist views of gender identity.

A second use of a theory of discourse for feminist politics is in understanding the formation of social groups. How does it happen, under conditions of inequality, that people come together, arrange themselves under the banner of *collective* identities, and constitute themselves as collective social agents? How do class formation and, by analogy, gender formation occur?

Clearly, group formation involves shifts in people's social identities and therefore also in their relation to discourse. One thing that happens here is that pre-existing strands of identities acquire a new sort of salience and centrality. These strands, previously submerged among many others, are reinscribed as the nub of new self-definitions and affiliations (see Jenson, 1989). For example, in the current wave of feminist ferment, many of us who had previously been 'women' in some taken-for-granted way have now become 'women' in the very different sense of a discursively self-constituted political collectivity. In the process, we have remade entire regions of social discourse. We have invented new terms for describing social reality, for example, 'sexism', 'sexual harassment', 'marital, date and acquaintance rape', 'labor force sex-segregation', 'the double shift', and 'wife-battery'. We have also invented new language games such as consciousness-raising and new, institutionalized public spheres such as the Society for Women in Philosophy (see Fraser, 1989; Riley, 1988). The point is that the formation of social groups proceeds by struggles over social discourse. Thus, a theory of discourse is useful here, both for understanding social groups and for coming to grips with the closely related issue of socio-cultural hegemony.

'Hegemony' is the Italian Marxist Antonio Gramsci's (1972) term for the discursive face of power. It is the power to establish the 'common sense' or 'doxa' of a society, the fund of self-evident descriptions of social reality that normally go without saying. This includes the power to establish authoritative definitions of social situations and social needs, the power to define the universe of legitimate disagreement, and the power to shape the political agenda. Hegemony, then, expresses the advantaged position of dominant social groups with respect to discourse. It is a concept that allows us to recast the issues of social identity and social groups in the light of societal inequality. How do pervasive axes of dominance and subordination affect the production and circulation of social meanings? How does stratification along lines of gender, race and class affect the discursive construction of social identities and the formation of social groups?

The notion of hegemony points to the intersection of power,

inequality and discourse. However, it does not entail that the ensemble of descriptions that circulate in society comprise a monolithic and seamless web, nor that dominant groups exercise an absolute, top-down control of meaning. On the contrary, 'hegemony' designates a process wherein cultural authority is negotiated and contested. It presupposes that societies contain a plurality of discourses and discursive sites, a plurality of positions and perspectives from which to speak. Of course, not all of these have equal authority. Yet conflict and contestation are part of the story. Thus, one use of a theory of discourse for feminist politics is to shed light on the processes by which the socio-cultural hegemony of dominant groups is achieved and contested. What are the processes by which definitions and interpretations inimical to women's interests acquire cultural authority? What are the prospects for mobilizing counter-hegemonic feminist definitions and interpretations to create broad oppositional groups and alliances?

I trust that the link between these questions and emancipatory political practice is obvious. A theory of discourse that lets us examine identities, groups and hegemony in the ways I have been describing would be a great aid to feminist practice. It would valorize the empowering dimensions of discursive struggles without leading to 'culturalist' retreats from political engagement.[3] In addition, the right kind of theory would counter the disabling assumption that women are just passive victims of male dominance. That assumption over-totalizes male dominance, treating men as the only social agents and rendering inconceivable our own existence as feminist theorists and activists. In contrast, the sort of theory I have been proposing would help us understand how, even under conditions of subordination, women participate in the making of culture.

Jacques Lacan and the Limits of Structuralism
In light of the foregoing, what sort of theory of discourse will be useful for feminist politics? What sort of theory can best meet our needs to understand identities, groups, hegemony and emancipatory practice?

In recent years, two general models for theorizing language have emerged in France. The first of these is the structuralist model, which studies language as a symbolic system or code. This model is derived from Saussure, presupposed in Lacan, and abstractly negated but not entirely superseded in deconstruction and in related forms of French women's writing. The second model, by contrast, I shall call the pragmatic model; it studies language at the level of discourses, as historically specific social practices of communication. This model is operative in the work of Mikhail Bakhtin, Michel Foucault, Pierre Bourdieu and in some but not all dimensions of the work of Julia Kristeva and Luce Irigaray. In this section, I shall argue that the first, structuralist model is not very useful for feminist politics.

Let me begin by noting that there are good prima facie reasons for feminists to be suspicious of the structuralist model. This model constructs its object of study by abstracting from exactly what we need to focus on, namely, the social practice and social context of communication. Indeed, the abstraction from practice and context are among the founding gestures of Saussurean linguistics. Saussure began by splitting signification into 'langue', the symbolic system or code, and 'parole', speakers' uses of language in communicative practice or speech. He then made the first of these, 'langue', the proper object of the new science of linguistics, and relegated the second, 'parole', to the status of a devalued remainder.[4] At the same time, Saussure insisted that the study of 'langue' be synchronic rather than diachronic; he thereby posited his object of study as static and atemporal, abstracting it from historical change. Finally, the founder of structuralist linguistics posited that 'langue' was indeed a single system; he made its unity and systematicity consist in the putative fact that every signifier, every material, signifying element of the code, derives its meaning positionally by way of its difference from all of the others.

Together, these founding operations render the structuralist approach of doubtful utility for feminist politics.[5] Because it abstracts from 'parole', the structuralist model brackets questions of practice, agency and the speaking subject. Thus, it cannot shed light on social identity and group formation. Moreover, because this approach brackets the diachronic, it will not tell us anything about shifts in identities and affiliations over time. Similarly, because it abstracts from the social context of communication, the model brackets issues of power and inequality. Thus, it cannot illuminate the processes by which cultural hegemony is secured and contested. Finally, because the model theorizes the fund of available linguistic meanings as a single symbolic system, it lends itself to a monolithic view of signification that denies tensions and contradictions among social meanings. In short, by reducing discourse to a 'symbolic system', the structuralist model evacuates social agency, social conflict and social practice.[6]

Let me now try to illustrate these problems by means of a brief discussion of the work of Jacques Lacan. Or rather, let me illustrate these problems by reconstructing and criticizing an ideal-typical reading of Lacan that I believe is widespread among English-speaking feminists. In so doing, I shall bracket the question of the fidelity of this reading, which could be faulted for exaggerating the centrality of phallocentrism to Lacan's view of the symbolic order and for over-emphasizing the influence of Saussure at the expense of other, countervailing influences, such as Hegel.[7] For my purposes, this ideal-typical, Saussurean reading of Lacan is useful precisely because it evinces with unusual clarity difficulties that beset many 'poststructuralist' theorists whose abstract attempts to break free of structuralism only render them all the more bound to it.

At first sight, this ideal-typical reading of Lacan seems to have some advantages for feminist theorists. By conjoining the Freudian problematic of the construction of gendered subjectivity to the Saussurean model of structural linguistics, it seems to provide each with its needed corrective. The introduction of the Freudian problematic promises to supply the speaking subject that is missing in Saussure and thereby to reopen the excluded questions about identity, speech and social practice. Conversely, the use of the Saussurean model promises to remedy some of Freud's deficiencies. By insisting that gender identity is *discursively* constructed, Lacan appears to eliminate lingering vestiges of biologism in Freud, to treat gender as socio-cultural all the way down, and to render it in principle more open to change.

However, these apparent advantages vanish upon closer inspection. Instead, it becomes clear that Lacan's theory is viciously circular. On the one hand, it purports to describe the process by which individuals acquire gendered subjectivity through their painful conscription as young children into a pre-existing phallocentric symbolic order. Here the structure of the symbolic order determines the character of individual subjectivity. But on the other hand, and at the same time, the theory purports to show that the symbolic order must necessarily be phallocentric since the attainment of subjectivity requires submission to 'the Father's Law'. Here, then, the nature of individual subjectivity, as dictated by an autonomous psychology, determines the character of the symbolic order.

One result of this circularity is an ironclad determinism. As Dorothy Leland (1991) has noted, the theory casts the developments it describes as necessary, invariant and unalterable. Phallocentrism, woman's disadvantaged place in the symbolic order, the encoding of cultural authority as masculine, the impossibility of describing a non-phallic sexuality, in short, any number of trappings of male dominance now appear as invariable features of the human condition. Women's subordination, then, is inscribed as the inevitable destiny of civilization.

I can spot several spurious steps in this reasoning, some of which have their roots in the presupposition of the structuralist model. First, to the degree Lacan has succeeded in eliminating biologism, and that is dubious for reasons I cannot take up here,[8] he has replaced it with psychologism, the untenable view that autonomous psychological imperatives given independently of culture and history can dictate the way they are interpreted and acted on within culture and history. Lacan falls prey to psychologism when he claims that the phallocentricity of the symbolic order is required by the demands of an enculturation process that is itself independent of culture.[9]

If one half of Lacan's circular argument is vitiated by psychologism, then the other half is vitiated by what I should like to call 'symbolicism'. By symbolicism, I mean, first, the homogenizing reification of diverse signifying practices into a monolithic and all-pervasive 'symbolic order' and, second, the endowing of that order with an exclusive and unlimited causal power to fix people's subjectivities once and for all. Symbolicism, then, is an operation whereby the structuralist abstraction 'langue' is troped into a quasi-divinity, a normative 'symbolic order' whose power to shape identities dwarfs to the point of extinction that of mere historical institutions and practices.

Actually, as Deborah Cameron (1985) has noted, Lacan equivocates on the expression 'the symbolic order'. Sometimes he uses this expression relatively narrowly to refer to Saussurean 'langue', the structure of language as a system of signs. In this narrow usage, Lacan would be committed to the implausible view that the sign system itself determines individuals' subjectivities independently of the social context and social practice of its uses. At other times, by contrast, Lacan uses the expression 'the symbolic order' far more broadly to refer to an amalgam that includes not only linguistic structures, but also cultural traditions and kinship structures, the latter mistakenly equated with social structure in general.[10] Here he conflates the ahistorical structural abstraction 'langue' with variable historical phenomena like family forms and child-rearing practices; cultural representations of love and authority in art, literature and philosophy; the gender division of labor; forms of political organization and of other institutional sources of power and status. The result is a notion of 'the symbolic order' that essentializes and homogenizes contingent historical practices and traditions, erasing tensions, contradictions and possibilities for change. It is a notion, moreover, that is so broad that the claim that *it* determines the structure of subjectivity is an empty tautology.[11]

The combination of psychologism and symbolicism in Lacan results in a theory that is of little use for feminist politics. To be sure, this theory offers an account of the discursive construction of social identity. However, it is not an account that can make sense of the complexity and multiplicity of social identities, the ways they are woven from a plurality of discursive strands. Granted, Lacan stresses that the apparent unity and simplicity of ego identity is imaginary, that the subject is irreparably split both by language and drives. But this insistence on fracture does not lead to an appreciation of the diversity of the socio-cultural discursive practices from which identities are woven. It leads, rather, to a unitary view of the human condition as inherently tragic.

In fact, Lacan differentiates identities only in binary terms, along the single axis of having or lacking the phallus. Now, as Luce Irigaray[12] has shown, this phallic conception of sexual difference is not an adequate basis for understanding femininity — nor, I would add, masculinity. Still less, then, is it able to shed light on other dimensions of social identities, including ethnicity, color and social class. Nor could the theory be emended to incorporate these manifestly historical phenomena, given its postulation of an ahistorical, tension-free 'symbolic order' equated with kinship.[13]

Moreover, Lacan's account of identity construction cannot account for identity shifts over time. It is committed to the psychoanalytic proposition that gender identity (the only kind of identity it considers) is basically fixed once and for all with the resolution of the Oedipus complex. Lacan equates this resolution with the child's entry into a fixed, monolithic and all-powerful symbolic order. Thus, if anything, he actually increases the degree of identity fixity found in classical Freudian theory. It is true, as Jacqueline Rose (1982) points out, that the theory stresses that gender identity is always precarious, that its apparent unity and stability are always threatened by repressed libidinal drives. But this emphasis on precariousness is not an opening onto genuine historical thinking about shifts in people's social identities. On the contrary, it is an insistence on a permanent, ahistorical condition, since on Lacan's view the only alternative to fixed gender identity is psychosis.

If the Lacanian model cannot provide an account of social identity that is useful for feminist politics, then it is unlikely to help us understand group formation. For Lacan, affiliation falls under the rubric of the imaginary. To affiliate with others, then, to align oneself with others in a social movement, would be to fall prey to the illusions of the imaginary ego. It would be to deny loss and lack, to seek an impossible unification and fulfilment. Thus, from a Lacanian perspective, collective movements would by definition be vehicles of delusion; they could not even in principle be emancipatory.[14]

Moreover, insofar as group formation depends on linguistic innovation, it is untheorizable from a Lacanian perspective. Since Lacan posits a fixed, monolithic symbolic system and a speaker who is wholly subjected to it, it is inconceivable how there could ever be any linguistic innovation. Speaking subjects could only ever reproduce the existing symbolic order; they could not possibly alter it.

It follows that one cannot even pose the question of cultural hegemony. There can be no question about how the cultural authority of dominant groups in society is established and contested, no question of unequal negotiations between different social groups occupying different discursive positions. On the contrary, on the Lacanian view there is simply '*the* symbolic order', a single universe of discourse that is so systematic, so all-pervasive, so monolithic that one cannot even conceive of such things as alternative perspectives, multiple discursive sites, struggles over social meanings, contests between hegemonic and counter-hegemonic definitions of social situations, conflicts of interpretation of social needs. One cannot even conceive, really, of a plurality of different speakers.

With the way blocked to a political understanding of identities, groups and cultural hegemony, the way is also blocked to an understanding of political practice. For one thing, there is no conceivable agent of such practice. None of the three moments that comprise the Lacanian view of the person can qualify as a political agent. The speaking subject is simply a grammatical 'I' wholly subjected to the symbolic order; it can only and for ever reproduce that order. The Lacanian ego is an imaginary projection, deluded about its own stability and self-possession, hooked on an impossible desire for unity and self-completion; it therefore can only and for ever tilt at windmills. Finally, there is the ambiguous Lacanian unconscious, sometimes an ensemble of repressed libidinal drives, sometimes the face of language as Other, but never anything that could count as a social agent.

This discussion shows, I think, that there are many things wrong with Lacan. I have focused here on conceptual as opposed to empirical issues, and I have not directly addressed the question, is Lacan's theory true? With respect to *that* question, I will note only that Lacan himself was remarkably unconcerned with empirical confirmation and that recent research on the development of subjectivity in infants and young children does not support his views. It now appears that even at the earliest stages children are not passive, blank slates on which symbolic structures are inscribed but, rather, active participants in the interactions that construct their experience (see, for example, Beebe and Lachman, 1988).[15]

Be that as it may, in focusing here on Lacan's conceptual shortcomings, I have stressed those deficiencies that have their roots in the presupposition of the structuralist conception of language. Lacan seemed to want to get beyond structuralism by introducing the concept of the speaking subject. This in turn seemed to hold out the promise of a way of theorizing discursive practice. However, as I hope I have shown, these promises have remained unfulfilled. The speaking subject introduced by Lacan is not the agent of discursive practice. It is simply an effect of the symbolic order conjoined to some repressed libidinal drives. Thus, the introduction of the speaking subject has not succeeded in dereifying linguistic structure. On the contrary, a reified conception of language as system has colonized the speaking subject.

Julia Kristeva: Between Structuralism and Pragmatics

So far, I have been arguing that the structural model of language is not especially useful for feminist politics. Now I want to suggest that the pragmatic model is more promising. Indeed, there are good prima facie reasons for feminists to prefer a pragmatic approach to the study of language. Unlike the structuralist approach, the pragmatic view studies language as social practice in social context. This model takes discourses, not structures, as its object. Discourses are historically specific, socially situated, signifying practices. They are the communicative frames in which speakers interact by exchanging speech acts. Yet discourses are themselves set within social institutions and action contexts. Thus, the concept of a discourse links the study of language to the study of society.

The pragmatic model offers several potential advantages for feminist politics. First, it treats discourses as contingent, positing that they arise, alter and disappear over time. Thus, the model lends itself to historical contextualization; and it allows us to thematize change. Second, the pragmatic approach understands signification as action rather than as representation. It is concerned with how people 'do things with words'. Thus, the model allows us to see speaking subjects not simply as effects of structures and systems, but rather as socially situated agents. Third, the pragmatic model treats discourses in the plural. It starts from the assumption that there is a plurality of different discourses in society, therefore a plurality of communicative sites from which to speak. Because it posits that individuals assume different discursive positions as they move from one discursive frame to another, this model lends itself to a theorization of social identities as non-monolithic. Next, the pragmatic approach rejects the assumption that the totality of social meanings in circulation constitutes a single, coherent, self-reproducing 'symbolic system'. Instead, it allows for conflicts among social schemas of interpretation and among the agents who deploy them. Finally, because it links the study of discourses to the study of society, the pragmatic approach allows us to focus on power and inequality. In short, the pragmatic approach has many of the features we need in order to understand the complexity of social identities, the formation of social groups, the securing and contesting of cultural hegemony, and the possibility and actuality of political practice.

Let me illustrate the uses of the pragmatic model for feminist politics by considering the ambiguous case of Julia Kristeva. Kristeva's case is instructive in that she began her career as a critic of structuralism and a proponent of a pragmatic alternative. However, having fallen under Lacan's sway along the way, she has not managed to maintain a consistently pragmatic orientation. Instead, she has ended up producing a strange, hybrid theory, one that oscillates between structuralism and pragmatics. In what follows, I shall argue that the politically fruitful aspects of Kristeva's thought are linked to its pragmatic dimensions, while the political impasses she arrives at derive from structuralist lapses.

Kristeva's intention to break with structuralism is most clearly and succinctly announced in a brilliant 1973 paper called 'The System and the Speaking Subject' (Kristeva, 1986). Here she argues that, because it conceives language as a symbolic system, structuralist semiotics is necessarily incapable of understanding oppositional practice and change. To remedy these lacunae, she proposes a new approach oriented to 'signifying practices'. These she defines as norm-governed, but not necessarily all-powerfully constraining, and as situated in 'historically determined relations of production'. As a complement to this concept of signifying practices, Kristeva also proposes a new concept of the 'speaking subject'. This subject is socially and historically situated, to be sure, but it is not wholly subjected to the reigning social and discursive conventions. It is a subject, rather, who is capable of innovative practice.

In a few bold strokes, then, Kristeva rejects the exclusion of context, practice, agency and innovation; and she proposes a new model of discursive pragmatics. Her general idea is that speakers act in socially situated, norm-governed signifying practices. In so doing, they sometimes transgress the established norms in force. Transgressive practice gives rise to discursive innovations and these in turn may lead to actual change. Innovative practice may subsequently be normalized in the form of new or modified discursive norms, thereby 'renovating' signifying practices.[16]

The uses of this sort of approach for feminist politics should by now be apparent. Yet there are also some warning signs of possible problems. First, there is Kristeva's antinomian bent, her tendency, at least in this early quasi-Maoist phase of her career, to valorize transgression and innovation per se irrespective of content.[17] The flip side of this attitude is a penchant for inflecting norm-conforming practice as negative *tout court*, irrespective of the content of the norms. Obviously, this attitude is not particularly helpful for feminist politics, since such politics requires ethical distinctions between oppressive and emancipatory social norms.

A second potential problem here is Kristeva's aestheticizing bent, her association of valorized transgression with 'poetic practice'. Kristeva tends to treat avant-garde aesthetic production as the privileged site of innovation. By contrast, communicative practice in everyday life appears as conformism *simpliciter*. This tendency to enclave or regionalize innovative practice is not useful for feminist politics. We need to recognize and assess the emancipatory potential of oppositional practice *wherever* it appears — in bedrooms, on shopfloors, in the caucuses of the American Philosophical Association.

The third and most serious problem that I want to discuss is Kristeva's additive approach to theorizing. By this I mean her penchant for remedying theoretical problems by simply *adding* to deficient theories instead of by scrapping or overhauling them. This, I submit, is how she ends up handling certain features of structuralism; rather than eliminating certain structuralist notions altogether, she simply adds other, anti-structuralist notions alongside of them.

Kristeva's additive, dualistic style of theorizing is apparent in the way she analyzes and classifies signifying practices. She takes such practices to consist in varying proportions of two basic ingredients. One of these is 'the symbolic', a linguistic register keyed to the transmission of propositional content via the observance of grammatical and syntactical rules. The other is 'the semiotic', a register keyed to the expression of libidinal drives via intonation and rhythm and not bound by linguistic rules. The symbolic, then, is the axis of discursive practice that helps reproduce the social order by imposing linguistic conventions on anarchic desires. The semiotic, in contrast, expresses a material, bodily source of revolutionary negativity, the power to break through convention and initiate change. According to Kristeva, all signifying practices contain some measure of each of these two registers of language, but, with the signal exception of poetic practice, the symbolic register is always the dominant one.

In her later work, Kristeva provides a psychoanalytically-grounded gender subtext to her distinction between the symbolic and the semiotic. Following Lacan, she associates the symbolic with the paternal, and she describes it as a monolithically-phallocentric, rule-bound order to which subjects submit as the price of sociality when they resolve the Oedipal complex by accepting the Father's Law. But then Kristeva breaks with Lacan in insisting on the underlying persistence of a feminine, maternal element in all signifying practice. She associates the semiotic with the pre-Oedipal and the maternal, and she valorizes it as a point of resistance to paternally-coded cultural authority, a sort of oppositional feminine beach-head within discursive practice.

Now, this way of analyzing and classifying signifying practices may seem at first sight to have some potential utility for feminist politics. It seems to contest the Lacanian presumption that language is monolithically phallocentric and to identify a locus of feminist opposition to the dominance of masculine power. However, on closer inspection, this appearance of political usefulness turns out to be largely illusory. In fact, Kristeva's analysis of signifying practices betrays her best pragmatic intentions. The decomposition of such practices into symbolic and semiotic constituents does not lead beyond structuralism. The 'symbolic', after all, is a repetition of Lacan's reified, phallocentric symbolic order. And while the 'semiotic' is a force that momentarily disrupts that symbolic order, it does not constitute an alternative to it. On the contrary, as Judith Butler (1991) has shown, the contest between the two modes of signification is stacked in favor of the symbolic: the semiotic is by definition transitory and subordinate, always doomed in advance to reabsorption by the symbolic order. Moreover, and more fundamentally problematic, I think, is the fact that the semiotic is defined parasitically over against the symbolic as the latter's mirror image and abstract negation. Simply adding the two together, then, cannot and does not lead to pragmatics. Rather, it yields an amalgam of structure and anti-structure. Moreover, this amalgam is, in Hegel's phrase, a 'bad infinity', since it leaves us oscillating ceaselessly between a structuralist moment and an anti-structuralist moment without ever getting to anything else.

Thus, by resorting to an additive mode of theorizing, Kristeva surrenders her promising pragmatic notion of signifying practice to a quasi-Lacanian neo-structuralism. In the process, she ends up reproducing some of Lacan's most unfortunate errors. She, too, often lapses into symbolicism, treating the symbolic order as an all-powerful causal mechanism and conflating linguistic structure, kinship structure and social structure in general (see, for example, Kristeva, 1982). On the other hand, Kristeva sometimes does better than Lacan in appreciating the historical specificity and complexity of particular cultural traditions; much of her later work analyzes cultural representations of gender in such traditions. Even here, however, she often lapses into psychologism; for example, she mars her potentially very interesting studies of cultural representations of femininity and maternity in Christian theology and in Italian Renaissance painting by falling back on reductive schemes of interpretation that treat the historical material as reflexes of autonomous, ahistorical, psychological imperatives like 'castration anxiety' and 'feminine paranoia'.[18]

All told, then, Kristeva's theory of discourse surrenders many of the advantages of pragmatics for feminist politics. In the end, she loses the pragmatic stress on the contingency and historicity of discursive practices, their openness to possible change. Instead, she lapses into a quasi-structuralist emphasis on the recuperating power of a reified symbolic order and thereby surrenders the possibility of explaining change. Likewise, her theory loses the pragmatic stress on the plurality of discursive practices. Instead, it lapses into a quasi-structuralist homogenizing and binarizing orientation, one that distinguishes practices along the sole axis of proportion of semiotic to symbolic, feminine to masculine, and thereby surrenders the potential to understand complex identities. Next, Kristeva loses the pragmatic stress on social context. Instead, she lapses into a quasi-structuralist conflation of 'symbolic order' with social context and thereby surrenders the capacity to link discursive dominance to societal inequality. Finally, her theory loses the pragmatic stress on interaction and social conflict. Instead, as Andrea Nye (1987) has shown, it focuses almost exclusively on *intra*subjective tensions and thereby surrenders its ability to understand *inter*subjective phenomena, including affiliation, on the one hand, and struggle, on the other.[19]

This last point can be brought home by considering Kristeva's account of the speaking subject. Far from being useful for feminist politics, her view replicates many of the disabling features of Lacan's. Her subject, like his, is split into two halves, neither of which is a potential political agent. The subject of the symbolic is an over-socialized conformist, thoroughly subjected to symbolic conventions and norms. To be sure, its conformism is put 'on trial' by the rebellious, desiring ensemble of bodily-based drives associated with the semiotic. But, as before, the mere addition of an anti-structuralist force doesn't lead beyond structuralism. The semiotic 'subject' can't itself be an agent of feminist political practice for several reasons. First, it is located beneath, rather than within, culture and society; so it is unclear how its practice could be *political* practice (Butler, 1991, makes this point). Second, it is defined exclusively in terms of the transgression of social norms; thus, it cannot engage in the reconstructive moment of feminist politics, a moment essential to social transformation. Finally, it is defined in terms of the shattering of social identity, and so it cannot figure in the reconstruction of the new, politically constituted, *collective* identities and solidarities that are essential to feminist politics.

By definition, then, neither half of Kristeva's split subject can be a feminist political agent. Nor, I submit, can the two halves joined together. They tend rather simply to cancel one another out, one forever shattering the identitarian pretensions of the other, the second forever recuperating the first and reconstituting itself as before. The upshot is a paralyzing oscillation between identity and non-identity without any determinate practical issue. Here, then, is another instance of a 'bad infinity', an amalgam of structuralism and its abstract negation.

If there are no individual agents of emancipatory practice in Kristeva's universe, then there are no such collective agents either. This can be seen by examining one last instance of her additive pattern of thinking, namely, her treatment of the feminist movement itself. This topic is most directly addressed in an essay called 'Women's Time' for which Kristeva is best known in feminist circles (in Kristeva, 1986). Here, she identifies three 'generations' of feminist movements: first, an egalitarian, reform oriented, humanist feminism, aiming to secure women's full participation in the public sphere, a feminism best personified perhaps by Simone de Beauvoir; second, a culturally-oriented gynocentric feminism, aiming to foster the expression of a non-male-defined feminine sexual and symbolic specificity, a feminism represented by the proponents of 'écriture féminine' and 'parler femme'; and finally, Kristeva's own, self-proclaimed brand of feminism — in my view, actually post-feminism — a radically nominalist, anti-essentialist approach that stresses that 'women' don't exist and that collective identities are dangerous fictions.[20]

Now, I want to argue that, despite the explicitly tripartite character of this categorization, there is a deeper logic in Kristeva's thinking about feminism that conforms to her additive, dualistic pattern. For one thing, the first, egalitarian humanist moment of feminism drops out of the picture, since Kristeva falsely — and astoundingly — assumes its programme has already been achieved. Thus, there are really only two 'generations' of feminism she is concerned with. Next, despite her explicit criticisms of gynocentrism, there is a strand of her thought that implicitly partakes of it — I mean Kristeva's quasi-biologistic, essentializing identification of women's femininity with maternity. Maternity, for her, is the way that women, as opposed to men, touch base with the pre-Oedipal, semiotic residue. (Men do it by writing avant-garde poetry; women do it by having babies.) Here, Kristeva dehistoricizes and psychologizes motherhood, conflating conception, pregnancy, birthing, nursing and child-rearing, abstracting all of them from socio-political context, and erecting her own essentialist stereotype of femininity. But then she reverses herself and recoils from her construct, insisting that 'women' don't exist, that feminine identity is fictitious and that feminist movements therefore tend toward the religious and the proto-totalitarian. The overall pattern of Kristeva's thinking about feminism, then, is additive and dualistic: she ends up alternating essentialist gynocentric moments with anti-essentialist nominalistic moments, moments that consolidate an ahistorical, undifferentiated, maternal feminine gender identity with moments that repudiate women's identities altogether.

With respect to feminism, then, Kristeva leaves us oscillating between a regressive version of gynocentric-maternalist essentialism, on the one hand, and a post-feminist anti-essentialism, on the other. Neither of these is useful for feminist politics. In Denise Riley's terms, the first *overfeminizes* women by defining us maternally. The second, by contrast, *underfeminizes* us by insisting that 'women' don't exist and by dismissing the feminist movement as a proto-totalitarian fiction.[21] Simply putting the two together, moreover, does not overcome the limits of either. On the contrary, it constitutes another 'bad infinity' and so, another proof of the uselessness for feminist politics of an approach that merely conjoins an abstract negation of structuralism to a structuralist model left otherwise intact.

Conclusion

I hope the foregoing has provided a reasonably vivid and persuasive illustration of my most general point, namely, the superior utility for feminist politics of pragmatic over structuralist approaches to the study of language. Instead of reiterating the advantages of pragmatic theories, I shall close with one specific example of their uses for feminist politics.

As I argued, pragmatic theories insist on the social context and social practice of communication, and they study a plurality of historically changing discursive sites and practices. As a result, these theories offer us the possibility of thinking of social identities as complex, changing and discursively constructed. This in turn seems to me our best hope for avoiding some of Kristeva's diffi-culties. Complex, shifting, discursively constructed social identities provide an alternative to reified, essentialist conceptions of gender identity, on the one hand, and to simple negations and dispersals of identity, on the other. They thus permit us to navigate safely between the twin shoals of essentialism and nominalism, between reifying women's social identities under stereotypes of femininity, on the one hand, and dissolving them into sheer nullity and oblivion, on the other.[22] I am claiming, therefore, that with the help of a pragmatic theory of discourse we can accept the critique of essen-tialism without becoming post-feminists. This seems to me to be an invaluable help. For it will not be time to speak of post-feminism until we can legitimately speak of post-patriarchy.[23]

Notes

I am grateful for helpful comments and suggestions from Jonathan Arac, David Levin, Paul Mattick Jr, John McCumber, Diana T. Meyers and Eli Zaretsky.

1. I group these writers together not because all are Lacanians — clearly only Kristeva and Lacan himself are — but rather because, disclaimers notwithstanding, all continue the structuralist reduction of discourse to symbolic system. I shall develop this point later in this essay.

2. Thus, the fund of interpretive possibilities available to me, a late twentieth-century American, overlaps very little with that available to the thirteenth-century Chinese woman I may want to imagine as my sister. And yet in both cases, hers and mine, the interpretive possibilities are established in the medium of social discourse. It is in the medium of discourse that each of us encounters an inter-pretation of what it is to be a person, as well as a menu of possible descriptions specifying the particular sort of person each is to be.

3. For the critique of 'cultural feminism' as a retreat from political struggle, see Alice Echols (1983).

4. For a brilliant critique of this move, see Pierre Bourdieu (1977). Similar objec-tions are found in Julia Kristeva's 'The System and the Speaking Subject', in Kristeva (1986), to be discussed below, and in the Soviet Marxist critique of Russian formalism from which Kristeva's views derive.

5. I leave it to linguists to decide whether it is useful for other purposes.

6. These criticisms pertain to what may be called 'global' structuralisms, that is, approaches that treat the whole of language as a single symbolic system. They are not intended to rule out the potential utility of approaches that analyze structural relations in limited, socially situated, culturally and historically specific sub-languages or discourses. On the contrary, it is possible that approaches of this latter sort can be usefully articulated with the pragmatic model discussed below.

7. For an account of the tensions between the Hegelian and Saussurean dimen-sions of Lacan's thought, see Peter Dews (1987).

8. Lacan's claim to have overcome biologism rests on his insistence that the

phallus is not the penis. However, many feminist critics have shown that he fails to prevent the collapse of the symbolic signifier into the organ. The clearest indication of this failure is his claim, in 'The Meaning of the Phallus', that the phallus becomes the master signifier because of its 'turgidity', which suggests 'the transmission of vital flow' in copulation. See Jacques Lacan (1982).

9. A version of this argument is made by Dorothy Leland (1991).

10. For an account of the declining significance of kinship as a social structural component of modern capitalist societies, see Linda J. Nicholson (1986).

11. In fact, the main function of this broad usage seems to be ideological. For it is only by collapsing into a single category what is supposedly ahistorical and necessary and what is historical and contingent that Lacan can endow his claim about the inevitability of phallocentrism with a deceptive appearance of plausibility.

12. See 'The Blind Spot in an Old Dream of Symmetry' in Luce Irigaray (1985). Here Irigaray shows how the use of a phallic standard to conceptualize sexual difference casts woman negatively as 'lack'.

13. For a brilliant critical discussion of this issue as it emerges in relation to the version of feminist psychoanalysis developed in the US by Nancy Chodorow, see Elizabeth V. Spelman (1988).

14. Even Lacanian feminists have been known on occasion to engage in this sort of movement-baiting. It seems to me that, in her introductory chapter to *The Daughter's Seduction*, Jane Gallop (1982) comes perilously close to dismissing the politics of a feminist movement informed by ethical commitments as 'imaginary'.

15. I am grateful to Paul Mattick Jr for alerting me to this work.

16. 'Renovation' and 'renewal' are standard English translations of Kristeva's term, 'renouvellement'. Yet they lack some of the force of the French. Perhaps this explains why readers have not always noticed the change-making aspect of her account of transgression, why they have instead tended to treat is as pure negation with no positive consequences. For an example of this interpretation, see Judith Butler (1991).

17. This tendency fades in her later writings, where it is replaced by an equally undiscriminating, even shrill, neo-conservative emphasis on the 'totalitarian' dangers lurking in every attempt at uncontrolled innovation.

18. See Kristeva, 'Stabat Mater' in Julia Kristeva (1986) and 'Motherhood According to Giovanni Bellini' in Julia Kristeva (1980).

19. The present account of Kristeva's philosophy of language is much indebted to Andrea Nye's (1987) brilliant critical discussion.

20. I take the terms 'humanist feminism' and 'gynocentric feminism' from Iris Young (1985). I take the term 'nominalist feminism' from Linda Alcoff (1988).

21. For the terms 'underfeminization' and 'overfeminization' see Denise Riley (1988). For a useful discussion of Kristeva's neo-liberal equation of collective liberation movements with 'totalitarianism', see Ann Rosalind Jones (1984).

22. This point builds on work that Linda Nicholson and I did jointly and that she is continuing. See Nancy Fraser and Linda Nicholson (1988).

23. I borrow this line from Toril Moi (1987).

References

Alcoff, Linda (1988) 'Cultural Feminism versus Poststructuralism: The Identity Crisis in Feminist Theory', *Signs: Journal of Women in Culture and Society* 13(3): 405–36.

Beebe, Beatrice and Frank Lachman (1988) 'Mother–Infant Mutual Influence and Precursors of Psychic Structure', in Arnold Goldberg (ed.), *Frontiers in Self Psychology, Progress in Self Psychology* 3. Hillsdale, NJ: The Analytic Press.

Bourdieu, Pierre (1977) *Outline of a Theory of Practice*. Cambridge: Cambridge University Press.

Butler, Judith (1991) 'The Body Politics of Julia Kristeva', in Nancy Fraser and Sandra Bartky (eds), *Revaluing French Feminism: Critical Essays on Difference, Agency, and Culture*. Bloomington IN: Indiana University Press.

Cameron, Deborah (1985) *Feminism and Linguistic Theory*. New York: St Martin's Press.

Dews, Peter (1987) *Logics of Disintegration: Post-structuralist Thought and the Claims of Critical Theory*. London: Verso.

Echols, Alice (1983) 'The New Feminism of Yin and Yang', in Ann Snitow, Christine Stansell and Sharon Thompson (eds), *Powers of Desire: The Politics of Sexuality*. New York: Monthly Review Press.

Fraser, Nancy (1989) 'Struggle over Needs: Outline of a Socialist-feminist Critical Theory of Late-capitalist Political Culture', in Nancy Fraser, *Unruly Practices: Power, Discourse and Gender in Contemporary Social Theory*. Minneapolis: University of Minnesota Press.

Fraser, Nancy and Linda Nicholson (1988) 'Social Criticism without Philosophy: An Encounter between Feminism and Postmodernism', *Theory, Culture & Society* 5(2–3): 373–94.

Gallop, Jane (1982) *The Daughter's Seduction: Feminism and Psychoanalysis*. Ithaca, NY: Cornell University Press.

Gramsci, Antonio (1972) *Selections from the Prison Notebooks of Antonio Gramsci*, ed. and trans. by Quinton Hoare and Geoffrey Nowell Smith. New York: International Publishers.

Irigaray, Luce (1985) *Speculum of the Other Woman*, trans. Gillian C. Gill. Ithaca, NY: Cornell University Press.

Jenson, Jane (1989) 'Paradigms and Political Discourse: Labour and Social Policy in the USA and France before 1914', Working Paper Series, Center for European Studies, Harvard University.

Jones, Ann Rosalind (1984) 'Julia Kristeva on Femininity: The Limits of a Semiotic Politics', *Feminist Review* 18: 56–73.

Kristeva, Julia (1980) *Desire in Language: A Semiotic Approach to Art and Literature*, ed. Leon S. Roudiez, trans. Alice Jardine, Thomas Gora and Leon Roudiez. New York: Columbia University Press.

Kristeva, Julia (1982) *Powers of Horror: An Essay on Abjection*, trans. Leon S. Roudiez. New York: Columbia University Press.

Kristeva, Julia (1986) *The Kristeva Reader*, ed. Toril Moi. New York: Columbia University Press.

Lacan, Jacques (1982) 'The Meaning of the Phallus', in Juliet Mitchell and Jacqueline Rose (eds), *Feminine Sexuality: Jacques Lacan and the École Freudienne*. New York: W.W. Norton.

Leland, Dorothy (1991) 'Lacanian Psychoanalysis and French Feminism: Toward an Adequate Political Psychology', in Nancy Fraser and Sandra Bartky (eds), *Revaluing French Feminism: Critical Essays on Difference, Agency and Culture*. Bloomington, IN: Indiana University Press.

Moi, Toril (1987) Lecture at conference on 'Convergence in crisis: Narratives of the history of theory'. Duke University (September 24–27).

Nicholson, Linda J. (1986) *Gender and History: The Limits of Social Theory in the Age of the Family*. New York: Columbia University Press.

Nye, Andrea (1987) 'Woman Clothed with the Sun', *Signs: Journal of Women in Culture and Society* 12(4): 664–86.

Riley, Denise (1988) *'Am I that name?' Feminism and the Category of 'Women' in History*. Minneapolis: University of Minnesota Press.

Rose, Jacqueline (1982) 'Introduction − II', in Juliet Mitchell and Jacqueline Rose (eds), *Feminine Sexuality: Jacques Lacan and the École Freudienne*. New York: W.W. Norton.

Spelman, Elizabeth V. (1988) *Inessential Woman*. Boston: Beacon Press.

Young, Iris (1985) 'Humanism, Gynocentrism and Feminist Politics', *Hypatia* 3, published as a special issue of *Women's Studies International Forum* 8(3): 173–83.

Nancy Fraser teaches at Northwestern University. Her latest book is *Unruly Practices* (University of Minnesota Press).

On the Sociology of Intellectual Stagnation: The Late Twentieth Century in Perspective

Randall Collins

Studies of intellectual life have preferred to focus on periods of creativity. Yet we recognize what is creative only in relative perspective, by contrast to what is regarded as lacking in creativity. Comparison of the dark side against the light, and against the grey between, is necessary for seeing the structural conditions associated with all of the varieties of intellectual life. A second reason for studying stagnation is perhaps of greater immediate significance. There is no guarantee that we ourselves — denizens of the late twentieth century — inhabit a period of creativity. There is some likelihood that future intellectual historians looking back will concentrate on the great ideas of the first third of the twentieth century, and regard the rest as a falling off into mediocrity.

How does such a falling off occur? I suggest a sociological answer; not by examining ourselves directly through the partisan fog of the present, but by looking in a more distant mirror: the end of the Christian Middle Ages. This period was widely regarded as stagnant and uncreative. Yet when we come close up to it we find that intellectual life was certainly not dead. It was merely unable to gain any impetus outside narrow circles, and the strongest message that comes through more broadly was a disparagement of its own knowledge. Here again we see the self-consuming autocriticism characteristic of the 'postmodernism' of our own times.

Almost all subsequent periods regarded late medieval philosophy as a period of stagnation. The Renaissance, especially the Italian intellectuals of the late 1400s and 1500s, viewed the preceding period as barbaric and pointed to the universities of their own times as exemplars of its most decadent phase. By the late 1300s, scholastic thinkers themselves felt their own intellectual culture was dead. In 1402 Jean Gerson, the last important philosopher at the University

Theory, Culture & Society (SAGE, London, Newbury Park and New Delhi), Vol. 9 (1992), 73-96.

of Paris for over a hundred years, condemned the rationalist philosophy of his predecessors. Echoing both nominalist and fideist themes, he declared that intellectuals engaged in arbitrary and absurd speculation; they followed pagan philosophy instead of penitence, humility and faith; their over-estimation of Reason was the source of heresies, like those which proceeded from the realist Bradwardine to Wyclif and Hus. Gerson's contemporary Peter of Candia, who became Pope in 1409, observed the factional wars of his time as ones which no one could expect to have any resolution. He considered various opinions, not citing them as authorities for arguments in the manner of the scholastics, but with detachment like that of a twentieth-century intellectual who falls back from participation into historiography. This sounds not unlike the 'end of philosophy' themes and the disparagement of 'foundationalism' of late twentieth-century intellectuals. We find a disturbing reason to be interested in the social causes of intellectual stagnation: the suspicion that we might be in a similar situation today.

My analysis here is taken from a larger work: a comparative sociological study of intellectual communities over very long periods of world history (Collins, forthcoming).[1] The focus necessarily is not upon the details but upon the overall structure. The skeleton of intellectual life, for my purposes, is the network structure among the leading intellectuals themselves: their groups, chains of masters and pupils, their rivalries and oppositions; and surrounding this skeleton, the organizations which provide the material support for the existence of intellectual activity. If there are sociological conditions which are associated with both the ups and downs of creativity, they should be apparent at this level as well as in the content of intellectual productions themselves.

Three Kinds of Intellectual Stagnation
Stagnation is not a simple condition; there seem to be at least three kinds.

Stagnation (A): Loss of Cultural Capital
Ideas may simply be forgotten; later intellectuals are unable to do what earlier ones could. Aristotle's doctrine was lost for several centuries after his death; the achievements of Stoic logic were forgotten by late antiquity, Megarian logic even sooner. In China, the sophisticated positions of the late Warring States period, especially Mohist logic and its rivals, were largely eclipsed by the religious Confucian-

ism of the Han dynasty. In the late T'ang, the metaphysical subtleties of the Consciousness-only philosophy, as well as most other schools, were lost among the Buddhists. And to leave philosophy for an area in which technical criteria of puzzle-solving are especially clear, the breakthrough into generalized and explicit algebraic methods achieved during the Sung and Yuan dynasties (*c*. 1050–1300) was lost in the Ming (1366–1644), so that later mathematicians could no longer understand the earlier texts (Ho, 1985: 69–70; Qian, 1985: 106). The loss of ideas makes us think of a Dark Age, brought about by destruction of material conditions of civilizations, such as the decline of Rome in the West. But these examples show that idea-loss can also happen within prosperous periods of high civilizations; indeed the loss of Greek culture had started in Rome long before the barbarian conquests.

Stagnation (B): Dominance of the Classics

An opposite form of stagnation occurs when the ideas of the greatest thinkers overshadow their successors. There is no new creativity, which necessarily would displace the old. Such a period should not be labelled as having a low level of culture; one might say that it stays at the peak: the ideas that are taught and circulated are the best yet achieved. It is an irony of the intellectual world that we are not satisfied with this. We admire creativity, but when great creativity gets its rewards we soon regard it as stagnation. There are two sides of creativity, the energy of creation and the visions it produces; in the long run each undermines the other. Since creativity is driven by chains of eminence, some earlier figures are bound to be overshadowed by their successors. The greatest rewards tend to go to those who are last in a dense and competitively balanced chain. This is why Hegel could say 'the owl of Minerva spreads its wings only with the falling of dusk'. Stagnation as well as creativity is at the heart of the network structure of intellectual life.

Historical comparisons show there is nothing automatic about this enshrinement of the classics. In India, where ideology strongly favoured immutable wisdom from the past, there were long periods of change in both Buddhist and Hindu camps. Greek philosophy, too, tended more to forget earlier doctrines than to repeat them; when it thought it was reiterating Pythagoras or Plato often it was grafting new doctrines onto them. In China, the enshrinement of Confucius, Lao Tzu and the ancient divination texts nevertheless went along with periods when there was considerable innovation disguised as commentaries on these texts. There is a trade-off between Stagnation (A) and Stagnation (B) — more precisely, at least one way in which old cultural capital is lost is through creative reinterpretation of it (although there are more extreme forms of forgetting, and other versions of creativity). A civilization may have episodes of either kind of stagnation. In China, after Chu Hsi had formulated his grand synthesis around 1200, Ch'eng/Chu Neo-Confucianism acquired a stranglehold upon Chinese intellectual life for over 300 years; to put the matter is a different light, Chinese intellectuals could rest serenely in enjoying the great philosophy that already existed.

Late Christendom exemplifies Stagnation (B) more than Stagnation (A). The achievements of Thomas Aquinas and Duns Scotus towered over constructive philosophy, just as those of Ockham did on the critical side. The late medieval scholastics enshrined an extremely high level of creativity; yet its very solidity eventually provoked an attack from advocates of intellectual movement. The textbooks of the 1500s and 1600s, especially those of the Spanish and French universities of the Counter-Reformation, came to represent sterility in the eyes of Francis Bacon and Descartes. One could also say that the Renaissance, which coincides with this stagnant period of medieval philosophy, provides only a rival stagnation of the same type (B), in its adulation of the ancient classics.

Stagnation (C): Technical Refinement

A third type of stagnation may indeed be no stagnation at all, but only the appearance of such. Intellectual life does not stop in its tracks, but its very progress breeds not respect but alienation. A common claim about late medieval philosophy has been the field had become too technical, over-refined, spinning angels dancing in conceptual air. Duns Scotus was aptly called Doctor Subtilis, the subtle doctor. The Renaissance humanists were particularly put out by Duns's style: both his neologisms in metaphysics (certainly not known in the days of Cicero!) and the long tortuous sentences with clause after clause of careful qualification. This is more than emblematic of the time. The writing of a centrally located philosopher is a precipitate of the energies and concepts built up by the intellectual community. Duns's abstractions and distinctions, his complicated and rarified world-view, and his patient tenacious threads of argument are the embodiment of the conflicting factions of philosophers who had been realigning for three intense generations, and driving up the level of abstraction and subtlety at every step.

The Scotists did not stop in their tracks after the death of the masters; they continued to defend and elaborate, now attempting alliances with nominalists, sometimes making anti-nominalist coalitions by playing down their differences with the Thomists. But the excitement of a new synthesis did not appear. The nominalists, loosely designated, were often very creative, by the standards of twentieth-century analytical philosophy.[2] But they are now specialized in logic or other technical subjects. Their work provides no strong focus for the intellectual field, no vortices of emotional energy. The technical innovations do not propagate very widely; they are no challenge to the image of the overpowering masters, no visible alternative to Stagnation (B). And in time, because such creativity does not attract followers, it cannot reproduce itself; it dries up, and the situation begins indeed to approach Stagnation (A).[3] By the time of the Renaissance, beginning in the 1400s in circles far outside the university world which had sustained medieval intellectual life, there is genuine loss of ideas and ignorance of what medieval philosophy was about. Duns Scotus, the Subtle Doctor, is on his way to being caricatured as the 'Dunce', the stupid pupil forced to sit in the corner wearing a 'dunce's cap'.

Reversal of the External Conditions

How does stagnation happen? In principle, it should be the result of the obverse of conditions required for creativity. If intellectuals are allowed to form a community, they automatically tend to develop issues and divide the attention space among factions. Creativity is the energy that builds up as this process continues over several generations of personal contacts within the network. External conditions determine when such a network structure comes into existence and how long it will last. The crucial conditions for creativity are those which sustain *multiple bases of intellectual conflict across a primary focus of attention*. Creativity depends upon a centre, criss-crossed by material resources that can uphold opposing factions; a small number of centres linked by intermobility of their participants can provide this necessary intermeshing of focus and conflict.

As long as this structural shape continues to exist, external conditions may intervene by destroying, prohibiting or promoting a particular faction. This in itself does not damage the creativity of the whole network, as it may rearrange intellectual space and set the stage for new internal alignments. Upheavals in the external bases of factions, destructive as they may be for the people within them, are not a bad thing for intellectual life as a whole, provided that the overall structure still contains multiple factions and a common focus of attention. Surrounding social conflict, organization-building and destruction — the rise and fall of schools and states, of religious factions and orders of monks, of the Papacy or the Caliphate — will in fact promote creativity by causing the realignment of factions. Creativity comes to an end when external conditions eliminate either the bases for multiple factions or the common centre.

Let us briefly survey the overall structure of the intellectual world in the creative and non-creative periods across Greek, Chinese, Islamic and Christian philosophy.

Greece
In the pre-Socratic period, creativity is centred at first in a network of cities on the Ionian coast, with Miletos at the core. Then the network migrates to a number of colonies in southern Italy and Sicily, where the main institutional continuity is provided by the Pythagorean brotherhood. There is also dispersion around the Aegean, to Abdera in the north as well as the medical schools at Cos and Cnidus in the southeast. It is possible that creativity would have dissipated, but geopolitical events now provided a centre. The Persian conquest of Ionia and the Greek coalition and counter-attack fostered migration, as did the democratic revolutions and the upsurge of tyrants; refugees and ambassadors formed the milieu for a cosmopolitan intellectual network which came to centre on the imperialist power at Athens. The metropolis is just that: it is a centre of intellectual attraction, filled almost entirely with foreigners. Socrates and Plato are virtually the only Athenians among the important intellectuals of their city for hundreds of years: Aristotle, Diogenes, Epicurus, Zeno and others come from the remote provinces. It is similar to medieval Paris during its great thirteenth century, when there is scarcely a Frenchman among the leading masters.

For a couple of generations, Athens is flanked by peripheral nodes at Megara, Elis, Cyrene, Cyzicus and elsewhere; these are specialized homes of particular schools, and almost all connected to the networks of the centre. Originally independent schools such as those of Abdera, Lampsacus and Mytilene reach their zenith when they finally establish their school in Athens, like that which made the Epicureans famous. The centre provides a focus of attention and the opportunity for the meshing of networks; creativity is sustained when there are multiple bases for contending factions. Athens at its height was cross-cut by a variety of schools, anchored in external differences in political support, religious orientation and lifestyle radicalism. Shifts in these external bases provided the ultimate forces that drove internal realignments in carving up intellectual space.

In the Hellenistic period, the external bases narrowed. Most of the peripheral nodes dropped out; the rival schools now, by and large, are based only in Athens, displacing those with an independent centre of support. There is one other centre of intersecting circles: Alexandria absorbs the medical schools from Cos and Cnidus, as well as Peripatetics and Stoics from Athens. For a century there is a balanced situation of creativity between the rivals, down to the generation of Chrysippus or Carneades. With the growing hegemony of Rome and the political collapse of Athens, by around 100 BC the material bases provided by the Athenian schools had disappeared. Intellectual centres migrate away, to Pergamum, Rhodes, Naples; but each of these fosters a single school, not a cosmopolitan centre and none survives more than a generation or two. Alexandria still functions institutionally, but is too isolated to sustain much creativity. Philosophy becomes largely absorbed by the practice of rhetoric, an occupation of municipal lawyers and wandering speech-makers: a base which provides neither centralization nor insulation for intellectuals to pursue autonomous concerns.

The coming of Christianity and other popular religious movements further decentralizes the intellectual world. The Gnostic sects are small and organizationally dispersed; the Christian church is more hierarchical, but its bases are geographically far-flung and dependent on regional political fortunes. The most creative period is the balance of rivalry when Christians enter the philosophical schools at Alexandria, provoking the great pagan synthesis of Plotinus and his followers. But both Christian philosophers and Plotinine pagans migrate away to the centres of political patronage, respectively to Syria and to Rome, whence the networks soon further disperse. By late antiquity, Athens and Alexandria have become not centres of intersecting factions, but local strongholds of a particular faction; elsewhere there are religious intellectuals active at Constantinople, Pergamum, Antioch, Milan, Carthage. Centralization is lost first, leading to the defocusing of intellectual life, the general loss of abstraction and the predominance of particularistic theology and magic. Later, the material bases for multiple factions are drastically curtailed, with the general material decline of the Empire; accumulated cultural capital is then largely forgotten.

China

In the early creative phase of the Warring States period, intellectuals circulate among the Chi-hsia Academy, the courts at Wei, Ping-yang and Ch'in. The greatest of these are centres of intersecting circles. Political and prestige rivalry between the major courts was overlaid by the autonomous organizational movements of Confucians and Mohists; these conditions fostered the growth of a third party of unaffiliated intellectuals who carved out a variety of positions across the turf provided by focus on the life of debate. Again, in the great period of Buddhist creativity, there is competition among several organized factions intersecting physically at a few places: the capital of the pro-Buddhist dynasties, especially the T'ang, with its court and great monasteries, counterbalanced by the great inter-sectarian monasteries at T'ien-tai, Lu-shan and Shao-lin ssu. A later period of creativity under the Sung dynasty was based upon intellectual exchange among factions centred at the two northern capitals, Lo-yang (the old capital and cultural centre for out-of-office officials) and Chang-an, where the ups and downs of Wang An-Shih's reform movement were taking place. Here was a multiple meshing among political/literary factions of the gentry, reforming and traditionalist officials of the examination system, and the quasi-religious schools of the Neo-Confucians and occultists. Under the Southern Sung dynasty, there were again interconnected rival centres: Chu Hsi's academy, which is the most successful of the private schools living off and simultaneously opposing the examination system; and the professors of the national university such as Liu Chiu-Yuan.

The stagnant periods of Chinese intellectual life are either dominated by a single centre, or are drastically dispersed. The huge but uncreative national university of the Han, reaching 30,000 students at its height, exemplifies the former. We see the dispersion and loss of focus in the later period of Ch'an Buddhism, when its monasteries proliferate across China but interconnections among its lineages fade away; it is then that Ch'an creativity gives way to its own version of scholasticism, making koans out of the exploits of its earlier leaders. The huge development of the material conditions of education under the Ming dynasty shows dispersion without creative focus. There are hundreds of thousands of students in small scattered schools, supporting an industry of printed books (Chaffee, 1985). The national university and the mass gatherings for the provincial and metropolitan examinations do not stimulate the debate of philosophical factions, but only the individual pursuit of scholastic forms.

Stagnation and Loss of a Centre in Islam

In Islam and Christendom, philosophy follows a similar pattern; conditions for rising creativity are followed by those of stagnation. As we have noted, the differences between the two regions are matters of degree, although they accumulate into differences in substance.

In the earliest period of the Islamic empire, the principal centres of philosophy were dispersed: Jundishapur in southwestern Persia where the pagan school of Athens had moved after being closed down in 529; Antioch, inheritor of the Alexandrian school after 718, before it moved on around 850 to Harran, in northern Syria, where a school of Sabian star-worshippers also existed; the Nestorian school at Nisibis in Syria (Nakosteen, 1964: 16–19; Watt, 1985: 37–9). These preserved the ancient cultural capital, but were not known for innovation. It was only when their scholars were gathered to Baghdad, for the Caliph's translation project and under other patrons, that the density needed for a creative network was achieved. During the great creative period of Islamic life, from 800 to 1000, virtually all the intellectuals were at Baghdad and at the port city, Basra, 300 miles down the Euphrates. It was a close network, with much movement between both places.

Baghdad and Basra provided the creative combination of a central focus of attention together with multiple bases of intellectual factions. These bases included the court as well as other aristocratic patrons supporting groups engaged in collecting libraries, translating foreign texts, and charitable hospitals where medicine was taught together with related Greek learning. On the side of 'ancient learning', there were rival groups of translators: the Jundishapur lineage exemplified by Hunayn, now at the House of Wisdom, as well as star-worshippers from Harran such as the family of Thabit ibn Qurra. Nestorian Christians, Sabians, Zoroastrians and Hindus crossed at this centre under Moslem sponsorship; the first great Muslim philosophers, al-Kindi and al-Farabi, were at the centre of these networks in Baghdad. Basra was the initial centre of philosophical creativity on the side of the 'Islamic sciences'; its mosque was where the rational theologians, including the Mu'tazilites and Ash'arites were formed; and Basra was home base of the secret society of the Pure Brethren. These networks also had branches in Baghdad, in the orbit of Greek *falsafah*. The early Sufis, too, though they were a dispersed collection of wanderers, made their greatest impact at Baghdad; this was the site of their most famous early representatives, al-Bistami, al-Junayd, and al-Hallaj.

The other important ingredient in the intellectual scene were the lineages of the teachers of jurisprudence (i.e. legal 'schools' in a metaphorical but not physical sense). Initially these were regionally based: Malik and his followers at Medina; al-Shafi'i in Egypt; Abu Hanifa at Kufa and Baghdad, yet other styles of interpretation in Syria, Persia and elsewhere (Lapidus, 1988: 164–5). There was a huge proliferation of such legal sects; it is estimated that by around 800 AD there were some 500 of them. By around 900 to 1000, some four or five schools took the lead; by the 1100s, acceptance of one of four schools had become the criterion of orthodoxy as a Muslim. The law schools were, by and large, a decentralizing agent, even when they had winnowed to a few lineages. In the creative period of philosophy, it was the Hanbalis who were most active as a scriptural, anti-rationalist opposition. This traditionalist lineage centred originally on Baghdad, in most immediate contact with the rational theologians.

A central point for these competing factions existed at Baghdad with an outlier at Basra. The sometimes violent conflicts among these groups did not threaten the overall structure as long as the general conditions remained intact. As the Baghdad Caliphate lost its political power, its importance as a patron of intellectual life declined, and the central focus where networks might confront one another began to disappear. For a time Nishapur, in eastern Persia near the Caspian Sea (two months' journey from Baghdad) became important, but mainly in theological studies; it was the main Ash'arite centre from 900 until about 1100. For a while some network connection was maintained between it and Baghdad; al-Ghazali, as well as some of his teachers, was active in both places. Intellectual life was now dispersing; even Nishapur no longer maintained any central focus for the theologians after 1100, who are found now in Ispahan, Kirman, Damascus, Jerusalem and elsewhere (Watt, 1985: 92).

The madrasas (colleges) which proliferated in every city after 1050 added to this dispersion. The factional competition between Sunnite and Shi'ite motivated many of these endowments. But the factions did not intersect institutionally; madrasas specialized in one or the other sect. In addition, they remained small, typically around 10–20 endowed students with a single professor, although some of the large colleges had as many as 75 students (Nakosteen, 1964: 42–4, 49–50; Makdisi, 1981: 31). At most, madrasas of the four legal schools might amalgamate physically into a single architectural complex. Large and internally differentiated faculties did not come into being. The expansion of Sufi orders in this period also enhanced dispersion; particular orders dominated in outlying regions such as Anatolia, Transoxiana, north Africa, India, as well as in Persia and the Middle East. Again there was little institutional point of inter-section among rival groups. The Sufi orders were largely based on lay members and thus compatible with other pursuits. The madrasas tended to become permeated with Sufism, which took the edge off the mysticism and subordinated it to traditionalism and law. The madrasas ended by producing a type not unlike the Confucian gentry, oriented to government and propriety but preserving a tinge of Taoist mysticism for their private lives.

The Spanish episode which was a temporary break in the later Muslim stagnation recapitulates the early creative structure. Cordoba and Toledo provided the focus for interconnected networks. As the centre of the western Caliphate, Cordoba contained the legal, theological and secular court networks characteristic of Baghdad of an earlier period. The balance existed for a relatively short time. As early as 950, the Caliph had imported a huge library from the east, competing with the eastern Caliphate for prestige as a centre of learning, and patronized Jewish scholars as a cosmo-politan counterweight to Muslim religious factions. The conserva-tive side was also strong; law was monopolized by the Malikites, the most literalist and anti-innovative of the law schools, being opposed even to *waqf* foundations which in the east had been used to endow madrasas (Makdisi, 1981: 238). Politics swung pro- and anti-secular learning; for a few generations after 1050, the balance of networks broke into creativity. Network density was enhanced while Toledo was a base where Christian translators, Jewish religious intellectuals and Arab scientists intermeshed. The Christian reconquest, which took this great city from the Arabs in 1085, at first added pluralism to the networks rather than destroying them. We find intellectuals of all three faiths moving about, stimulating one another around the twin hubs, Toledo and Cordoba. Other cities and their schools fed into these networks: Almeria, Seville, Granada, Lucena, all close to Cordoba in the south. After 1200, the structure is lost. Cordoba falls to the Christians in 1236; the Jewish/Arab networks no longer link; the translators move on to Italy. Its structural bases gone, the Spanish Golden Age was over. Thenceforward neither Muslims, Christians nor Jews show much philosophical creativity in Spain.

Which type of stagnation characterizes the later age of Islam? In some respects there is a loss of cultural capital (Stagnation A). Ibn Rushd's great achievement in freeing Aristotle from neo-Platonism, and his own constructive philosophy, were largely unknown in the east (Fakhry, 1983: 275). Mu'tazili rational theology is driven out as well. In so far as there is adulation of the classics (Stagnation B), it is in the realm of the religious texts of Islam, and in a narrow aspect of philosophy: the studies of logic which became incorporated as adjuncts to legal argument in the madrasas. Even here there is some movement: commentaries and supercommentaries added onto the texts to be mastered by students.

The consensus of most historians is that these commentaries are unoriginal and pedantic. But it is possible, as Hodgson argues, that they merely have not received attention from Western scholars, and that technical advances are buried within. Around 1450, in Shiraz (Persia) al-Dawwani included in his supercommentaries on school logic a solution to the liar's paradox that anticipates Russell's theory of types (Hodgson, 1974, Vol. 2: 472); and there may be more advances of this sort. But surely this was at least Stagnation (C), focusing on technicalities too refined to come to wider notice. Al-Dawwani's reputation was largely as a religious moralist, while his technical creativeness had little following. In the social organization of the intellectual world, flashes of brilliance had no reflection; the illusory stagnation of technical refinement led into the real stagnation of classicism and loss of past achievements.

Centre and Disintegration in Christendom

In European Christendom we can follow the steps by which the central focus of intellectual life built up. There is nothing inherent about the initial attraction of Paris. In the Carolingian period, the networks tended to be further east: at Fulda and the Palatine court of the Emperor, as well as the court at Laon. The schools of Italy were active by 1000, though their most famous members moved north. An early dialectician like Anselm of Besate wandered from Parma to Mayence; Lanfranc from Bologna to Bec in Normandy. Rosecelin taught at Compiège, at Loches and Tours on the lower Loire, at Besancon near the Alps (Gilson, 1944: 233–4). Abelard is famous for his travels around 1100–1140, but now the net is confined to northern France, and he spent increasing time in Paris. Chartres was a rival centre for several generations in the 1100s, but its network flowed away into Paris by the end of the century. The advantage of Paris was that it provided in close compass multiple bases for intellectual life. It included the rival jurisdictions of the cathedral, the religious abbeys, the patronage of the monarchy and eventually of the Pope (Ferruolo, 1985: 16–17). Italy, despite its lead both in classical learning and later as a place for Arabic translations, became peripheral to the network centred on Paris. The teachers from Bec, Laon, Chartres and Tours found maximal attention by congregating in Paris. By 1200, their intersection promoted the organization of the university.

The height of creativity, from 1230 to about 1360, was a time when the optimal background conditions existed. Paris provided the focus, but it was balanced and fed by other universities and schools linked by migrating teachers and students. There was an especially important exchange of masters between Paris and Oxford; both had the rare privilege of faculties of theology, due to the political importance of the French and English kings to the papacy.[4] Cologne with its Dominican house of studies was a third outlier, with strong network ties to Paris. For a generation in the early 1300s, the papal court at Avignon became a fourth centre, but full of scholars with Paris and Oxford connections. The highly creative philosophers were those in geographical overlaps, belonging to several major centres; Grosseteste, Bacon, Albertus, Aquinas, Ockham, Eckhart had been at two, Scotus at three. These figures incorporated the intellectual representations of the intersecting centres in their own persons.

At the same time, the centres contained multiple grounds of factionalism. There were the rival Orders of Franciscans and Dominicans; there were internal organizational conflicts within the most powerful Order, the Franciscans; there was the jealousy of secular theologians over the privileges of the Orders at the universities; there was a struggle for control and autonomy between theological and arts faculties. Conflicts took place across multiple dimensions. The two great Orders, emerging in the 1220s, by 1231 laid claim to two theology chairs at Paris. In 1255 the secular theology masters tried to have the mendicant Orders forbidden from lecturing at Paris; it was only through the intervention of the Pope that in 1257 Bonaventure and Aquinas were confirmed in their chairs — the latter surrounded by armed bodyguards to protect him from the seculars (Gilson, 1944: 438; Hyman and Walsh, 1983: 505). This was the setting in which the secular theologian Henry of Ghent attacked Aquinas at Paris in the 1270s, and Aquinas had attacked the claims of the Arts Masters to independence from theological orthodoxy. Around 1315, the Chancellor Henry of Harclay attacked the Dominicans for attempting to teach at Oxford without receiving a local MA; soon after, Harclay's probable student William of Ockham attacked the Realism of the theological philosophy which was now the official doctrine of the Orders. Such external bases of factional struggle within the university provided part of the energy of intellectual creation.

The inner differentiation of the university, and its autonomous field of intellectual combat, were two important ingredients of creativity. But they were effective only when combined with the centralization which brought all the networks together. For the life of philosophy, the university structured around the higher faculty of theology was the key. Paris was not the only place where a university corporation was formed. Law teachers and students were forming guilds at Bologna by around 1100. Parallel with Paris in the late 1100s, universities were also growing up at Oxford, Montpellier and Salerno, the latter two predominantly medical. With the exception of Oxford, which became a network satellite of the Paris metropolis, these other universities had almost no impact on the world of philosophy of this period. The same was true in the 1200s, when universities were formed at Naples and Padua (along with smaller ones) in Italy; at Salamanca and Valladolid (again with smaller ones) in Spain; Cambridge in England; Toulouse, Angers and Orleans in France itself. Many of the smaller schools specializing in law did not even have arts faculties (Cobban, 1988: 3). As far as philosophy was concerned, the other universities acted at best as feeders for higher studies at Paris.

After 1300, the situation began to change. Intellectual life dispersed to many places, both inside and outside the universities. Especially in the late 1300s and the 1400s, we find independent mystics in Germany and the Netherlands, humanists in Italy, Jews in southern France and Italy; Averroists in the medical and legal faculties in Italy, where philosophy had previously shown little penetration; nominalists are prominent in the universities in Germany. After 1350, Oxford no longer stands out, and the Paris networks are fading.

The decline of abstract philosophy was not due to the decline of the university itself. On the contrary, this was a period of accelerating growth of the university system as a whole (see Table 1). By the end of the 1200s, there were eighteen universities, twelve of them major in size and importance. By 1400 there were thirty-four universities, eighteen of them major; by 1500 there were fifty-six. Even more universities were founded, but many of them failed. The failure rate went up during these centuries; between 1300 and 1500, about half of all university foundations were failures.[5] The market for educational credentials was expanding explosively, but at the same time flooding the market, raising risks of failure and losing its former prestige.

More universities existed but they were becoming smaller. Paris at its height around 1280–1300 had some 6000–7000 students; the number began falling in the 1300s and fell below 3000 by 1450 (enrolment data from Rashdall, 1936, Vol. II: 149, 171, 178–91; Stone, 1974: 91; Simon, 1966:245). Bologna rivalled the size of Paris in the early 1200s but fell behind thereafter. Oxford may have had a maximum of 3000 students in the 1200s; there were an estimated 1500 in 1315 and fewer than 1000 in 1438; by 1500–1510, the yearly average was down to 124. Toulouse may have had 2000 students at its height; this fell to 1380 teachers and students in 1387 and below 1000 in the 1400s. Avignon (founded in 1303) and Orleans had 800–1000 students, mainly in law, in the 1390s; these numbers fell off drastically in the following century. The smaller French and Italian universities never had more than a few hundred students at their height, and they often closed for lack of students.

Proliferation of universities was especially rapid in Italy and Spain, and here the failure rates were highest; Italy had an overwhelming 80 percent failure rate in the 1300s and 1400s. France, too, experienced considerable numbers of foundings; it reached a failure rate of at least 78 percent in the 1400s. Expansion in Germany and in central and far northern Europe was more successful. Here there was less initial competition over students. The first university in the region was founded at Prague in 1347, which carried on successfully with some 1500 students until the early 1400s. Vienna, Cologne and Leipzig succeeded to the leadership, with as many as 1000 students

TABLE 1
University Foundations and Failures, 1000–1600 AD

Total	Italy	France	Britain	German Empire, Scandinavia Low Countries	Iberia
1000s					
F = 1	F = 1				
f = 0					
T = 1M					
1100s					
F = 6	F = 3	F = 2	F = 1		
f = 17%	f = 1				
T = 5M	T = 2M	T = 2M	T = 1M		
1m	1m				
1200s					
F = 19	F = 8	F = 5	F = 1		F = 5
f = 37%	f = 3	f = 2			f = 2
T = 12M	T = 4M	T = 4M	T = 2M		T = 2M
6m	4m	1m			1m
1300s					
F = 34	F = 15	F = 5	F = 1	F = 10	F = 3
f = 47%	f = 12	f = 1	f = 1	f = 2	
T = 18M	T = 4M	T = 5M	T = 2M	T = 6M	T = 2M
14m	7m	4m		2m	3m
1400s					
F = 41	F = 5	F = 9	F = 3	F = 15	F = 9
f[a] = 48%	f = 4	f = 7		f = 4	f = 5
T = 22M	T = 5M	T = 5M	T = 2M	T = 8M	T = 2M
34m	7m	6m	3m	11m	7m
1500s					
F = 54	F = 5	F = 4	F = 2	F = 18	F = 25
f = 31%	f = 2	f = 1		f = 2	f = 12
T = 23M	T = 4M	T = 4M	T = 3M	T = 9M	T = 3M
70m	11m	9m	4m	26m	20m
Totals 1000–1600					
F = 155	F = 37	F = 25	F = 8	F = 43	F = 42
f = 39%	f = 60%	f = 44%	f = 13%	f = 19%	f = 45%

Sources: Rashdall 1936: Shepherd, 1964: No. 100: *The Cambridge Modern History Atlas*, 1912, Map 9; Kagan (in Stone, 1974: 355–405).
Key: F = foundations; f = failures; T = total in existence at end of century; M = major universities; m = minor universities.
[a] Includes 'paper universities' given legal charters, but which did not actually come into existence.

at various times in the 1400s. The smaller German universities ranged from 80 to 400 students, hitting their peaks around 1450–80 and declining thereafter.

One might expect to associate this institutional growth with intellectual creativity, but the opposite happened. Significant networks were not maintained; a central focus was lost. None of the new universities acquired anything like the drawing power that Paris once commanded. Instead of a structure in which multiple bases of factionalism intersected at a centre, factionalism itself became geographically localized. Intellectual borders hardened; conflict no longer produced creative realignments, but merely a habitual reiteration of dividing lines. Partly responsible was a decline in the internationalism of the old High Medieval centres, set in motion by external political forces. Already in 1303 the French king was putting pressure on the Paris theologians to support him in conflict with the Pope; foreign scholars who refused, including Duns Scotus, temporarily left Paris (Gilson, 1944: 710–11). There was a growing tendency for scholars to stay at home; now the French–English wars restricted Englishmen studying or teaching in France, and vice versa. This nationalism was a new development, since earlier wars had not disturbed the unity of Christendom; it was the new efforts of the rulers to control the now highly-developed church bureaucracy that was removing the institutions of religious learning as a neutral meeting place. The Papacy responded to slights in one place by licensing universities elsewhere; for instance in 1316, the Pope licensed Toulouse to teach theology, overturning the monopoly of Paris theologians in France. In 1359 a theological faculty was granted to a new university at Florence, although it failed quickly for lack of students; in 1364 the pre-eminent legal university, Bologna, finally was granted a theological faculty (Cobban, 1988: 144). The schism in the Papacy, in which rival Popes existed almost every year from 1378 to 1449, fostered yet further foundations and rivalries.

Nationalism and local factionalism made a self-reinforcing spiral. Previously the Paris masters had the right, granted by the Pope, to teach in all universities without re-examination; now this was contested by Oxford and Montpellier. Universities now tended to break apart along intellectual lines (de Wulf, 1947, Vol. 3: 50–196). Strong nominalist universities included Vienna (founded in 1365), where the curriculum required only nominalist texts; Heidelberg (founded in 1386); Erfurt (1392); Cracow (1397); Leipzig (1409). Cologne, where the old Dominican school was displaced by a degree-granting university in 1388, was a stronghold of Thomism. At Louvain, founded about 1425, the statutes prohibited the teaching of 'nominalists' including Ockham and Buridan. The nominalists were periodically forced out, leaving Paris in 1407 and returning in 1437 after Paris was recaptured by the English; in 1474 Louis XI banned nominalism, though rescinding the edict in 1481. Oxford on the other hand became strongly nominalist. The Orders, once centres of creativity, now were frozen in their official doctrines. The Dominicans, who had made Thomism compulsory in 1309, were increasingly barred from England by the strength of the Franciscans. Dominican life on the continent became uneasy as well: they left Paris in 1387, returning in 1403 as the result of changing fortunes in the Hundred Years War. The stronghold of Thomism became primarily the universities of Spain, where the Counter-Reformation eventually added its weight to make it virtually the criterion of faith against heretics; by the same token, it became anathema to Protestants.

The universities now were intellectual fortresses. Change came no longer by internally-generated creativity, but when a school was taken by storm when external politics changed. The very labels 'nominalist', 'realist', 'Scotist' had hardened in this period, from the inchoate movements of the earlier period, into names hurled in battle. The humanists, who treated all the 'schoolmen' as an item of satire, brought no relief, but only an additional faction when they entered the universities.

Academicization as a Two-edged Sword

We face a disturbing paradox. Schools provide the material base and the insulation from lay conceptions which allow intellectuals to pursue their own ideas. But schools are also places of routine and pedantry. Formalism develops for its own sake; texts are memorized and covered with commentaries; refinements become narrow and trivial. We see this in the Christian universities after 1300. Even the surge of new foundations in this period does not breathe fresh life into learning. The Islamic madrasas have a similar scholasticism from the outset; their expansion brings activity only in the form of piling up supercommentaries upon traditional texts. In Greco-Roman antiquity too, the level of support for formal education does not correlate with the times of creativity; the municipal schools of 250–500 AD, with their high salaries and their representation of the rival philosophies, repeat the traditional positions in set rhetorical forms. All these educational systems centre on dialectic and debate, but without promoting innovation; the contest itself becomes a static form of training and display.

Neither madrasas nor Greek schools were universities in the European sense. Academic institutions in China came closer to this structure. The Imperial university of the Han, and especially its expansion in the T'ang and subsequent dynasties, had a differentiated faculty and trained for a series of academic degrees. It was involved in much the same credentialling dynamics for bureaucratic careers found in medieval Christendom. But the prosperous periods of the university tended to be intellectually the most stagnant. The height of student population in the Han is the time when Confucianism was formalized into textual orthodoxy; the huge examination system of the Ming enforced Neo-Confucianism as an endless set of standard exercises. Similarly, Buddhist intellectual life was stifled after the late T'ang when the government required formal examinations for certificates to become a monk.

The tendency of schools, with their formal curricula and examinations, is conservative. Yet sometimes the schools are the center of creativity. We see this when formal schooling was first institutionalized in Athens and in Alexandria, and there are later moments of upsurge especially at the latter. In China, the creative period of Neo-Confucianism is connected to the development of private schools and the movement to reform the university and the official examinations. The forming of the European schools in the 1100s is the milieu for creativity; in the next century the process of formalization in the university, the piling up of authorities and proofs known as 'scholasticism', was the vehicle for the higher development of philosophy. Only in the Islamic madrasas is a creative phase missing; even here one can point to al-Ghazali's sophisticated destruction of philosophy, formulated at the great government-sponsored madrasa in Baghdad within the first generation of its foundation.

Academicization is a two-edged sword. The material base that schools provide for intellectual life can be positive or negative in supporting creativity. The tendencies to rote learning, narrow technique and a routine of exercises and exams are always present. When they are overlaid by the energies of building new career paths and reorganizing intellectual space, the result is creative breakthroughs in the realm of higher abstractions. It is only when a fine balance holds among intersecting factions at a focus of attention that creativity exists. Disturbing the balance or removing the focus, one may be left with the material institutions and large numbers of intellectuals, but settled into scholastic routine. With this comes the stagnation of classics and technicalities, and eventually an atmosphere in which the more creative high points become forgotten. Stagnation in all its forms is a danger of academic success.

Coda: The Intellectual Demoralization of the Late Twentieth Century

De te fabula narratur. What we see around ourselves in recent decades has been an enormous expansion of cultural production. There are over one million publications annually in the natural sciences, over 100,000 in the social sciences and comparable amounts in the humanities (de Solla Price, 1986: 266). To perceive the world as a text is not too inaccurate a description, perhaps not of the world itself, but of the life position of intellectuals: we are almost literally buried in papers. As the raw size of intellectual production goes up, the reward to the average individual goes down, at least in the realm of pure intellectual rewards of being recognized for one's ideas and of seeing their impact upon others. The pessimism and self-doubt of the intellectual community under these circumstances is not surprising.

Which of the three types of stagnation do we exemplify? Loss of cultural capital (Stagnation A), certainly: the inability of late twentieth-century intellectuals to build constructively on the achievements of their predecessors. Simultaneously there exists a cult of the classics (Stagnation B): the historicism and footnote-scholarship of our times, in which doing intellectual history becomes superior to creating it. (This very paper is self-exemplifying in this respect.) And also we have the Stagnation (C) of technical refinement: to take just a few instances, the acute refinements and formalisms of logical and linguistic philosophy have gone on apace in little specialized niches; in the same way among all factions of the intellectual world today we find the prevalence of esoterica, of subtleties and of impenetrable in-group vocabularies. As with the nominalists and other scholastics of the fourteenth and fifteenth centuries, today's intellectual technicalities sometimes offer a high level of insight in their own spheres, but they are over-refined to travel well outside.

In our own day as at the end of medieval Christendom, all three types of stagnation exist and interact. The underlying cause lies not with any individual failure, nor with the quality of our ideas, but with the structure of intellectual communities and their material foundations. As before, Dark Ages of the mind are not necessarily ushered in by material collapse, but can occur in times of material abundance; a major cause is overabundance and dispersion of the material means of intellectual production. Our structural condition as intellectuals can be summarized in the phrase: loss of a centre of intersecting conflicts, loss of the small circle of circles at which our arguments can be focused. It is not a centre of agreement that is lacking; creative intellectual periods never had that. What is lost is a nexus in the sense of a network of places where disagreements are tightly and creatively focused.

This structural condition, which has been growing more acute since 1950, is based on the enormous expansion and decentralization of the academic world which has taken place since that time. The US, which began this process somewhat earlier than other industrial powers, has more than 3000 colleges and universities, and scores of them are in the running for the claim to be centres of intellectual productivity. Expansions comparable in direction if not in sheer volume took place in the decades after 1950 in France, Germany, the UK and Italy, with similar decentralizing effects. This expansion is structurally based and likely to continue, with temporary variations in pace, over the long-term future. Education has become connected to opportunities for employment, both in the form of state-enforced licenses and as informal emblems of social status; it now expands autonomously through the dynamics of a currency-like credential inflation driven by the competition for more schooling, and the resulting rise of credential requirements for employment. The relations between the supply and demand for education are circular and self-reinforcing, and the prospects for further expansion are limited only by the economic productivity of the surrounding base (on the dynamics of this process see Collins, 1979; Ramirez and Boli-Bennett, 1982; Bourdieu, 1988).

The production of academic intellectuals rides upon this wave of credential inflation. With expansion of demand for lower level degrees and certificates, there comes an increase in the numbers of higher degree holders to train those of the next rank down; thus we have the massive expansion in the number of PhDs. And since these scholars struggle for positions by using their reputations for productivity in scientific or scholarly publications, the output of scholarly products necessarily follows the same inflationary path as the competition for lower levels of academic degrees. The productivity of scholarly researchers constitutes a further superordinate market upon the expansion of higher education. As each level of education becomes saturated and deflated in value, superordinate markets for cultural credentials are added beyond them.

Analogous processes take place in non-academic spheres of cultural production. In the realm of pop culture, there has been a huge expansion of commercial markets for recorded music and films and for live performances and broadcasts; these in turn give rise to superordinate markets for the status-bearing accoutrements connected to rock and film stars, ranging from apparel to gossip. In this atmosphere of superordinate arenas of cultural production pyramiding upon one another, it is not surprising that the content of modern culture has become both self-reflective and ironic. We see this both in the pop culture, with its themes of privatized alienation and showy nihilism, and in the successive waves of ironicization among intellectuals of which postmodernism is only the latest. The content of the 'postmodern' message is to deny objective truth; this might be seen as an ideology of cultural producers in a highly pyramided market structure, where nothing in sight seems to touch solid earth. Such a structure of cultural production is bound to be self-conscious, and to make its self-consciousness a major item for cultural circulation. In one sense, these various alienated modernisms are correct reflections upon the culture-producing structures in which they originate. From a larger viewpoint, these structures are objectively real, as the present-day extension of long-term struggles which constitute the dynamism of markets (see Collins, 1990).

The historical ups and downs in cultural production that we characterize as creativity and stagnation are themselves the results of underlying changes in the material conditions which support intellectual production. The connection is not a simple linear one; as we have seen, the optimum of creativity occurs not when the material bases for intellectuals are most abundant, but when there is a fine balance between a few rival centres of intellectual life, tied together into a single network. This is what we have lost today. Whether it will come back again in the future depends upon further restructurings of that organizational base.

Notes

1. The scholarly apparatus used in charting networks and organizational bases of intellectuals is far too large to be cited here. What follows contains perforce only fragmentary documentation; details on sources are available in the larger work.

2. This is emphasized throughout the *Cambridge History of Later Medieval Philosophy*, Cambridge 1982. The creativity of the nominalists apparently lasted two generations, dissipating by the late 1300s. It is possible that later advances occurred but have been ignored by historians, since this period of late scholasticism has not been much studied. In any case, this obliviousness to nominalist innovation started very early, with its contemporaries.

3. The sheer complexity of argument tended to bury it. The works of Dullaert of Ghent, at Paris in the early 1500s

> summarize in great detail (and usually with hopelessly involved logical argument) the teachings of Oxford 'calculatores' such as Thomas Bradwardine, William Heytesbury, and Richard Swineshead; of Paris 'terminists' such as Jean Buridan, Albert of Saxony, and Nicole Oresme; and of Italian authors such as James of Forli, Simon of Lendenaria, and Peter of Mantua — while not neglecting the more realist positions of Walter Burley and Paul of Venice. The logical subtlety of Dullaert's endless dialectics provoked considerable adverse criticism from Vives [Dullaert's student] and other humanists . . . (*Dictionary of Scientific Biography* Vol. 9: 237)

Two generations later, the leading Aristotelean in Italy, Jacopo Zabarella at the great University of Padua, discusses Aristotelean physics in complete ignorance of the critical advances in the work of the Merton and the Buridan–Oresme groups (*Encyclopedia of Philosophy* Vol. 8: 366).

4. Cambridge also had a theology faculty, although not an important one; this was apparently due to its origin in a migration of masters from Oxford in 1209.

5. The failure rate for the 1200s is skewed upwards by several failures in the 1290s; prior to that point the success rate was quite high. Estimates of undercounting of 'paper universities' which received charters but failed to come into existence probably make the failure rate for the 1400s 10–15 percent too low (see Rashdall, 1936, Vol. II: 325–31).

References

Bourdieu, Pierre (1988) *Homo Academicus*. Stanford: Stanford University Press.

Chaffee, John W. (1985) *The Thorny Gates of Learning in Sung China*. Cambridge and New York: Cambridge University Press.

Cobban, Alan B. (1988) *The Medieval English Universities*. Berkeley: University of California Press.

Collins, Randall (1979) *The Credential Society: An Historical Sociology of Education and Stratification*. New York: Academic Press.

Collins, Randall (1990) 'Market Dynamics as the Engine of Historical Change', *Sociological Theory* 8: 111–35.

Collins, Randall (forthcoming) *The Causes of Philosophies. A Sociological Theory of Intellectual Change*.

Fakhry, Majid (1983) *A History of Islamic Philosophy*. New York: Columbia University Press.

Ferruolo, Stephen C. (1985) *The Origins of the University. The School of Paris and their Critics 1100–1215*. Stanford: Stanford University Press.

Gilson, Etienne (1944) *La Philosophie au moyen age des origines patristiques à la fin du 14e siécle*. Paris: Payot.

Ho, Peng Yoke (1985) *Li, Qi & Shu. An Introduction to Science and Civilization in China*. Hong Kong: Hong Kong University Press.

Hodgson, Marshall G.S. (1974) *The Venture of Islam*, 3 volumes. Chicago: University of Chicago Press.

Hyman, Arthur and James J. Walsh (1983) *Philosophy in the Middle Ages*. Indianapolis: Hackett.

Lapidus, Ira M. (1988) *A History of Islamic Societies*. Cambridge and New York: Cambridge University Press.

Makdisi, George (1981) *The Rise of Colleges. Institutions of Learning in Islam and the West*. Edinburgh: Edinburgh University Press.

Nakosteen, Mehdi (1964) *History of Islamic Origins of Western Education*. Boulder: University of Colorado Press.

Qian, Wen-yuan (1985) *The Great Inertia, Scientific Stagnation in Traditional China*. London: Croom Helm.

Ramirez, Francisco O. and John Boli-Bennett (1982) 'Global Patterns of Educational Institutionalization', in Philip Altbach (ed.) *Comparative Education*. New York: Macmillan.

Rashdall, Hastings (1936) *The Universities of Europe in the Middle Ages*. Oxford: Oxford University Press.

Shepherd, William R. (1964) *Historical Atlas*. New York: Barnes and Noble.

Simon, J. (1966) *Education in Tudor England*. Cambridge and New York: Cambridge University Press.

de Solla Price, Derek J. (1986) *Little Science, Big Science and Beyond*. New York: Columbia University Press.

Stone, Lawrence (1974) *The University in Society*. Princeton: Princeton University Press.

Watt, W. Montgomery (1985) *Islamic Philosophy and Theory*. Edinburgh: Edinburgh University Press.

de Wulf, Maurice (1947) *Histoire de la philosophie medievale*. Paris: Vrin.

Randall Collins is Professor of Sociology at the University of California, Riverside.

From Industrial Society to the Risk Society: Questions of Survival, Social Structure and Ecological Enlightenment

Ulrich Beck

Are Risks Timeless?

Aren't risks at least as old as industrial society, possibly even as old as the human race itself? Isn't all life subject to the risk of death? Aren't and weren't all societies in all epochs 'risk societies'?

On the contrary, should we not (or must we not) be discussing the fact that since the beginning of industrialization, threats — famines, epidemics or natural catastrophes — have been continually reduced? To list only a few key words: the reduction of infant mortality, the 'bonus years' (Imhof), the achievements of the welfare state, the enormous progress in technological perfection over the past hundred years. Isn't the Federal Republic of Germany, in particular, an Eldorado of bureaucratically organized care and caution?

Certainly there are 'new risks', such as nuclear power, chemical and biotechnical production and the like. But, considered mathematically or physically, are these not dangers of great scope, but also of exceedingly small, actually negligible probability? Looking at them coolly and rationally, does that not imply that they should be given a lesser status than long accepted risks, such as the incredible carnage on the highways or the risks to smokers?

Certainly, ultimate security is denied to us human beings. But is it not also true that the unavoidable 'residual risks' are the downside of the opportunities — for prosperity, relatively high social security and general comfort — that developed industrial society offers to the majority of its members in a historically unparalleled manner? Is the dramatization of such risks not in the end a typical media spectacle, ignoring established expert opinion, a 'new German anxiety', as untenable and just as short-lived as the debacle regarding the

Theory, Culture & Society (SAGE, London, Newbury Park and New Delhi), Vol. 9 (1992), 97–123

'railroad sickness' from the end of the preceding century?

And finally, aren't risks a central concern of the engineering and physical sciences? What business has the sociologist here? Isn't that once again typical?

The Calculus of Risk: Predictable Security in the Face of an Open Future

Human dramas — plagues, famines and natural disasters, the looming power of gods and demons — may or may not quantifiably equal the destructive potential of modern mega-technologies in hazardousness. They differ essentially from 'risks' in my sense since they are not based on decisions, or more specifically, decisions that focus on techno-economic advantages and opportunities and accept hazards as simply the dark side of progress. This is my first point: risks presume industrial, that is, techno-economic decisions and considerations of utility. They differ from 'war damage' by their 'normal birth', or more precisely, their 'peaceful origin' in the centres of rationality and prosperity with the blessings of the guarantors of law and order. They differ from pre-industrial natural disasters by their origin in decision-making, which is of course never conducted by individuals but by entire organizations and political groups.[1]

The consequence is fundamental: pre-industrial hazards, no matter how large and devastating, were 'strokes of fate' raining down on mankind from 'outside' and attributable to an 'other' — gods, demons or Nature. Here too there were countless accusations, but they were directed against the gods or God, 'religiously motivated', to put it simply, and not — like industrial risks — politically charged. For with the origin of industrial risks in decision-making the problem of social accountability and responsibility irrevocably arises, even in those areas where the prevailing rules of science and law permit accountability only in exceptional cases. People, firms, state agencies and politicians are responsible for industrial risks. As we sociologists say, the social roots of risks block the 'externalizability' of the problem of accountability.[2]

Therefore, it is not the number of dead and wounded, but rather a social feature, their industrial self-generation, which makes the hazards of mega-technology a political issue. The question remains however: must one not view and assess the past 200 years as a period of continual growth in calculability and precautions in dealing with industrially produced insecurities and destruction? In fact, a very promising approach, and one barely explored to date, is to trace the (political) institutional history of evolving industrial society as the conflict-laden emergence of a system of rules for dealing with industrially produced risks and insecurities (see Ewald, 1986; Evers and Nowotny, 1987; Böhret, 1987; Lau, 1988).

The idea of reacting to the uncertainties that lie in opening and conquering new markets or in developing and implementing new technologies with collective agreements — insurance contracts for instance, which burden the individual with general fees just as much as they relieve him from dramatic damage cases — is hardly a new social invention. Its origins go back to the beginnings of intercontinental navigation, but with the growth of industrial capitalism, insurance was continually perfected and expanded into nearly all problem areas of social action. Consequences that at first affect only the individual become 'risks', systematically caused, statistically describable and in that sense 'predictable' types of events, which can therefore also be subjected to supra-individual and political rules of recognition, compensation and avoidance.

The calculus of risks connects the physical, the engineering and the social sciences. It can be applied to completely disparate phenomena not only in health management — from the risks of smoking to those of nuclear power — but also to economic risks, risks of old age, of unemployment, of traffic accidents, of certain phases of life and so forth. In addition, it permits a type of 'technological moralization' which no longer need employ moral and ethical imperatives directly. To give an example, the place of the 'categorical imperative' is taken by the mortality rates under certain conditions of air pollution. In this sense, one could say that the calculus of risk exemplifies a type of ethics without morality, the mathematical ethics of the technological age. The triumph of the calculus of risks would probably not have been possible if fundamental advantages were not tied to it.

The first of these lies in the fact that risks open the opportunity to document statistically consequences that were at first always personalized and shifted onto individuals. In this way they are revealed as systematic events, which are accordingly in need of a general political regulation. Through the statistical description of risks (say in the form of accident probabilities) the blinkers of individualization drop off — and this is not yet sufficiently the case with environmental diseases such as pseudo-croup, asthma or even cancer. A field for corresponding political action is opened up: accidents on the job, for instance, are not blamed on those whose health they have already ruined anyway, but are stripped of their individual origin and related instead to the plant organization, the lack of precautions and so on.

A second advantage is closely connected to the first: insurance payments are agreed on and guaranteed on a no-fault basis (setting aside the extreme cases of gross negligence or intentional damage). In that way, legal battles over causation become unnecessary and moral outrage is moderated. Instead, an incentive for prevention is created for businesses, in proportion to the magnitude of the insurance costs — or perhaps not.

The decisive thing, however, is ultimately that in this manner the industrial system is made capable of dealing with its own unforeseeable future. The calculus of risks, protection by insurance liability laws and the like promise the impossible: events that have not yet occurred become the object of current action — prevention, compensation or precautionary after-care. As the French sociologist François Ewald (1986) shows in detailed studies, the 'invention' of the calculus of risks lies in making the incalculable calculable, with the help of accident statistics, through generalizable settlement formulae as well as through the generalized exchange principle of 'money for damages'. In this way, a norm system of rules for social accountability, compensation and precautions, always very controversial in its details, creates present security in the face of an open uncertain future. Modernity, which brings uncertainty to every niche of existence, finds its counter-principle in a *social compact against industrially produced hazards and damages*, stitched together out of public and private insurance agreements.

Politically and programmatically, this pact for the containment and 'just' distribution of the consequences of the standard industrial revolution is situated somewhere between socialism and liberalism, because it is based on the systematic creation of consequences and hazards, but at the same time involves individuals in preventing and compensating for them. The consensus that can be achieved with it always remains unstable, conflict-laden and in need of revision. For that very reason, however, it represents the core, the inner 'social logic' of the consensus on progress, which — in principle — legitimated techno-economic development in the first phase of industrialism. Where this 'security pact' is violated wholesale, flagrantly and systematically, the consensus on progress itself is consequently at stake.

Risk and Threat: On the Overlapping of Normal and Exceptional Conditions

My decisive idea, and the one that leads us further, is that this is precisely what has happened in a series of technological challenges with which we are concerned today — nuclear power, many types of chemical and bio-technological production as well as the continuing and threatening ecological destruction. The foundations of the established risk logic are being subverted or suspended.[3]

Put another way, since the middle of this century the social institutions of industrial society have been confronted with the historically unprecedented possibility of the destruction through decision-making of all life on this planet. This distinguishes our epoch not only from the early phase of the industrial revolution, but also from all other cultures and social forms, no matter how diverse and contradictory these may have been in detail. If a fire breaks out, the fire brigade comes; if a traffic accident occurs, the insurance pays. This interplay between beforehand and afterwards, between the future and security in the here and now, because precautions have been taken even for the worst imaginable case, has been revoked in the age of nuclear, chemical and genetic technology. In all the brilliance of their perfection, nuclear power plants have suspended the principle of insurance not only in the economic, but also in the medical, psychological, cultural and religious sense. *The residual risk society has become an uninsured society*, with protection paradoxically diminishing as the danger grows.

There is no institution, neither concrete nor probably even conceivable, that would be prepared for the 'WIA', the 'worst imaginable accident', and there is no social order that could guarantee its social and political constitution in this worst possible case.[4] There are many, however, which are specialized in the only remaining possibility: denying the dangers. For after-care, which guarantees security even against hazards, is replaced by the dogma of technological infallibility, which will be refuted by the next accident. The queen of error, science, becomes the guardian of this taboo. Only 'communist' reactors, but not those in West Germany, are empirical creations of the human hand which can toss all their theories onto the scrap-heap. Even the simple question 'What if it does happen after all?' ends up in the void of unpreparedness for after-care. Correspondingly, political stability in risk societies is the stability of not thinking about things.

Put more precisely, nuclear, chemical, genetic and ecological mega-hazards abolish the four pillars of the calculus of risks. First, one is concerned here with global, often irreparable damage that can no longer be limited; the concept of monetary compensation therefore fails. Second, precautionary after-care is excluded for the worst imaginable accident in the case of fatal hazards; the security concept of anticipatory monitoring of results fails. Third, the 'accident' loses its delimitations in time and space, and therefore its meaning. It becomes an event with a beginning and no end; an 'open-ended festival' of creeping, galloping and overlapping waves of destruction. But that implies: standards of normality, measuring procedures and therefore the basis for calculating the hazards are abolished; incomparable entities are compared and calculation turns into obfuscation.

The problem of the incalculability of consequences and damage becomes clear with particular vividness in the lack of accountability for them. The scientific and legal recognition and attribution of hazards takes place in our society according to the principle of causality, the polluter-pays principle. But what strikes engineers and lawyers as self-evident, even virtually demanded by ethics, has extremely dubious, paradoxical consequences in the realm of mega-hazards. One example: the legal proceedings against the lead crystal factory in the community of Altenstadt in the Upper Palatinate (reported in *Der Spiegel* 46, 1986: 32ff).

Flecks of lead and arsenic the size of a penny had fallen on the town, and fluoride vapours had turned leaves brown, etched windows and caused bricks to crumble away. Residents were suffering from skin rashes, nausea and headaches. There was no question where all of that originated. The white dust was pouring visibly from the smokestacks of the factory. A clear case. A clear case? On the tenth day of the trial the presiding judge offered to drop charges in return for a fine of DM 10,000, a result which is typical of environmental crimes in the Federal Republic (1985: 13,000 investigations, twenty-seven convictions with prison terms, twenty-four of those suspended, the rest dropped).

How is that possible? It is not only the lack of laws and not merely the legendary shortcomings in applying them which protect the criminals. The reasons lie deeper and cannot be eliminated by the staunch appeals to the police and the law-makers that issue ever more loudly from the ranks of the environmentalists. A conviction is blocked by the very thing that was supposed to achieve it: the strict application of the (individually interpreted) polluter-pays principle.

In the case of the lead crystal factory, the commission of the crime could not be and was not denied by anyone. A mitigating factor came into play for the culprits: there were three other glass factories in the vicinity which emitted the same pollutants. Notice: the more pollution is committed, the less is committed.

More precisely: the more liberally the acceptable levels are set, the greater the number of smokestacks and discharge pipes through which pollutants and toxins are emitted, the lower the 'residual probability' that a culprit can be made responsible for the general sniffling and coughing, that is to say, the less pollution is produced. Whereas at the same time — one does not exclude the other — the general level of contamination and pollution is increasing. Welcome to the real-life travesty of the hazard technocracy![5]

This organized irresponsibility is based fundamentally on a confusion of centuries. The hazards to which we are exposed date from a different century than the promises of security which attempt to subdue them. Herein lies the foundation for both phenomena: the periodic outbreak of the contradictions of highly organized security bureaucracies and the possibility of normalizing these 'hazard shocks' over and over again. At the threshold of the twenty-first century, the challenges of the age of atomic, genetic and chemical technology are being handled with concepts and recipes that are derived from early industrial society of the nineteenth and the early twentieth centuries.[6]

Is there an operational criterion for distinguishing between risks and threats? The economy itself reveals the boundary line of what is tolerable with economic precision, through the refusal of private insurance. Where the logic of private insurance disengages, where the economic risks of insurance appear too large or too unpredictable to insurance concerns, the boundary that separates 'predictable' risks from uncontrollable threats has obviously been breached again and again in large and small ways.

Two types of consequences are connected in principle to this overstepping of the bounds. First, the *social* pillars of the calculus of risks fail; security degenerates into mere technical safety. The secret of the calculus of risks, however, is that technical *and* social components work together: limitation, accountability, compensation, precautionary after-care. These are now running in neutral, and social and political security can be created solely by means of a contradictory maximizing of technical superlatives.

Second, a central part of this political dynamic is the social contradiction between highly developed safety bureaucracies on the one hand, and the open legalization of previously unseen, gigantic threats on the other, without any possibility of after-care. A society which is oriented from top to toe toward security and health is confronted with the shock of their diametrical opposites, destruction and threats which scorn any precautions against them.

Two contrary lines of historical development are converging in late twentieth-century Europe: a level of security founded on the perfection of techno-bureaucratic norms and controls, and the spread and challenge of historically new hazards which slip through all the meshes of law, technology and politics. This contradiction, which is not of a technical, but a social and political character, remains hidden in the 'confusion of centuries' (Günther Anders). And this will continue so long as the old industrial patterns of rationality and control last. It will break up to the extent that improbable events become probable. 'Normal catastrophes' is the name Charles Perrow (1982) gives in his book to this predictability with which what was considered impossible occurs — and the more emphatically it is denied, the sooner, more destructively and shockingly it occurs. In the chain of publicly revealed catastrophes, near-catastrophes, whitewashed security faults and scandals the technically centred claim to the control of governmental and industrial authority shatters — quite independently of the established measure of hazards: the number of dead, the danger of the contaminations and so on.

The central social-historical and political potential of ecological, nuclear, chemical and genetic hazards lies in the collapse of administration, in the collapse of techno-scientific and legal rationality and of institutional political security guarantees which those hazards conjure up for everyone. That potential lies in the unmasking of the concretely existing anarchy which has grown out of the denial of the social production and administration of mega-hazards.[7]

Hazards of the nuclear and chemical age, therefore, have a social as well as a physical explosiveness. As the hazards appear, the institutions which are responsible for them, and then again not responsible, are pressed into competition with the security claims they are compelled to issue, a competition from which they can only emerge as losers. On the one hand, they come under permanent pressure to make even the safest things safer; on the other hand, this overtaxes expectations and sharpens attention, so that in the end not only accidents, but even the suspicion of them, can cause the façades of security claims to collapse. The other side of the recognition of hazards is the failure of the institutions that derive their justification from the non-existence of hazard. That is why the 'social birth' of a hazard is an event which is equally improbable and dramatic, traumatic and unsettling to the entire society.

Precisely because of their explosiveness in the social and political space, hazards remain distorted objects, ambiguous, interpretable, resembling modern mythological creatures, which now appear to be an earthworm, now again a dragon, depending on perspective and the state of interests. The ambiguity of risks also has its basis in the revolutions which their official unambiguity had to provoke. The institutions of developed industrial society — politics, law, engineering sciences, industrial concerns — accordingly command a broad arsenal for 'normalizing' non-calculable hazards. They can be under-estimated, compared out of existence or made anonymous causally and legally. These instruments of a symbolic politics of detoxification enjoy correspondingly great significance and popularity (this is shown by Fischer, 1989).

Ministers of the Environment, no matter what their party affiliation, are not to be envied. Hampered by the scope of their ministry and its financial endowment, they must keep the causes largely constant and counter the cycle of destruction in a primarily symbolic fashion. A 'good' minister of the environment ultimately is the one who stages activities in a publicity-grabbing way, piling up laws, creating bureaucratic jurisdictions, centralizing information. He may even dive into the Rhine with a daredevil smile or try a spoonful of contaminated whey powder, provided the media eyes of a frightened public are trained upon him. Dogged adherence to a line must be sold with the same TV smile and 'good arguments' as a 180-degree shift in direction. First the nuclear reprocessing plant at Wackersdorf is flogged through with police power, only to have to shout 'April Fools!' after others who obviously know more about it have turned it down.

But gradually, one accident at a time, the logic of the institutionalized non-management of problems can turn into its opposite: what does probability-based safety — and thus the entire scientific diagnosis — mean for the evaluation of the worst imaginable accident, whose occurrence would leave the experts' theories intact but destroy their lives?

Sooner or later the question will arise as to the value of a legal system that regulates and pursues every detail of the technically manageable minor risks, but legalizes the mega-hazards by virtue of its authority, to the extent they cannot be minimized technically, and burdens everyone with them, including those who resist?

How can a democratic political authority be maintained which must counter the escalating consciousness of hazards with energetic safety claims, but in that very process puts itself constantly on the defensive and risks its entire credibility with every accident or sign of an accident?

The Role of Technology and the Natural Sciences in the Risk Society

There is a public dispute over a new ethics of research in order to avoid incalculable and inhuman results. To limit oneself to that debate is to misunderstand the degree and type of involvement of the engineering sciences in the production of hazards. An ethical renewal of the sciences, even if it were not to become entangled in the thicket of ethical viewpoints, would be like a bicycle brake on an intercontinental jet, considering the autonomization of technological development and its interconnections with economic interests. Moreover, we are not concerned merely with the ethics of research, but also with its logic and with the unity of culprits and judges (experts) of the engineering sciences in the technocracy of hazards.

An initial insight is central: in matters of hazards, no one is an expert — particularly not the experts. Predictions of risk contain a double fuzziness. First, they presume cultural acceptance and cannot produce it. There is no scientific bridge between destruction and protest or between destruction and acceptance. Acceptable risks are ultimately accepted risks. Second, new knowledge can turn normality into hazards overnight. Nuclear energy and the hole in the ozone layer are prominent examples. Therefore: the advancement of science refutes its original claims of safety. *It is the successes of science which sow the doubts as to its risk predictions.*

But conversely, it is also true that acute danger passes the monopoly of interpretation to those who caused it, of all people. In the shock of the catastrophe, people speak of rem, Becquerels or ethylene glycol as if they know what such words mean and they must do so in order to find their way in the most everyday matters. This contradiction must be exposed: on the one hand the engineering sciences involuntarily enact their own self-refutation in their contradictory risk diagnoses. On the other, they continue to administer the privilege handed down to them from the Kaiser's days, the right to determine according to their own internal standards the global social question of the most intensely political nature: how safe is safe enough?

The power of the hard sciences here rests on a simple social construct. They are granted the binding authority — binding for law and politics — to decide on the basis of their own standards what the 'state of technology' demands. But since this general clause is the legal standard for safety, private organizations and committees (for instance, the Society of German Engineers, the Institute for Standards) decide in Germany the amount of hazards to which everyone can be subjected (see Wolf, 1987).

If one asks, for instance, what level of exposure to artificially produced radioactivity must be tolerated by the populace, that is, where the threshold of tolerance separating normality from hazardousness is situated, then the Atomic Energy Act gives the general answer that the necessary precautions are to correspond to 'the state of technology' (Sec. 7 II No. 3). This phrase is fleshed out in the 'Guidelines' of the Reactor Safety Commission — an 'advisory council' of the Ministry of the Environment in which representatives of engineering societies hold sway.

In air pollution policy, noise protection and water policy one always finds the same pattern: laws prescribe the general programme. But anyone who wishes to know how large a continuing ration of standardized pollution citizens are expected to tolerate needs to consult the 'Ordinance on Large Combustion Facilities' or the 'Technical Instructions: Air Quality' and similar works for the (literally) 'irritating' details.

Even the classical instruments of political direction — statutes and administrative regulations — are empty in their central statements. They juggle with the 'state of technology', thus undercutting their own competence, and in its place they elevate 'scientific and technical expertise' to the throne of the civilization of threat.

This *monopoly of scientists and engineers in the diagnosis of hazards*, however, is simultaneously being called into question by the 'reality crisis' of the natural and engineering sciences in their dealings with the hazards they produce. It has not been true only since Chernobyl, but there it first became palpable to a broad public: safety and probable safety, seemingly so close, are worlds apart. The engineering sciences always have only probable safety at their command. Thus, even if two or three nuclear reactors blow up tomorrow, their statements remain true.

Wolf Häfele, the dean of the German reactor industry, wrote in 1974:

> It is precisely the interplay between theory and experiment or trial and error which is no longer possible for reactor technology . . . Reactor engineers take account of this dilemma by dividing the problem of technical safety into sub-problems. But even the splitting of the problem can only serve to approximate ultimate safety . . . The remaining 'residual risk' opens the door to the realm of the 'hypothetical' . . . The interchange between theory and experiment, which leads to truth in the traditional sense, is no longer possible . . . I believe it is this ultimate indecisiveness hidden in our plans which explains the particular sensitivities of public debates on the safety of nuclear reactors. (Häfele, 1974)

What one hears here is nothing less than the contradiction between experimental logic and atomic peril. Just as sociologists cannot force society into a test tube, engineers cannot let people's reactors blow up all around them in order to test their safety, unless they turn the world into a laboratory. Theories of nuclear reactor safety are testable only after they are built, not beforehand. The expedient of testing partial systems amplifies the contingencies of their interaction, and thus contains sources of error which cannot themselves be controlled experimentally.

If one compares this with the logic of research that was originally agreed upon, this amounts to its sheer reversal. We no longer find the progression, first laboratory then application. Instead, testing comes after application and production precedes research. The dilemma into which the mega-hazards have plunged scientific logic applies across the board; that is, for nuclear, chemical and genetic experiments *science hovers blindly above the boundary of threats*. Test-tube babies must first be produced, genetically engineered artificial creatures released and reactors built, in order that their properties and safety can be studied. The question of safety, then, must be answered affirmatively before it can even be raised. The authority of the engineers is undermined by this 'safety circle'.

Through the anticipation of application before it has been fully explored, science has itself abolished the boundary between laboratory and society (Beck, 1988: Ch. 5; Kohn and Weyer, 1989). Along with that, the conditions of freedom of research have shifted. Freedom of research implies freedom of application. Today, anyone who demands or grants only freedom of research abolishes research. The power of technology is based in its command of practice.

Engineers can directly apply things, where politics must first advise, convince, vote and then push them through against resistance. This makes technology capable of conducting a policy of the *fait accompli*, which not only puts all the others under constant pressure to react, but also puts them at the mercy of the engineers' judgment for assessment and avoidance of disaster. This power grows with the velocity of the innovations, the lack of clarity regarding their consequences and hazards, and it grows even though the credibility of technological promises of safety is thereby undermined.

Where the monopoly of technology becomes a monopoly on concealed social change, it must be called into question and cancelled by the principle of division of powers — like the earlier 'legal transcendence of the sovereign'. Internally, this implies a redistribution of the burdens of proof and, externally, the liberation of doubt (see Beck, 1988: Ch. 8; 1990). In all central social issues and committees relative to technological development, systematic alternatives, dissenting voices, dissenting experts and an interdisciplinary diversity would have to be combined. The exposure of scientific uncertainty is the liberation of politics, law and the public sphere from their patronization by technocracy.

The Ecological Conflict in Society

If the risk society does not mean only a technical challenge, then the question arises: what political dynamics, what social structure, what conflict scenarios arise from the legalization and normalization of global and uncontrollable systematic threats? To reduce things to an admittedly crude formula: hunger is hierarchical. Even following the Second World War, not everyone went hungry. Nuclear contamination, however, is egalitarian and in that sense 'democratic'. Nitrates in the ground water do not stop at the general director's water tap (see Beck, 1986: 48ff).[8]

All suffering, all misery, all violence inflicted by people on other people to this point recognized the category of the Other — workers, Jews, blacks, asylum seekers, dissidents and so forth — and those apparently unaffected could retreat behind this category. *The 'end of the Other', the end of all our carefully cultivated opportunities for distancing ourselves, is what we have become able to experience with the advent of nuclear and chemical contamination.* Misery can be marginalized, but that is no longer true of hazards in the age of nuclear, chemical and genetic technology. It is there that the peculiar and novel political force of those threats lies. Their power is the power of threat, which eliminates all the protective zones and social differentiations within and between nation states.

It may be true that in the storm tide of threat 'we're all in the same boat', as the cliché goes. But, as is so often the case, here too there are captains, passengers, helmsmen, engineers and men and women overboard. In other words, there are countries, sectors and enterprises which *profit* from the production of risk, and others which find their economic existence threatened together with their physical well-being. If, for instance, the Adriatic or the North Sea dies or they are perceived socially as 'hazardous to health' — this difference is cancelled with respect to economic effects — then it is not just the North Sea or the Adriatic which die, along with the life those seas contain and make possible. The economic life in all the towns, sectors and coastal countries that live directly or indirectly from the commercialization of the sea is also extinguished. At the apex of the future, which reaches into the horizon of the present day, industrial civilization is transformed into a kind of 'world cup' of the global risk society. Destruction of nature and destruction of markets coincide here. It is not what one has or is able to do that determines one's social position and future, but rather where and from what one lives and to what extent others are permitted in a prearranged unaccountability to pollute one's possessions and abilities in the guise of 'environment'.

Even passionate denial, which can certainly count on full official support, has its limits. The revenge of the abstract expert dispute on hazards is its geographic concretion. One can dispute everything, operating the official whitewashing machinery in high gear. That does not prevent, but only accelerates the destruction. In this way, 'toxin-absorbing regions' come into being, crossing national boundaries and old institutional lines of conflict, creating geographical positions whose 'fate' coincides with the industrial destruction of nature (see Beck, 1988: 247ff.).

The greenhouse effect, for example, will raise temperatures and sea levels around the world through the melting of the polar icecaps. The period of warming will submerge entire coastal regions, turn farmland into desert, shift climatic zones in unpredictable ways and dramatically accelerate the extinction of species. *The poorest in the world will be hit the hardest*. They will be least able to adapt themselves to the changes in the environment. Those who find themselves deprived of the basis of their economic existence will flee the zone of misery. A veritable Exodus of eco-refugees and climatic asylum-seekers will flood across the wealthy North; crises in the Third and Fourth Worlds could escalate into wars. Even the climate of world politics will change at a faster pace than is imaginable today. So far, all these are just projections, but we must take them seriously. When they have become reality, it will already be too late to take action.

Many things would be easier here if those countries on the way to industrialization could be spared the mistakes of the highly industrialized countries. But the unchecked expansion of the industrial society is still considered the *via regia* that promises the mastery of many problems — not only those of poverty — so that the prevailing misery often displaces the abstract issues of environmental destruction.

'Threats to nature' are not only that; pointing them out also threatens property, capital, jobs, trade union power, the economic foundation of whole sectors and regions, and the structure of nation states and global markets. Put another way: there is a major distinction between the conflict field of wealth production, from which the nineteenth century derived the experience and premises of industrial and class society, and the conflict field of hazard production in the developed nuclear and chemical age, to which we are only just beginning to become sensitive in sociology. It probably lies in the fact that wealth production produced the antagonisms between capital and labour, while the systematic chemical, nuclear and genetic threats bring about polarizations between capital and capital — and thus also between labour and labour — cutting across the social order. If the social welfare state had to be forced through against the concerted resistance of the private investors, who were called on to pay in the form of wage and fringe-benefit costs, then *ecological threats split the business camp*. At first glance, it is impossible to discern where and how the boundary runs; or more accurately, who receives the power, and from where, to cause the boundary to run in what way.

While it may still be possible to speak of the 'environment' on the level of an individual operation, this talk becomes simply fictitious on the level of the overall economy, because there a type of 'Russian roulette' is being played behind the increasingly thin walls of the 'environment'. If it is suddenly revealed and publicized in the mass media that certain products contain certain 'toxins' (information policy is receiving a key importance considering the fact that hazards are generally imperceptible in everyday life), then entire markets may collapse and invested capital and effort are instantly devalued.

No matter how abstract the threats may be, their concretizations are ultimately just as irreversible and regionally identifiable. What is denied collects itself into geographical positions, into 'loser regions' which have to pay the tab for the damage and its 'unaccountability' with their economic existence. In this 'ecological expropriation', we are facing the historical novelty of a devaluation of capital and achievement, while relationships of ownership and sometimes even the characteristics of the goods remain constant. Sectors that had nothing or very little causally to do with the production of the threat — agriculture, the food industry, tourism, fisheries, but also retail trade and parts of the service industry — are also among those most affected.

Where the (world) economy splits into risk winners and risk losers — in a manner difficult to define — this polarization will also make its mark upon the structure of employment. First, new types of antagonisms that are specific to countries, sectors and enterprises arise between groups of employees and correspondingly within and between trade union interest organizations. Second, these are, so to speak, third-hand antagonisms, derived from those between factions of capital, which turn the 'fate of workers' into 'fate' in a further and fundamental dimension. Third, with the intensified consciousness of the corresponding lines of conflict, a sector-specific alliance of the old 'class opponents', labour and capital, may arise. The consequence may be a confrontation between this union-management bloc and other mixed factions over and above the divisions of class differences which have been narrowed under the pressure of 'ecological politicization'.[9]

One has to wonder what an ecological labour movement would really mean. The production and definition of hazards aims largely at the level of products, which escapes almost completely from the influence of the works councils and workers' groups and falls completely under the jurisdiction of management. And this is still at the intra-organizational level. Hazards are produced by business operations, to be sure, but they are defined and evaluated socially — in the mass media, in the experts' debate, in the jungle of interpretations and jurisdictions, in courts or with strategic-intellectual dodges, in a milieu and in contexts, that is to say, to which the majority of workers are totally alien. We are dealing with 'scientific battles' waged over the heads of the workers, and fought out instead by intellectual strategies in intellectual milieux. The definition of hazards eludes the grasp of workers and even, as things stand, the approach of trade unions for the most part. Workers and unions are not even those primarily affected; that group consists of the enterprises and management. But as secondary targets they must count on losing their jobs if worst comes to worst.

Even a latent risk definition hits them in the centre of their pride in achievement, their promise of a usable commodity. Labour and labour power can no longer conceive of themselves only as the source of wealth, but must also be perceived socially as the motive force for threat and destruction. The labour society is not only running out of labour, the only thing which gives meaning and solidity to life, as Hannah Arendt puts it ironically, it is also losing even this residual meaning.

Somewhat crudely, one can say in conclusion: what is 'environment' for the polluting industry, is the basis of economic existence for the affected loser regions and loser sectors. The consequence is: political systems in their architecture as nation states on the one hand, and large-scale ecological conflict positions on the other, become mutually autonomous and create 'geopolitical' shifts which place the domestic and international structure of economic and military blocs under completely new stresses, but also offer new opportunities. *The phase of risk society politics which is beginning to make itself heard today in the arena of disarmament and detente in the East–West relationship can no longer be understood nationally, but only internationally, because the social mechanics of risk situations disregards the nation state and its alliance systems.* In that sense, apparently iron-clad political, military and economic constellations are becoming mobile, and this forces or, better, permits, a new 'European global domestic policy' (Genscher).

Political Reflexivity: The Counterforce of Threat and the Opportunities for Influence by Social Movements

Where progress and fate appear interwoven, the goals of social development are spelled antithetically from the highest to the lowest floor. This is certainly not the first conflict which modern societies have had to master, but it is one of the most fundamental. Class conflicts or revolutions change power relations and exchange elites, but they hold fast to the goals of techno-economic progress and clash over mutually recognized civil rights. The double face of 'self-annihilating progress', however, produces conflicts that cast doubt on the social basis of rationality — science, law, democracy. In that way, society is placed under permanent pressure to negotiate foundations without a foundation. It experiences an institutional destabilization, in which all decisions — from local government policy on speed limits and 'parking lots' to the manufacturing details of industrial goods to the fundamental issues of energy supply, law and technological development — can suddenly be sucked into fundamental political conflicts.

While the façades remain intact, quasi-governmental power positions arise in the research laboratories, nuclear power plants, chemical factories, editorial offices, courts and so on, in the milieu of hazards dependent on definitions and publicity. Put another way: as the contradictions of the security state are stirred up, systems come to require action and become subject-dependent. The courageous Davids of this world get their chance. The colossal interdependence of threat definitions — the collapse of markets, property rights, trade union power and political responsibility — brings about key positions and media of 'risk-definition' which cross the social and professional hierarchy.

On the one hand, one can use all one's powers of conviction to pile up arguments for the institutional non-existence of suicidal threats, one need not deny one iota of hope to the institutional hegemony, one can even draw on the distraction of the social movements and the limitations of their political effectiveness, and one must still recognize with equal realism: all this is countered by the opposing power of threat. It is constant and permanent, not tied to interpretations denying it, and even present in places demonstrators have long since abandoned. The probability of improbable accidents grows with time and the number of implemented mega-technologies. Every 'event' arouses memories of all the other ones, not only in Germany, but all over the world.

Different types of revolutions have been contrasted: coups d'état, the class struggle, civilian resistance and so on. They all have in common the empowering and disempowering of social subjects. Revolution as an autonomized process, as a hidden, latent, permanent condition, in which conditions are involved against their own interests, while political structures or property and power relations remain unchanged — this is a possibility which so far, to my knowledge, has neither been taken into consideration nor thought through. But it is precisely this conceptual scheme into which the *social power of threat* fits. It is the product of the deed, requiring no political authorization and no authentication. Once in existence, awareness of it endangers all institutions — from business to science, from law to politics — which have produced and legitimated it.

Everyone asks: from where will the opposing forces come? It is probably not very promising to place large or small ads for the missing 'revolutionary subject' in hip papers of the subculture. It feels good, of course, to appeal to reason with all the strictness at one's command, and it can do no harm, for the very reason that a realistic view of experience has shown that it leaves few traces behind. One could also found another circle for the solution of global problems. Certainly, it is to be hoped that political parties will catch on.

If all this does not suffice to stimulate alternative political action however, then there remains the knowledge of the activatable political reflexivity of the hazard potential.[10] Three Mile Island, Chernobyl, Hanau, Biblis, Wackersdorf and so forth: the global experiment of nuclear energy (toxic chemistry) has by now taken over the roles of its own critics, perhaps even more convincingly and effectively than the political counter-movements could ever have managed on their own. This becomes clear not only in the worldwide, unpaid negative advertising at peak news times and on the front pages of papers, but also in the fact that everyone between the Alpine chalets and the North Sea mud flats now understands and speaks the language of the nuclear critics. Under the dictates of necessity, people have passed a kind of crash course in the contradictions of hazard administration in the risk society: on the arbitrariness of acceptable levels and calculation procedures or the unimaginability of the long-term consequences and the possibilities of making them anonymous through statistics. They have learned more information, more vividly and more clearly than even the most critical critique could have ever taught them or demanded of them.

The most enduring, convincing and effective critics of nuclear energy (or the chemical industry and so forth) are not the demonstrators outside the fences or the critical public (no matter how important and indispensable they may be). The most influential opponent of the threat industry is the threat industry itself.

To put it differently, the power of the new social movements is not based only on themselves, but also on the quality and scope of the contradictions in which the hazard producing and administering industries are involved in the risk society. Those contradictions become public and scandalous through the needling activities of the social movements. Thus, there is not only an autonomous process of the suppression of dangers, but also opposite tendencies to uncover this suppression, even though they are much less marked and always dependent on the civil courage of individuals and the vigilance of social movements. Catastrophes that touch the vital nerves of society in a context of highly developed bureaucratic safety and welfare arouse the sensationalist greed of the mass media, threaten markets, make sales prospects unpredictable, devalue capital and set streams of voters in motion. Thus the evening news ultimately exceeds even the fantasies of countercultural dissent; daily newspaper reading becomes an exercise in technology critique.

This oppositional power of the unintended revelation of hazards depends of course on overall social conditions, which have so far been fulfilled in only a few countries: parliamentary democracy, (relative) independence of the press, and advanced production of wealth in which the invisible threat of cancer is not overridden for the majority of the populace by acute undernourishment and famine.

In the co-operation from within and without over and above the boundary lines of the subsystems there are in this sense also symptoms of a strength, which have so far remained almost unnoticed. The socially most astonishing, most surprising and perhaps least understood phenomenon of the 1980s in West Germany is the unexpected renaissance of an 'enormous subjectivity' — inside and outside the institutions (see Beck, 1986: Chs 2 and 4; Beck and Beck-Gernsheim, 1990). In this sense it is not an exaggeration to say that *citizens' groups have taken the initiative thematically in this society.* It was they who put the themes of an endangered world on the social agenda, against the resistance of the established parties. Nowhere does this become so clear as in the spectre of the 'new unity' which is haunting Europe. The compulsion to perform ecological lip-service is universal. It unites the Christian Social Union with the Communists, and the chemical industry with its Green critics. All products, absolutely all products, are 'safe for the environment' to say the least. There are rumours that the chemical concerns plan to take out full-page ads announcing themselves as a registered conservation association.

Admittedly this is all just packaging, programmatic opportunism, and perhaps really intentional rethinking now and then. The actions and the points of origin of the facts are largely untouched by it. Yet it remains true: the themes of the future, which are now on everyone's lips, have not originated from the farsightedness of the rulers or from the struggle in parliament — and certainly not from the cathedrals of power in business, science and the state. They have been put on the social agenda against the concentrated resistance of this institutionalized ignorance by the entangled, moralizing groups and splinter groups fighting each other over the proper way, split and plagued by doubts. *Democratic subversion has won a quite improbable thematic victory.* And this in Germany, rupturing with an authoritarian everyday culture which, historically, has enabled all official nonsense and insanity with its anticipatory obedience.

Even the surprising aspect of the events in Eastern Europe is after all the rebellion of the really existing individuals against a 'system' that had allegedly dominated them into the very capillaries of daily life. The tiny groups of avowed civil libertarians swell into popular movements that redraw the plans of the civic structure. It is not only the planned economy which is bankrupt. Systems theory, which conceives of society independent of subjects, has also been thoroughly refuted. In a society devoid of consent, revealed as virtually legitimatory, even a gust of wind that brings on the call for freedom can topple the powerful like a house of cards. The soft — orientations, hopes, ideas, people's interests — triumphs over the hard — the organizations, the established, the powerful, and the armed. Eastern Europe is one big citizens' group exulting in a success that is overrunning it.

The differences between protesting citizens in the East and the West are evident and have often been mentioned, but this is less true of the considerable common ground they share. Both are oriented to the grassroots, non-parliamentary, not tied to any particular class or party, and programmatically diffuse or even fragmented. Their Horatio Alger careers in both places are also similar: criminalized, fought, patronized but in the end part of party programmes and inaugural speeches. This has happened with environmental issues, women's issues and the peace movement, now outstripped by the galloping democratization in Eastern Europe. The 'democracy issue' has reawakened — in the struggles over there for the most basic human rights, here for the enforcement of rights that were only granted partially even in our countries (Rödel et al., 1989). The question, however, of how the universal challenge of an industrial system producing wealth *and* destruction is to be solved democratically remains completely open, both theoretically and practically.

The Utopia of Ecological Democracy

Europe is called to a new social project and has already set off on it. The East–West antagonism as an ideological fortress mentality is breaking up on both sides. The international themes of the risk civilization could move into the resulting vacuum. One sign of this is the pressure for global arrangements which technology, science and business produce. Another is the dawning of the large and small, the creeping and the galloping suicidal hazards everywhere in the world, and a final sign comes from the elevated standards of promised safety and rationality in developed welfare state capitalism.

These are the horrendous opportunities that offer themselves to a European global domestic policy, not only in the foundation and building of the 'European house', but also by the highly industrialized countries assuming a large portion of the costs for the necessary corrective measures. In the place where the dynamic of industrial development had its origin, in Europe, enlightenment on and against industrial society could also begin. This project of an ecological enlightenment would have to be designed and fought for both on the macro and micro levels. Even in everyday life, because the threats overturn well-worn routine everywhere and represent a spectacular challenge for civil courage — at jobs in industry, in the practices of doctors where people come with their fears and questions, in research which can block off or reveal, in the courts, in the monitoring of the administration and, not least, in the editorial offices of the mass media, where the invisible can be made culturally discernible. There are many concrete concerns in the relationship of the 'European house' to its neighbours on this planet. Among them is the impossibility of appearing any longer with the self-confidence of the donating wealthy, but rather admitting our destructive industrial role and correcting it in thought and action.

The technological project, the technological dogmatism of industrialism must not simply be extended to the ecological crisis, lest an ever more perfect technocracy result from the public dramatization of the dangers. *Industrial society has produced a 'truncated democracy', in which questions of the technological change of society remain beyond the reach of political-parliamentary decision-making.* As things stand, one can say 'no' to techno-economic progress, but that will not change its course in any way. It is a blank check to be honoured — beyond agreement or refusal. That is a manufactured 'natural force' in civilization, an 'industrial middle ages', that must be overcome by more democracy — the production of accountability, redistribution of the burdens of proof, division of powers between the producers and the evaluators of hazards, public disputes on technological alternatives (see Beck, 1988: Ch. 7)[11]. This in turn requires different organizational forms for science and business, science and the public sphere, science and politics, technology and law, and so forth.

The ecological extension of democracy then means: playing off the concert of voices and powers, the development of the independence of politics, law, the public sphere and daily life against the dangerous and false security of a 'society from the drawing board'.

My suggestion contains two interlocking principles: first, carrying out a division of powers and second, the creation of a public sphere. Only a strong, competent public debate, 'armed' with scientific arguments is capable of separating the scientific wheat from the chaff and allowing the institutions for directing technology — politics and law — to reconquer the power of their own judgement.

The means: with regard to all issues that are central to society dissenting voices, alternative experts, an interdisciplinary variety and, not least, alternatives to be developed systematically must always be combined. The public sphere in co-operation with a kind of 'public science' would be charged as a second centre of the 'discursive checking' of scientific laboratory results in the crossfire of opinions. Their particular responsibility would comprise all issues that concern the broad outlines and dangers of scientific civilization and are chronically excluded in standard science. The public would have the role of an 'open upper chamber'. It would be charged to apply the standard, 'How do we wish to live?' to scientific plans, results and hazards.

That presupposes that research will fundamentally take account of the public's questions and be addressed to them and not just multiply our common problems in an economic short circuit with industry. Perhaps it would be possible that through these two steps — an opening of science from within and the filtering out of its limitations in a public test of its practice — that politics and science could successively hone their direction-finding and self-monitoring instruments — instruments that are now largely inactive.

The cultural blindness of daily life in the civilization of threat can ultimately not be removed; but culture 'sees' in symbols. The images in the news of skeletal trees or of dying seals have opened people's eyes. Making the threats publicly visible and arousing attention in detail, in one's own living space — these are cultural eyes through which the 'blind *citoyens*' can perhaps win back the autonomy of their own judgement.

To conclude with a question: what would happen if radioactivity itched? Realists, also called cynics, will answer: people would invent something, perhaps a salve, to 'turn off' the itching. A good business then. Certainly, explanations would soon arise and would enjoy great public effect: they would claim that the itching had no meaning, that it might be correlated to other factors besides radioactivity, and that it was harmless in any case, unpleasant but provably harmless. If everyone ran around scratching themselves and with rashes on their skin, and if photo sessions with fashion models as well as management meetings of the united denial institutes took place with all participants scratching themselves, it would have to be assumed that such explanations would have little chance of surviving. In that case, nuclear policy as well as dealings with modern megahazards in general, would confront a completely changed situation: the object being disputed and negotiated would be culturally perceptible.[12]

That is precisely where the future of democracy is being decided: are we dependent in all the details of life and death issues on the judgement of experts, even dissenting experts, or will we win back the competence to make our own judgement through a culturally created perceptibility of the hazards? Is the only alternative still an authoritarian technocracy or a critical one? Or is there a way to counter the incapacitation and expropriation of daily life in the civilization of threat?

Translated by Mark Ritter

Notes

This essay is a revised and expanded version of a text entitled 'Risk Society: Questions of Survival, Social Structure and Ecological Enlightenment' ('Risikogesellschaft. Überlebensfragen, Sozialstruktur und ökologische Aufklärung') which appeared in *Aus Politik und Zeitgeschicte* B (36/1989): 3-13.

1. Niklas Luhmann (1990) has pointed out this difference between pre-industrial hazards, which are not controllable, but also not caused by decisions, and industrial risks, which come from decisions and considerations of utility. Here Luhmann, the

systems theorist, ascribes the decisions exclusively to individuals, who otherwise are never presented as within organizations and bureaucracies in his theory.

2. This occurs in a historical amalgam of nature and society, where even natural catastrophes such as floods, landslides and so on, which are apparently externally caused, appear to be caused by human beings (see Beck, 1988: Ch. 2).

3. This idea was first worked out in case studies of major accidents by Lagadec (1987), deepened by Ewald (1986) and Perrow (1988); the argument was also developed in the German linguistic area by Evers and Nowotny (1987). For details, see Beck (1988) and Lau (1988).

4. In this respect the disputes over so-called 'catastrophic medicine' have an exemplary character.

5. The debate over the duties and function of law in risk societies has increased accordingly in recent years. See Wolf (1987 and 1988); Meyer-Abich and Schefold (1986); Ritter (1987); Blanke (1986); Heinz and Meinberg (1988); Calliess (1981); Bruggemeier (1988).

6. Later on we will not be concerned only, nor primarily, with issues of a new ethics of civilizational action, but with the fact that the established categories and criteria for institutional action stem from a different world.

7. Until Chernobyl, protection against catastrophes, for example, was planned only within a radius of 29 km around a power plant; foreign accidents were officially excluded (cf. Czada and Drexler, 1988; Gottweis, 1988).

8. The conflicts and crises of classical industrial society have not ended after all, so that realistically, overlaps will occur between the social structure and conflict dynamics of industrial and risk society. These are excluded here.

9. 'That there are symptoms of such a bloc-formation is seen in the West German nuclear industry following Chernobyl: works councils and employers' representatives jointly defended prevailing West German energy policy against any change of course' (Schumann, 1987). Contrary to the prevailing assumptions, Heine and Mautz (1989) in a corresponding study on 'industrial workers contra environmentalism', reach the conclusion: 'With the trend to professionalization of production work in the chemical industry, chemical workers could in future constitute a growing potential of ecologically vigilant production workers, who are capable of reflecting critically upon the ecological conditions and consequences of their own labour, and represent a supporting force for ecologically motivated political interventions.' (1989: 187)

10. This view is based generally on the theoretical distinction between simple and reflexive modernization, which has not yet been adequately worked out. To put it crudely, simple modernization runs within the framework of categories and principles of industrial society. In the second case, however, we are concerned with a phase of social transformation in which, by dint of its own dynamics, modernization changes its shape within industrial society. Class, stratum, occupation, sex roles, businesses, sectoral structure and in general the presuppositions and the course of 'natural' techno-economic progress are all affected. The world of classical industrial society is becoming just as much a tradition to be run over and demystified as, in the nineteenth century, industrial modernization ran over and demystified status-based feudal society. Unconsciously, acting against its own plan, modernization is undercutting modernization. In that way however, restratifications in social structures arise, along with power shifts, new lines of conflict, possibilities and constraints for coalitions. Social movements, the public sphere, ethics, the civil courage of

individuals and the networks of differential politics get their chances to exert historical influence (cf. Beck, 1986: 176ff.; Ch. 7, 8).

11. The arguments developed in Beck (1988) are often misunderstood as suggested political solutions, whereas they actually aim to stimulate institutional re-learning by political means.

12. In figurative terms: making radioactivity itch is a central task of political education in the risk society (cf. Claussen, 1989; Ackermann et al., 1988).

References

Ackermann, H. et al. (eds) (1988) *Technikentwicklung und politische Bildung.* Opladen: Westdeutscher Verlag.

Beck, U. (1986) *Risikogesellschaft. Auf dem Weg in eine andere Moderne.* Frankfurt/Main (English translation forthcoming from Sage Publications 1992).

Beck, U. (1988) *Gegengifte. Die organisierte Unverantwortlichkeit.* Frankfurt/Main: Suhrkamp. (English translation forthcoming, 1992, Polity.)

Beck, U. (1990) 'Praxis als Forschung', *Forschungsjournal Neue Soziale Bewegungen* 3(1).

Beck, U. and E. Beck-Gernsheim (1990) *Das ganz normale Chaos der Liebe.* Frankfurt: Suhrkamp.

Blanke, T. (1986) 'Autonomie und Demokratie', *Kritische Justiz* 4: 406–22.

Böhret, C. (ed.) (1987) *Herausforderungen an die Innovationskraft der Verwaltung.* Opladen: Leske & Budrich.

Bruggemeier, G. (1988) 'Umwelthaftsrecht. Ein Beitrag zum Recht in der "Risikogesellschaft"', *Kritische Justiz* 2: 209–30.

Calliess, R.-P. (1981) 'Strafzweck und Strafrecht. 40 Jahre Grundgesetz – Entwicklungstendenzen vom freiheitlichen zum sozial-autoritären Rechtsstaat?', *Neue Juristische Wochenschrift* 21: 1338–43.

Claussen, B. (1989) 'Politische Bildung in der Risikogesellschaft', *Aus Politik und Zeitgeschichte, B* 36.

Czada, R. and A. Drexler (1988) 'Konturen einer politischen Risikoverwaltung', *Österreichische Zeitschrift für Politikwissenschaft* 1: 52ff.

Evers, A. and H. Nowotny (1987) *Über den Umgang mit Unsicherheit.* Frankfurt: Suhrkamp.

Ewald, F. (1986) *L'Etat Providence.* Paris.

Fischer, J. (1989) *Der Umbau der Industriegesellschaft.* Berlin.

Gottweis, H. (1988) 'Politik in der Risikogesellschaft', *Österreichische Zeitschrift für Politikwissenschaft* 1: 3ff.

Häfele, W. (1974) 'Hypotheticality and the New Challenges: The Pathfinder Role of Nuclear Energy', *Minerva* 12(1): 313ff.

Heine, H. and R. Mautz (1989), *Industriearbeiter contra Umweltschutz.* Frankfurt: Campus.

Heinz, G. and U. Meinberg (1988) 'Empfehlen sich Änderungen im strafrechtlichen Umweltschutz, insbes. in Verbindung mit dem Verwaltungsrecht. Gutachten D für den 57. Dt. Juristentag', in Staendige Deputation des Dt. Juristentages (ed.) *Verhandlungen des 57. Dt. Juristentages in Mainz,* Vol. I. Part D.

Kohn, W. and J. Weyer (1989) 'Gesellschaft als Labor', *Soziale Welt* 3: 349–73.

Lagadec, P. (1987) *Das grosse Risiko.* Nördlingen: Greno (French original 1982).

Lau, C.H. (1988) 'Risikodiskurse', *Soziale Welt* 3: 418–36.

Luhmann, Niklas (1990) 'Die Moral des Risikos und das Risiko der Moral', in G. Bechmann (ed.) *Risiko und Gesellschaft*. In press.

Meyer-Abich, K.M. (1989) 'Von der Wohlstands- zur Risikogesellschaft', *Aus Politik und Zeitgeschichte* B 36: 3ff.

Meyer-Abich, K.M. and B. Schefold (1986) *Die Grenzen der Atomwirtschaft*. Munich.

Perrow, C. (1988) *Normale Katastrophen*. Frankfurt: Campus.

Ritter, E.H. (1987) 'Umweltpolitik und Rechtsentwicklung', *Neue Zeitschrift für Verwaltungsrecht* 11: 929–38.

Rödel, U., G. Frankenberg and H. Dubiel (1989) *Die demokratische Frage*. Frankfurt/Main: Suhrkamp.

Schumann, M. (1987) 'Industrielle Produzenten in der ökologischen Herausforderung', Research proposal, Göttingen.

Wolf, R. (1987) 'Die Antiquiertheit des Rechts in der Risikogesellschaft', *Leviathan* 15: 357–91.

Wolf, R. (1988) '"Herrschaft kraft Wissen" in der Risikogesellschaft', *Soziale Welt* 2: 164–87.

Ulrich Beck is Professor of Sociology at Bamberg/München. His book *Risikogesellschaft* (1986) will appear in English translation as *The Risk Society* (Sage, 1992).

Beyond Social Movements?

Alain Touraine

Introduction

All of us employ the term 'social movements' in such different ways
that our debates are often artificial. Even more clearly, historical
analyses of the current situation of any given country and of factors
favourable or unfavourable to the formation of social movements
are almost meaningless. One must therefore replace this exceedingly
vague expression by a precise representation of social dynamics.
Without in any way attempting to impose one conception over
against others, I wish to examine the historical context of that conception of social life which views it as simultaneously collective
action, operation of society on itself, and organized around a central social conflict, opposing those who direct the self-production
and transformation of society and those who are subjected to its
effects. This conception cannot be identified with a particular current of thought. Rather, Marxist and post-Marxist thought has long
been one of the most widespread expressions of this representation.
One encounters this representation every time that the notion of
social class is employed (at least as this notion is customarily used
in Europe), but also every time that society is defined as
industrial — that is, by a mode of production. This is the case even
when these expressions are in no way associated with a Marxist form
of thought. The question which arises with respect to countries
which have been considerably influenced by socialist, communist or
anti-imperialist forms of thought, is : can the idea of a central social
conflict — which I here identify with the recognition of social
movements — survive what now appears as the irremediable decline
of historicist thought, that is, of a form of thought which defined
the social actor by his position in a social progress opposed by the
forces of conservatism and of reaction. This is the essential point:
it is surely impossible to dissociate the concept of social movement,

Theory, Culture & Society (SAGE, London, Newbury Park and New Delhi),
Vol. 9(1992), 125–145.

thus defined, from the representation of social life as, simultaneously, a set of cultural representations through which society produces itself and all the aspects and consequences of a central social conflict. Thus, the notion of social movement, as used here, designates a general representation of social life rather than a particular type of phenomenon. This representation differs both from the liberal image of society as a marketplace and from the identification of society with a central power or a set of mechanisms implacably bent on maintaining the established social order. One can, of course, reject this representation of social life at the outset. But one cannot deny that it has been very influential, especially in the twentieth century, which has been largely dominated, at the international level, by the association of Marxist parties and movements of social and, especially, national, liberation. Our thought is dominated by the crumbling of communist and nationalist regimes which claimed to be the heirs and representatives of these social and nationalist, anti-capitalist and anti-imperialist, movements. This collapse has rapidly attained almost all regions of the world: Central and Eastern Europe first and foremost, but also the Soviet Union and China (though the latter remains subject to a repressive regime), and the greater part of Latin America. It has attained yet other regions, including especially the Islamic world, where Marxist-inspired revolutionary parties, formerly so powerful in Syria, Egypt, Turkey and even Iran, have been destroyed or greatly weakened. In many countries, including especially those of Western Europe, references to Marxism have disappeared over a period of a few years. These references had been extremely frequent and formed a kind of catechism, usually an intolerable one. Yet suddenly, any serious consideration of the thought of Marx and his successors, and even of the traditions of the workers' movements and socialism, seems to take place in a vacuum. Fukuyama's article merits its success, because the question it poses is formulated in the very terms of historicism and, more precisely, of Hegelian thought. Doesn't historicism lead to its logical conclusion, the end of history? Put more simply, is it not striking that the collapse of communist and nationalist regimes appears not as the victory of one camp over the other, but rather as the triumph of reality over artifice, of social life itself over the authoritarian discourses that claimed not only to control it but to define it? Shouldn't the crisis of these political voluntarisms, of these modernizing, voluntarist and authoritarian states, intellectually imply the elimination of a whole set of notions, including those of social class, modes of production, historical phases and social movement in the sense indicated above (actor in a central social conflict through which the major orientations of a culture are transformed into social, political and economic organization).

This question should not be rejected or discarded through over-hasty answers. One must study the principal forms assumed by the decomposition of this historicist representation of social life prior to deciding whether nothing of it should survive, or whether, on the contrary, the concept of social movement can be separated out of, or even reinforced and deepened by, the crisis of historicism.

I. Triumphal Integration

The most obvious form taken by the crisis of the notion of social movement is the replacement of a bipolar image of society by that of a system maintained and reinforced by integrative mechanisms and the corresponding mechanisms of marginalization and social exclusion.

At the most readily observable level, many social analysts have long indicated that an organization of labour based on a direct conflict between the logic of managers and the logic of workers defending their individual and collective autonomy has been replaced by a system based on the circulation of information, so that work has increasingly become a position in a system of communication rather than a principle of autonomy and subjectivity. The world of employees is not that of workers. In particular, it is markedly different from that of qualified workers of the classic period of industry. Occupation was a fundamental principle of the autonomy of those workers in business enterprises where the various types of salary based on productivity placed workers in direct conflict with executives and management, as the thought and activity of Taylor himself very clearly indicate.

The transformation is even more apparent in the field of consumption. Our societies are decreasingly pyramidal, and one can no longer speak of a workers' or proletarian culture, as Maurice Halbwachs did, in a non-Marxist sense, shortly after the Second World War. We live in industrialized countries, in societies dominated by a feebly differentiated middle class, bounded on top by the world of the rich and extremely rich (who define themselves by their position in a market rather than by their professional roles), and below by the world of the temporarily or permanently excluded — the unemployed, sick or handicapped, isolated old people, ethnic and other minorities, etc.

More generally, isn't it obvious that the American concept of 'minority' has by and large replaced the European concept of social class? For example, in France, a country where Marxist-inspired discourse has been frequent, attention focuses not on socio-economically deprived minorities, but on the rejection of ethnic minorities (including many immigrant workers) by a significant fraction of the population. It is remarkable that in France, attempts to develop a workers' movement claiming the 'right to be different' were very rapidly brushed aside in favour of anti-racialist campaigns aimed at better integration of the newcomers in the nation, rather than concentrating on their differences and conflicts with socially and culturally more privileged categories. From a purely descriptive point of view, one observes that in many countries, including France, manual workers are increasingly unlikely to identify them-selves with the working class. Thus, one encounters in France a situation that took place much earlier in the United States.

One should emphasize that the vision of society as a social body or as a mass society appears — with very different connotations — among both conservative and radical thinkers. Isn't the opposition to both social democratic and communist themes — and thus denial of the capacity for collective action of the exploited masses — the very definition of leftism? This naturally leads to rejection of the notion of social movement and even that of class. The form of leftism which has had the greatest impact is the Castrist and Guevarist theory of *foco* and guerrilla struggle. These are based on the idea that a country defined by its dependence on foreign imperialism cannot develop mass action, nor even an avant-garde party. It must therefore rely on the action of mobile guerrillas, who will ultimately topple the corrupt power, then transform themselves into a Leninist-type party leading to mass mobilization. This hyper-Leninism results, tragically, in a complete break with mass move-ments and in adventures like those of Guevara in Bolivia. Of course, leftist thought may lead to support of political regimes utterly dedicated to the pursuit of integration and the rejection of deviant minorities, where internal social conflicts and, more broadly, social movements, are not recognized. In a less politicized form, limited to an ideological representation, structural-Marxist thought (as it has sometimes been labelled) has analysed society as a discourse of domination and unveiled the mechanisms by which the system imposes its own interests on its members and prevents conflict formation. Reference to conflicts is purely artificial, because the actors are necessarily submissive and only marginals can be aroused to revolt, as Marcuse and, a generation later, Foucault attempted. In the West, including Latin America, it is the theme of social integration that has dealt the heaviest blows to the theme of social struggle and social movements. It is as if the nineteenth century believed that the oppressed could liberate themselves, whereas twentieth-century thinkers are primarily impressed by the weakness of particular actors vis-a-vis the capacities for domination and manipulation of both absolute power and mass culture. It seems that today we think more readily in terms of social contradictions, exclusion and minorities than in terms of conflict, domination and social movements.

Liberal Fragmentation

The classical image of social movements, as developed in European thought since the nineteenth century, is linked to the image of social life as a society of production. We haven't yet — at least in this part of the world — become aware of the profound transformation of our analytical tools implied by the transition from a society of production to one of consumption. The worker is defined, first and foremost, by his place in the division of labour and the social relations of production. The consumer can surely be defined, as we have just recalled, by the type and degree of his participation in what some call values and others systems of social control, but this image is almost worthless, as it cannot explain the real operation of consumer society. Consumer society is based on demands which are also needs, and these cannot be reduced to the quest for status, as some superficial critics and commentators have claimed. These needs are centred on the individual himself, on his desire to affirm himself, to please or be attractive to others, to develop his experience of time and space, to ensure his health and the education of his children, etc. Consumption leads to the introduction into social life of demands that are by no means always social, and are sometimes even anti-social, inasmuch as the eroticization of numerous consumer goods suggests the pertinence of Freudian analyses. Therefore, consumer identity is no longer fully defined by social relations. Consequently, the demands or requests of the consumer are no longer organized around a central principle. In contrast, at the beginning of this century, one could still believe that workers' claims found specific expression in the domains of lodging, education and culture as well as in the political order and in unions. How could the patient, the parent of a schoolchild, the tourist, the TV viewer, and the automobile buyer have the same interests, and why should they find themselves in the same camp, facing the same adversaries?

The business enterprise — from the workshop to the entire system of capitalist production — was the natural and obvious adversary of popular movements. Yet, we everywhere observe a remarkably rapid and profound transformation of the image of the business enterprise. In the United States, the captains of industry have long been the heroes of popular imagination. However, this has not been the case in Europe nor in many other parts of the world, since business was defined above all as a social actor whose interests were assumed to be opposed to those of the workers. But today, in numerous countries, businesses have ceased to be social actors and have become purely economic actors, defined by their position in the national and, especially, international market, rather than by their role in relations of social production. Business is not the basic cell of post-industrial society; modern businesses are like the regiments that protect the frontiers of society from foreign invasion and provide their country with a strong position in the international marketplace. Here too, we have difficulty in adjusting our representations to such fundamental transformations. One still hears, on all sides, that business is the place where workers and, especially, managers, must invest their efforts. Yet, the principal characteristic of the present situation is the dissociation of the world of business, the professional world in general, and the world of culture. The success of business no longer depends on its ethic, Protestant or otherwise, but on its ability to develop strategy and to mobilize its financial, and also its technical and human, resources.

Thus, a great gulf is created between the two actors of industrial society — business and the worker — previously so close that they were almost entirely defined by their mutual relations and conflicts. The worker has been transformed into a consumer, and what was an organization in the sociological sense of the word has truly become a business, defined by its position in the capital, goods and services markets.

Daniel Bell (1976), in a well-known book, *The Cultural Contradictions of Capitalism*, stressed the dissociation of norms and values concerning production, consumption and politics in American society. How can we fail to see that he was right? We have just examined this dissociation in the spheres of production and consumption. This dissociation is equally striking in the realm of politics. Traditions inherited from the nineteenth century have defined democracy as — above all — representative. Yet, as the twentieth century draws to a close, the notion of representative democracy is in deep crisis almost everywhere. It is losing ground not to participatory democracy — which negatively evokes revolutionary and populist regimes — but to the more modest conception of a democracy defined by institutional rules. This kind of democracy doesn't guarantee power-sharing by all, but at least it safeguards against its illegitimate appropriation by a man, a governing apparatus or a privileged social category. In other words, the main problem facing democracy is no longer its struggle against the ruling classes, nor the opposition of an all-powerful elite and a dependent mass, but its struggle against the various types of totalitarianism that have so brutally dominated the twentieth century. The nineteenth century was characterized by a great increase in power sharing. The late twentieth century is primarily preoccupied with the attempt to create limits to power, which so often tends to become absolute and to speak in the name of the society it devours. Hannah Arendt was surely the great initiator of this reversal in our thinking about democracy, of the affirmation that the problems of order and political liberty are more fundamental than social problems and, in any case, are not dominated by them. This non-social, non-representative concept of democracy, which was so strongly held by Isaiah Berlin and Karl Popper, but also — in a very different spirit — by Claude Lefort, no longer sees the political order as the stake in what are ultimately work conflicts. Thus, the vast domain of political analysis is separated, by a single stroke, from the study of conflicts and social movements.

Should this new form of thought be labelled liberal? To me, this term seems adequate, since the essence of liberal thought does not consist in a positive affirmation nor in the definition of a central goal, but rather in the refusal of any central principle of analysis and action. According to the liberals, such principles inevitably transform themselves into a central power — a power that is more ideological than political or economic, and therefore constitutes an insurmountable obstacle to the respect and development of freedoms.

Even if we do not feel satisfied with this critical vision, how can we fail to see that we have entered — probably for a long time — what may be labelled a liberal climate? This, after having lived — for a very long time and in the great majority of the world's countries — in a social-democratic or socialist climate; that is, with the idea that the intervention of a central power, based on the increasing political participation of the masses, would reinforce freedoms and help them penetrate the sphere of work. Today, all forms of state intervention are called into question, not only in the countries formerly labelled socialist — who strive to rid themselves of this appellation as a sick person seeks to rid himself of infectious disease — but also in the democratic countries, where the Welfare State — the principal political invention of the nineteenth-century West — is accused of impotence, and even of the maintenance and reinforcement of social inequalities. How can one fail to recognize — whatever our political positions — that the theme of social movements (as I defined it at the outset) was closely associated with the theme of the necessity of state intervention? As if the ultimate justification of social movements, which may initially be violent, is the progress of social security programmes, which always depend on the state and efficiently limit the risks and inequalities which strike most dramatically the feeblest and the poorest. The interest in social movements would not have been as great, had it not always been linked to the desire for reform. Conversely, even the partisans of the most moderate forms of industrial democracy, such as the English Fabians or the German theorists of the Weimar Republic, or even the yet more moderate defenders of *Sozialmark-twirtschaft*, have always kept in mind that behind these policies, however moderate, there lurks the profile of the workers' movement and its class organizations.

How can we fail to conclude that in a newly liberal world, the very idea of a social movement becomes meaningless, because social movements are not conceivable without the recognition that social relations of production have a central role in determining political choices and relations? Once again, the debates about social movements would be of very little significance if they didn't call into question not only particular phenomena but a general representation of social life.

The Destructive Effect of the State on Social Movements
It has been very frequently observed that the idea of 'social movement' is more appropriate to countries that have experienced genuine capitalist development than to others. This observation is

of critical importance. It reminds us that social movements oppose the actors of civil society, and thus presuppose not only that civil society is distinct from the state, but also — and this goes much further — that modernization processes are subordinate to the functioning of an already modern society; or — to cite the simplest and most extreme formulation — that modernization is endogenous. Isn't this the very definition of Western rationalism, for which modernization is nothing other than the triumph of reason over tradition, of instrumental thought over religious belief, of achievement over ascription? It is only in so far as the modernization effort *is* the functioning of modernity that there appears sufficient space for social movements. On the contrary, wherever development has been exogenous rather than endogenous, wherever modernity has been imposed and primitive accumulation (to use Marx's term) clearly dissociated from capitalist accumulation properly speaking — in brief, wherever the inception of the modernization process has been due to war, conquest or the expropriation of significant social, regional or national categories, the state and the relationships of dominance, alliance and protection created by it replace the civil space of social movements.

Whereas the nineteenth century was marked by the development of capitalist economic centres, especially those of the Victorian economy, the twentieth century has been marked by the entry of non-modern countries into the modernization process. These countries were non-modern both because they had maintained social, religious or economic organizations that opposed the formation of endogenous actors of modernization, and because colonization had maintained or even re-established structures of command and control that favoured the subordination of local society to the colonial order, rather than colonial society's capacity for self-modernization. If the central figure of the nineteenth century was the bourgeoisie, then the central figure of the twentieth century was the state, whether revolutionary, nationalist, socialist or communal. In the central countries, growth in wealth and the actions undertaken by the workers' movement, in all its forms, led to the rapid institutionalization of labour conflicts and therefore to a normal decline in the social movements which accompanied the first industrialization. In the rest of the world, however, the state replaced social movements and generally considered them its principal enemies. It is no accident that the most important revolution of the twentieth century, the Soviet revolution, was led by the Bolsheviks who, on the eve of the revolution, still constituted a small minority among Russian labour movements, then in full development, and that the first victims of the new Soviet power came from what was then called the workers' opposition. In communist regimes, unions are the part of the political system most strictly subordinated to the central power. This allows us to appreciate the extraordinary newness of the Polish Solidarity movement, which appeared in 1980, for it is simultaneously a labour, democratic and nationalist movement.

How could the social movements have survived the tentacular development of the totalitarian state? And, now that the totalitarian power is crumbling or called into question, how can the opposition speak in the name of social movements? It is evident that the idea of democracy is the only direct and efficient antidote to totalitarian power.

It is perhaps too early to propose analyses of post-communist societies, and of what will happen in post-nationalist societies. But we already know enough to realize that these regimes do not box in or crush social movements or, more generally, social actors. Rather, they pervert them, or even destroy or dissolve them. The horses do not race the day the barriers are raised, because they have been locked up for too long. They lacked oxygen, many have died, and others don't have the strength to run or are afraid of the whippings they used to receive. True, when totalitarian regimes crumble, persons, groups and organizations that have struggled for a long time, at the cost of great sacrifices, seem ready to occupy the place of the collapsed powers; but the testimony of these individuals and groups shows us that we must be prudent in assessing the capacity of the new regimes to produce new actors and new social movements. In most cases, the chief factor is the desire to be completely rid of the old system, and therefore, to adopt a clearly liberal position, giving priority to political liberty and the market economy, considered as the only efficient means of eliminating *nomenklatura* and totalitarianism. In both cases, chaos is the dominant note: the decomposition of the old system does not automatically lead to the formation of a new system. In a third set of cases — this is especially true of ones characterized by deep political and economic crisis — the actors formed are defensive, populist and nationalist rather than offensive. They are incapable of directing social relations (particularly those involved in production) and become absurdly irrational. These are not statements of extreme pessimism, but of realism. They recognize the testimony of the most incontrovertible witnesses, who have declared the extraordinary difficulty of the renaissance and recreation of social actors in regimes whose very essence was the destruction of these actors — whose policy was to let the state bureaucracy devour, pervert or reduce them to slavery. In writing these lines, I in no way give up hope that actors and social movements will be recreated: that would contradict the hopes of so many of the participants in liberation struggles around the world. But one cannot accept a superficial image of social movements as a quasi-mechanical phenomenon. The same holds true of the study of the conditions of return to a market economy. To cite two, particularly clear, examples: neither in the Soviet Union nor in Poland do we witness the rise of a new generation of entrepreneurs. The ruins of an administered economy lead more easily to disorder, a black market and speculation than to investment efforts and the reconstitution of a price system, that is, to the rational allocation of a market economy.

How can we fail to conclude that the grandiose image of a society that results from conflicts and negotiations among social movements, adversaries and yet partners in the social construction of the same cultural orientations and actors in the same civil society, has been dealt a severe, most would say a deadly, blow? On the one hand, the liberal explosion has suppressed every central principle of regulation of social life. On the other hand, the totalitarian or post-totalitarian systems have destroyed the plurality of actors and refused to allow any autonomy to negotiations, social conflicts and political debates. Caught between these two extremes, the idea of social movement is lost. In this respect, it is similar to the various forms of social and industrial democracy, which increasingly tend to forget their origins in struggle and to transform themselves into corporatisms, that is, to integrate themselves into the reductive apparatus of the state.

The Return of Social Movements?

Can civil society, defined as the social space of production of social life by work and the creation of cultural values, reconstitute the two fronts which, as we have just described, have been destroyed? Can civil society free itself from the control of the state on the one hand and, on the other, can it reconstruct itself beyond the increasing diversity of demands on the market? This question is of interest not only to those who seek to defend analysis in terms of social movements. One may well consider that the question raised is that of the very existence of sociology. The manifest decline of sociological thought is due to invasion of its field of study by two intellectual approaches very different from its own. It cannot be sufficiently stressed that the response to totalitarianism is, neither theoretically nor practically, a social one. The response to totalitarianism can only be a political one, based on reflection about the concept of democracy. Thus, the field of sociology is invaded by political philosophy, which is making a remarkable intellectual come-back. The other aspect of the situation is more complex because, as we have seen, criticism of the notion of 'social movement' comes from two seemingly unrelated perspectives, whose attacks are in fact co-ordinated and complementary. On the one hand, a strictly liberal form of thought attempts to reduce sociological analysis to economic analysis, that is to rational — which is not to say transparent — choices in the marketplace. According to the other point of view, society is an organized apparatus of self-control, and social behaviours are merely effects of the system — false consciousness. This radical separation of meaning and consciousness occults not only the idea of social movement but also that of social actor, and more generally, the whole field of sociology, especially as defined by Weber. Put more simply, whether one believes in the implacable logic of systems or, on the contrary, seeks to liberate oneself from such logics, one no longer formulates one's analysis or one's action in social terms. One refers either to institutional rules or to properly individualistic demands. Social space tends to fragment or disappear, and the most pessimistic are convinced that public space — *öffentlichkeit* — dissolves under the blows of mass politics, and especially mass culture. The mass media are merely the most visible aspects and the best-organized power centres of mass culture.

It would be an exaggeration to claim that one can only save sociological analysis by reconstructing thinking about social movements. Many would prefer to stop half-way, and not to accept the most demanding and critical proposition of a sociology of social movements: the idea that we must always think of social systems as organized around a central conflict. But in reality, tomorrow as well as yesterday, it is probably the most radical thought, the one which does not fear the introduction of the most exacting hypothesis — that of a principle of integration and centring of social conflicts, which has the best chances of playing a central role in the reconstruction of sociological analysis. If such an awakening does not take place, sociological analysis may disintegrate completely, to be absorbed partly by economic analysis and partly by political philosophy.

Let us successively examine the three fronts on which sociological analysis is attacked. Does each of them show signs of the reconstruction of an analysis in terms of social movements?

Current historical circumstances oblige us to give priority to the theme of the totalitarian state or, more precisely, to the downfall of modernizing, authoritarian, voluntarist states. Our prudent, critical remarks should not make us lose sight of the nature of the upheavals that we are observing. More concretely, isn't the appeal to a Western democratic model the most striking characteristic of post-communist societies? Aren't these countries, which so ardently wish to move to democracy, capable of rediscovering the sources of representative democracy, even though there exists today the danger of a more or less brutal break between an extreme economic liberalism and a fairly aggressive nationalist populism? Isn't democratization the specific characteristic of the political transformation process in these countries; that is, democratization in the sense of the reconstruction of institutional forms of political liberty, is the initial condition for the renaissance of social actors and the debates among them, debates which, in the first instance, concern ways of avoiding a negative break between extreme economic liberalism and a populism that cannot achieve the economic reconstruction of the country. Isn't this power game, which we have so often considered a degeneration of the democratic process when observing Western countries, not also a phase of democratization in countries emerging from totalitarian regimes? The democratic game can only develop completely if it combines and opposes forces that consider themselves responsible for the economic life of the country, its national existence and the defence of specific social interests. Let us note that democracy's institutional frame has reconstituted itself, without major difficulties, in Czechoslovakia, Hungary, Poland and East Germany, that it has partially reconstituted itself in the Soviet Union and even in Bulgaria. For now, Romania is the only country of the region where it is not yet possible to speak of the re-establishment of a democratic regime. Whatever its limits, the functional differentiation of social actors is progressing: the intellectuals and managers are freeing themselves from the administrative and ideological logic of the state, unions are reconstituting themselves, enterprises are being created, cultural life is admirably enriched. Would it be anticipating observable reality too much to say that the political and social life of these countries is organized around the choice — both political and social in character — between the dissociation of political and economic liberalism, on the one hand, and the reconstruction of socio-economic actors, on the other? These developments are not the harbingers of social movements, but they are signs of the transition from purely institutional democracy to the formation of choices that could make this democracy representative.

What is already manifest in post-communist Central Europe is a tendency in other parts of the world. The situation in the new Latin American democracies is assuredly confused. Nevertheless, it is clear to all that the present conjuncture, which exacerbates populist-type demands on the state, renders a populist policy absolutely impossible. If this contradiction isn't recognized, it quickly leads to increase in social demands that cannot be satisfied, and thus to hyper-inflation. But although this is the image that first meets the eye, it is far from realistic. On the contrary, one can say that the major countries of Latin America are already engaged in the chaotic because extremely difficult, but tenacious, search for different ways of combining an open economic policy with the struggle against the growing menace of internal social dualism. In many countries, this orientation is labelled social democratic. But in fact, this term can be applied to situations as different as those of Mexico, Argentina, Brazil, Chile and Costa Rica — to mention only the clearest-cut. In other words, the current development of Latin America is dominated by the formation of opposed and complementary social actors: exporters and the urban masses. These social actors can certainly engage in civil war, as they did for such a long time in Argentina, leading it to disaster. But they may also, often in a similarly excessive manner, strive not to choose between equally catastrophic unilateral solutions. Sociologists cannot be satisfied with aggressively superficial images that reduce the history of Latin America to an irrational tumult. The smallest effort at observation allows us to see the operation of the difficult process — always at risk of failure — of the formation of new social actors, or even of new social movements, and therefore of a political process having a certain representative character.

It's much easier to answer those who consider that industrialized democratic societies are systems of integration that eliminate any possibility of movement of social actors. First, because this image, which had so much success in the 1970s, has been largely eroded by the neo-liberal vision which we have already evoked, and to which we shall soon return. Isn't it paradoxical to view societies in accelerated transformation, whose economic, social and political systems are assuredly more flexible and open than any others, as self-controlled systems for the transmission of inheritances, for the reproduction of inequalities and privileges? Isn't it irresponsible to say, with Marcuse, that societies of pure tolerance exercise a self-control as tight as that of totalitarian state societies? But these remarks are insufficient, since they address only the most excessive, exaggeratedly critical theories of social integration. It's more important to underline, for those who insist on the end of social bipolarity and the increasing integration of mass society, that this integration is much more limited than they claim. In fact, our societies are engaged in a race for change and, as in any running team, the stiffer the competition, the more numerous the obstacles to be overcome, the greater also the distances separating the runners. Today, we realize that equality of opportunity has made far less progress than expected, that most of the professions in which women have acquired an important role are ones in decline and that the decision centres remain overwhelmingly masculine; that the equalizing effects of schools, even when free and secular, are feeble or nil; that the redistribution of revenues effected by social security systems is much weaker than one could hope and sometimes non-existent. The theme of inequality thus again becomes the basis of an analysis in terms not only of social distance but of social conflicts. On condition, however, that this observation be strictly limited to the domain to which it applies: the management of change. This is what distinguishes that present analysis from earlier analyses, which dealt with the whole of social structure, and more particularly with the production system.

This leads us to the final field of debates and to the most critical interrogation, concerning the renaissance — possible or improbable — of social movements. Is our consumer society one in which individuals throw their demands at a market that, for all its rigidities and deviations, attempts to respond to them, or is it still a society based on production, with social relations of production at its core? It has been quite some time since Toffler (1980) made an important contribution to this discussion by creating the term *prosumer*, which encountered considerable success. He meant to say that the production system which we are, by and large, embarked upon makes us not only into consumers of goods, but — as consumers — operators of the system. Clearly, the patient is not merely a consumer of the hospital, the pupil or student a mere consumer of education, and — must one add — the TV viewer a mere consumer of television programmes, even if a certain logic tends to reduce him to this role. To take the most dramatically obvious example, the patient is placed in a hospital to which he both brings and opposes his will to autonomy, liberty and identity, though he also accepts and positively values the technical logic of health care. Sociologists and other observers, but also politicians and labour leaders, have come late to the recognition of the extreme importance of political opinion in post-industrial countries of tensions, conflicts and compromises between the logic of health care and that of the patient. Some superficial minds have contrasted qualified scientific medicine and 'natural' medicine. This reaction is fully analogous to that of the Luddites at the beginning of the industrial revolution. But, just as the workers' movement could only constitute itself once industry was accepted (which allowed contestation of relations of property and social control), so it is that genuine social conflict among administrative, technical and corporative logics only appears when the positive functions of science applied to medicine are recognized. This development has created a new political arena. So far, this arena hasn't found a specific form of expression, but it is extremely important to public opinion, as indicated by the success of certain television programmes and, in some countries, by the extreme development of juridical conflicts among patients, hospitals and doctors.

We are even less advanced in the realm of other cultural industries, such as schools and universities on the one hand, and the mass media on the other. Nevertheless, numerous sociological studies have already shown that we must replace the weak theme of socialization by a much richer and more readily observable one: the growing distance between the socializing and educative function of schools and universities and the psychological and cultural universe of pupils and students. This dissociation, which found such dramatic expression in the student movements of the 1960s, seems to have been forgotten, despite the fact that it is continuously reinforced and creates a world of misunderstandings and psychological crises to which teachers generally are extremely sensitive. It is more difficult to find clear formulations of conflicts of interest and orientation in the mass media, as the public is dispersed and has little means of influencing the centres that create the programmes.

In these three cases, how can we fail to recognize the competition and conflict between two logics? As so many critics have pointed out, one logic is that of reinforcement of the system, of maximization of the production of goods of general value, such as money, power and information. The other logic is the increasing reference, in the cultural industries, to the effort made by each individual to construct and defend his individuality. Let's call 'subject' the individual's effort to construct him or herself as an individual, rather than as a subordinate in a logic of order, whatever that order may be. We know only too well that this appeal to the individual can autodestruct if the individual defines himself as devoid of content, or may on the contrary nourish a new populism, or even new forms of cultural, national or other fundamentalisms. But already, in the post-industrial societies, that is, the ones where the cultural industries have acquired a dominant role, public opinion is structured by the debate between what may be labelled a logic of the marketplace — which is also a logic of power and accumulation — and a logic of individual liberty, which cannot be reduced to the affirmation of a self-destructive narcissism, nor to the return to cultural and ethnic roots in which the individual is suppressed in favour of a return to religions and theocracies.

These social movements, which develop in the cultural industries, may combine with the policies of struggle against exclusion and for equality evoked above. However, they are of a different nature, which shows the degree to which political action and social movement remain separated. A social movement doesn't speak in the name of a collectivity, it speaks either in the name of a ruling category or in that of a directed category, that is, in all cases, in the name of a category defined by dominance and power relations. All these movements present themselves as representatives and defenders of cultural movements recognized by all. Those who direct the great cultural industries speak in the name of individualism, because they put science in the service of medical care, education and information. They speak of creativity, liberation and liberty of choice, while constructing health, education and information systems aimed at maximizing 'output', i.e. developing as much as possible the quantity of medical, pedagogical and general information in circulation. In the other camp, one also speaks of individualism, of liberty and of movement, but in a more defensive and more 'utopian' manner, for here one speaks not merely for the individual, but in the name of his or her ability and desire to defend his or her individuality, his or her subjectivity. The essential point I wish to stress here is that these new movements differ from earlier, better-known ones not only by their nature, but above all by the break they establish between the social sphere, become increasingly moral, and the sphere of the state and strictly political action. The workers' movement in its central aspect — that is, the labour unions — was always a political actor and had a vision of reality well expressed by the term 'socialism'. In fact, union action was almost always subordinated to political action because, as we have seen, the working class was defined not as subjectivity but as agent in the implementation of an historical necessity. This mixture of subjectivity and objectivity, of voluntarist action and historical necessity, is disappearing. Simultaneously, social movements free themselves from the tutelage of a political party. This situation is not one of unmitigated advantages, since the political parties and the relationship to the state unified movements, each of which had its own specificities and usually also defended more limited interests. Today, the integration of different movements is no longer operated by the relationship to the state: it must operate directly, and this is much more difficult and involves considerable risk of fragmentation. Yet, how can one fail to see that this is how the autonomy — indeed preponderance — of civil society affirms itself, and that there already exists a commonness of orientation among different movements? One must stress the majority role of women in these new movements, characteristic of professions in which women are highly represented for traditional reasons. These are the sectors involving services to people, assured by women in the traditional society; when these services entered the sphere of market relations, women continued to assure them. But the fact that this situation is rooted in traditional society doesn't prevent these social formations, found in the sphere of services to persons, from contesting many principles which were and still are at the core of the most radical feminist movements, those which refuse to separate or oppose equality of opportunity and recognition of the biocultural specificity of women.

One should add that between the domain of social movement and that of centralized political action — action directly controlled by the state — there tends very quickly to develop a level intermediary between the social system and the political system, and that one should here call the level of public opinion or *öffentlichkeit*. I am not referring merely to television and the major presses, but primarily to organizations of influence-brokering and sometimes even of decision-making, which are distinct from political organizations and, in particular, from parliaments and elected local authorities. It is at this level, that of the pre-political expression and debates of social movements, that the theme of consensus or communication appears. This theme is none other than the direct recognition, by the groups involved, of the similitude of their cultural orientations and therefore of the existence of cultural stakes accepted by all the groups. To cite only one example, but the most important one: committees on biomedical ethics have been constituted in many countries. These committees do not seek to achieve compromises between the suppliers and users of health care, but to identify the common orientations, the fundamental ethical principles which can form the basis of relationships between the parties.

This transformation of the relationships between social movements and political action is so profound that it has prevented many observers from recognizing the existence of the new social movements for, as Charles Tilly put it, these do not have the same 'repertory' as the older movements. For those, the essential matter was the control of power, and images of violence were considered the most symbolic: the occupation of the Bastille or the Winter Palace, mass demonstrations often violently dispersed by the police, occupations of factories and the theme of the general strike. The new social movements seem as pacific and as interested in consciousness-raising as the others were violent and interested in the control of power. In brief, the old social movements were associated with the idea of revolution, the new ones are associated with the idea of democracy. Consequently, the idea of democracy can no longer be fully defined by institutional rules. One cannot consider democratic a regime that is not interested in the rights of the personal subject, which we again call, as in the eighteenth century, the rights of man. However, these are no longer seen as the rights — always linked to duties — of citizens, but as the rights of the individual over against encroaching political power.

Such analyses should, of course, circumvent the most usual risks of error. The fact that certain demands have taken shape recently doesn't mean that they constitute new social movements. Some currents of opinion and anti-establishment campaigns are not part of the core of the new social movements as defined above. In particular, following the 1960s and the major student movements, many Western countries have seen the formation of leftist-inspired, regionalist, anti-nuclear, and also feminist movements, which are not clearly social movements. In some cases, these were highly politicized and ideological forms of old social movements on the verge of disappearance. Italian and German terrorism is a case in point. These had recourse to physical violence to awaken a working class which they continued to consider as the revolutionary actor par excellence; but this actor had been fooled, manipulated and put to sleep, so that it was necessary to bring it brutally back to consciousness of its true interests. The terrorists looked towards a working class which, as they defined it, had long since ceased to exist, probably just as the anarchists, who became involved in a series of terrorist incidents at the end of the nineteenth century, looked towards a world on the borderline of crafts and industry, which had, by that time, given way in most places to extensive industrialization and mass production. In many countries, the 1970s were characterized by intermediary movements which voiced these new demands, in reality more cultural than economic, though they were expressed in the vocabulary of the old social movements. The student movements provide the clearest examples. I have analysed the French movement of May 1968 in these terms, showing the opposition between their content, which was new, and their Trotskyist or Maoist language, which made them seem reminiscent of the pre-revolutionary period in Russia. This contradiction is very similar to the one between the content and the language of the revolution of 1848 or of the Paris Commune. As Marx admirably showed, the new contents, that is, workers' claims, were subordinated to the exhausted old language of the French Revolution, almost a century earlier. All these contradictory movements crumbled or divided rapidly, so that by the end of the 1970s, many thought that it was time to abandon all reference to social movements, because we live in a type of society that leaves no room for a general but concentrated contestation of the principal forms of social organization. Isn't it necessary, today, to revise this judgement? Mustn't we go beyond the enthusiasm provoked by the collapse of the communist regime and the democratic liberation of peoples subjected to a doubly foreign yoke? Shouldn't we study the appearance of new social movements, and consequently, of new reform strategies in the industrialized and democratic countries themselves?

Some believe that history has reached its end. One could say, on the contrary, that the river of history, which had been lost in the bogs and meanders of totalitarianism and frozen in the discourse of the state, has returned to its bed and resumed its flow towards one or several futures. For it is only when a society is capable of debating its choices, of recognizing the complementarity of cultural orientations common to most and clearly opposed social interests, that it may have a history. History, which almost stopped in the East, may also halt in the West, if we make the marketplace into a prince as absolute as a political committee, if we believe that the lucid knowledge of the interests of each determines the organization of society by a cascade of rational choices and political compromises. One must, on the contrary, rediscover the existence and efficacity of social actors, East, West and South; one must therefore strive to understand how history, far from having reached its conclusion, resumes its march.

References

Bell, D. (1976) *The Cultural Contradictions of Capitalism*. London: Heinemann.
Toffler, A. (1980) *The Third Wave*. London: Collins.

Alain Touraine is Director of the Centre d'Analyse et d'Intervention Sociologiques, Paris.

Disaggregating the Idea of Capitalism

Dennis Wrong

The term 'capitalism' did not become widely used until the beginning of the present century when, as Fernand Braudel (1986: 237) writes, 'it fully burst upon political debate as the natural opposite of socialism'. Werner Sombart was mainly responsible for launching it in academic circles where it very shortly afterwards received an additional impetus from Max Weber's famous essay (1930), originally written in criticism of Sombart, and the debate over the Protestant ethic thesis that ensued. Although often believed to have been the major formulator and disseminator of the idea of capitalism as a historically distinctive economic system, Karl Marx never used the term, usually describing the social order shaped by the economic processes that were the subject of his most voluminous and influential writings as 'bourgeois society'. Nor did Adam Smith ever use the word. The Russian Revolution of October 1917 was largely responsible for securely establishing 'capitalism' as the name of the dominant order in the West that the Bolsheviks aspired to overthrow and replace with 'socialism', pictured as a vastly superior and radically different alternative.

This record contains many ironies and paradoxes. Most obviously, the common name for the old system doomed to perish came into general use nearly a century *after* the invention and spread of the name signifying both the social movement striving to overthrow it and the new order designed to supplant it. This might be regarded as an instance of Karl Mannheim's claim that conservative thought only achieves articulation in response to a prior ideological — in his terminology, utopian — assault upon the existing order it wants to affirm. However, 'capitalism' was never a concept favored by its defenders. It has nearly always been used pejoratively. The historian Fritz Stern (1987: 235) recently wrote:

Theory, Culture & Society (SAGE, London, Newbury Park and New Delhi), Vol. 9 (1992), 147–158

The detractors of capitalism are legion, its defenders few and uncertain. Stereotypes prevail: Capitalism involves alienation, exploitation, class conflict. Historically it is seen as the triumph of a corrupt and spineless bourgeoisie, ruthless in its pursuit of profit and in its repression of the class it lives off . . .'

Reviewing the much earlier seventeenth and eighteenth-century use of 'capitalist' to describe rich men and financial manipulators, Braudel (1986: 235) remarked, 'The word is never, the reader will have noticed, used in a friendly sense.' Braudel went on to recount how, converted into an 'ism', it became a 'political word' readily 'incorporated into the Marxist model', ultimately giving rise to a 'post-Marxian orthodoxy' in which 'we are not allowed to talk about capitalism before the end of the eighteenth century, in other words before the industrial mode of production' (Braudel, 1986: 238).

I remember C. Wright Mills in the late 1940s commenting on an article in *Fortune* that urged spokesmen for American business unapologetically to call the system they upheld 'capitalism' instead of resorting to euphemisms like 'free enterprise'. Mills saw this as an example of the growing realism of those he then described as 'sophisticated conservatives', an early approximation as a group to what he later named the 'power elite'. Mills overlooked that the article was probably written by one of several Trotskyist intellectuals on the magazine's staff, who undoubtedly saw himself as engaged in subtle ideological subversion in offering such terminological advice to the class enemy.

Even if Marx neither invented nor used the term, the essence of his work was to insist, against the classical economists, that the mode of production dominated by the use of money as capital was not simply equivalent to political economy as such; it was, on the contrary, no more than a transitory product of history rather than the embodiment of timeless natural laws analogous to those of Newtonian mechanics. But, though transitory, economic systems, or modes of production, generated classes in conflict over material interests that were the prime movers of history itself. Everything else in a society, its legal, political, religious and cultural institutions and values, constituted a superstructure shaped by the base of the economy, or the forces and relations of production.

The idea of 'capitalism' as a specific kind of economic system distinct from primitive communism, slavery, feudalism and the future prospect of socialism and full communism attracted comparative historians like Sombart and Weber. Yet these scholars were primarily interested in exploring the complex links between capitalism as an economic system and class structures, religious beliefs, legal systems and forms of government, as well as such relative cultural intangibles as moral outlooks and mentalities (*mentalités*). Paradoxically, if they borrowed the notion of capitalism as a particular kind of economic system from Marxism, they also enlarged it into a more comprehensive entity by aggregating it with non-economic, even primarily psychological, social and cultural phenomena. At the same time, they criticized or denied the causal priority ascribed by Marxists to economic forces, giving at least equal weight to such non-economic factors as the Protestant ethic, Roman law, urban political autonomy or an underlying rationalizing spirit or *Geist* pervading all spheres of social life, in accounting for the genesis of capitalism itself. Capitalism as a generic term for modern society owes as much to the historians and sociologists who were critics of Marxism as to Marxism itself.

An additional paradox is that Marx's preferred term for the post-feudal era, 'bourgeois society', essentially referred to a correlate of capitalism, namely, the class that became its historical carrier and achieved social dominance under its aegis, rather than to the mode of production itself. Bourgeois society is, therefore, an aggregative concept. Of all the various 'post' labels that have been so popular in recent years — post-industrial, post-materialist, post-capitalist, postmodern — post-bourgeois is the only one that is not unavoidably controversial because of a vagueness verging on vacuity that lends itself to arbitrary interpretation. Post-bourgeois at least suggests the disappearance of a bounded, residentially located, historical social class with a cultural profile of its own. But the disappearance of the class in no way entails the disappearance of capitalism, the mode of production associated with the rise of the class and both reflecting and shaping its style of life. The bourgeoisie dissolves, its distinctive values are partly negated and even reversed, partly diffused to everyone, but capitalism expands into a world system and with the collapse of communism overcomes the most formidable threat to its survival.

Apart from the overall issue of economic determinism or the economic interpretation of history, the changing historical context of capitalism necessitates continual consideration of which non-economic values and institutions are compatible with it, which limit or even threaten it, and which constitute necessary or sufficient conditions for its birth, growth and survival. The emergence of highly successful capitalist economies in the non-Western societies bordering the China Sea gives added importance to such assessments. Peter Berger (1986: 15–31) devotes much attention to the new East Asian capitalisms in a book whose declared purpose is to disaggregate *modernity* as the central historical experience of the West over the past two centuries by analytically separating from it capitalism as an economic system, granting that the latter's rise was part of the great transformation that created the modern West.

At the beginning of the century Max Weber (1930: 181–2) maintained that the persistence and future development of capitalism did not depend on the waning spirit of religious asceticism that had contributed to its birth: 'Victorious capitalism, since it rests on mechanical foundations, needs its support no longer.' Whether capitalism complements, or even undergirds, democratic government and the civil freedoms basic to the liberalism of the great eighteenth and nineteenth-century political revolutions, or whether it undermines them by concentrating power in the hands of a new ruling class, has been the subject of intense debate ever since socialist ideologies and movements became leading contenders for political power. 'Socialism' was originally coined as the antithesis not of capitalism but of 'individualism', which was coined at roughly the same time in the early nineteenth century. Individualism as a general moral and cultural outlook has long been regarded as both a cause and a consequence of capitalist economies. Recently, however, the existence of any necessary association between capitalism and individualism has been questioned, whatever connection may have existed at the historical conjuncture when capitalism as a new mode of production came into being. It has even been argued that 'the capitalist mode of production does not have any necessary ideological conditions of existence' (Abercrombie et al., 1986: 190). (Ideological here essentially means 'cultural'.)

All of these interpretations amount to efforts to disaggregate the social wholes — social formations, as structuralist Marxists call them — that include capitalist economies in order to determine which links between capitalism and other phenomena are intrinsic and which are merely extrinsic or historically contingent. One is moved to insist that an economy is an economy is an economy: it is meant to put food on the table, not to advance the telos of history, measure up to an ideal, express the moral or aesthetic spirit of a people, function harmoniously as part of a larger integrated social system, nor to create modernity so that modish pontifications in bad prose about something called 'postmodernity' can be turned out by professors.

The pairing of capitalism with socialism as its opposite leads to major misconceptions. The fundamental asymmetry between capitalism and socialism is often overlooked, especially at the level of political and ideological debate. Capitalism is not a theory — it is a condition. Both capitalism and socialism are conceptions of economic systems, but capitalism as a system was only discovered after the fact by the classical political economists, the last of whom, it has rightly been observed, was Karl Marx. Capitalism is a system of unintended consequences both in its origins and in its workings. Braudel once exclaimed, 'The best thing about capitalism is that no one invented it!' Or, as Ernest Gellner (1974: 183) mordantly put it, 'where it does not exist, no one will bother to invent it'. Capitalism is what we have, what we got stuck with; socialism, on the other hand, is an ideal, an ideology or utopia awaiting realization.

It is remarkable how often these painfully obvious and banal observations are ignored by both the eulogists and the critics of capitalism. The rise of capitalism is sometimes described as if benevolent or malevolent men had planned and instituted it at a determinate moment in history. Adam Smith is praised or blamed for having actually invented the market rather than for merely having first fully expounded how it worked to connect supply and demand.[1]

But capitalism is nothing but an economic system which has the palpable advantage but also the ideological disadvantage of actually existing, warts and all. Socialism by contrast has from its beginnings been a project, a shared ideal, something to be built by strenuous political mobilization and collective effort. Socialism possesses 'mythic superiority' over capitalism, as Peter Berger (1986: 194–209) puts it. It is seen — like freedom, democracy, nationhood — as incarnating ultimate values whereas capitalism is judged by its inevitably uneven economic results as solely of instrumental value. No one, as Schumpeter pointed out long ago, has ever died for capitalism. To be sure, there have been visionaries of an ideal or utopian capitalism — one thinks of Milton Friedman — but controversy over the merits of capitalism has always chiefly focused on its actual failures and achievements.

The mythic or utopian aura of socialism was only very partially dissipated by successful communist revolution in Russia. Nevertheless, since 1917 and especially since Stalin's dictatorship socialism as an economic system has faced the same problem of aggregation and disaggregation that capitalism has long confronted. To what extent did Soviet totalitarianism result from the centralized economy or from traditional Russian autocracy? Is it possible to combine socialist economics and political democracy? Long before the collapse of communism in 1989, at the very least since Khrushchev's famous 'secret speech' of 1956, a majority of socialists in the West have firmly dissociated their ideal from the model of Soviet communism. The New Left of the 1960s was an effort to cleanse socialism from the taint of association with the Soviet experience, although many of its partisans briefly invested illusory hopes in the 'actually existing' Third World socialisms of Cuba, China under Mao, North Vietnam and, somewhat later, Nicaragua. Yet the very term 'actually existing socialism' (*real existierender Sozialismus*) was the ironic coinage of a refugee from East Germany on encountering the utter indifference of the West German radical left to the regimes on the other side of the Berlin Wall.

The familiar contrast between capitalism as the status quo and socialism as the obvious alternative to it has been suddenly reversed with the collapse of communism in Central Europe and the Soviet Union. As the current joke has it, socialism is the longest route between capitalism and capitalism. The attempt by formerly communist states to initiate a transition from a command to a market economy in which private enterprise plays a leading role is altogether unprecedented. Is it possible to 'build capitalism' from the top down? How can a new entrepreneurial class of private owners of the means of production be created or recruited out of whole cloth in a short period of time? To what extent will a privatized *nomenklatura* form part of such a class? A few Marxists have already exhibited the stirrings of a tendency to invoke the capitalist aspirations of the delegitimated *nomenklatura* to account for the almost total lack of resistance, even of a non-violent sort, to the popular uprisings against communism in its entirety in Central Europe and the feeble and ultimately fruitless opposition to the continuing efforts to modify it fundamentally in the Soviet Union. There have also been voices on the left contending rather pathetically that the peoples of Central Europe may have wanted democracy and national self-determination but they have not been clamoring for the 'restoration of capitalism'. True enough, but, as we have seen, with the doubtful exception of a few ideologues of neo-classical economics, no one values capitalism for its own sake. The rebels against communism, however, have certainly wanted the economic results of capitalism in the form of a higher standard of living and greater consumer choice. Moreover, the manifest economic deficiencies of state socialism are what finally brought about its collapse.

As these recent events strongly suggest, capitalism as an economic system is not a uniform entity but a complex of inter-dependent attributes. In addition to detaching it from the changing historical contexts of non-economic institutions and cultural traits in which it has been embedded over the several centuries of its existence, its strictly economic features also need to be disaggregated and regarded as capable of independent variation. The almost universal declarations by leaders of the erstwhile Soviet bloc nations that they seek to establish a 'market economy' suggest this, as does the fact that all member parties of the Socialist International in the Western democracies (and in Israel and Japan) now assert their belief in free markets and their rejection of such traditional socialist objectives as central planning and the nationalization of major economic enterprises. The Italian Communist Party, now renamed, has also followed this route to acceptance of a mixed economy with a strong private sector and abandonment of socialism as a goal representing a radical alternative to capitalism.

I shall eschew yet another formal definition of capitalism and confine myself simply to listing its attributes that should be disaggregated from the total complex with which it is usually identified. They are: free market pricing, production for profit, competition between independent producers, a free labor market, and private ownership of the means of production. The free market is obviously the most important. Doubtless, as asserted by a woman in a Jules Feiffer cartoon, 'free market' is a 'better-sounding name' than 'capitalism', given the negative overtones that cling to the latter. But the use of market as a euphemism notwithstanding, the notion of 'market socialism' is not a contradiction in terms, nor even an oxymoron. There is an intellectual tradition affirming it in economic theory and it has recently been advocated by a number of Polish, Czech and Hungarian economists as well as by Alec Nove (1983) in his influential book *The Economics of Feasible Socialism*. In addition to his theoretical analysis, Nove assesses the experiences of Hungary and Yugoslavia, where reform-minded communist regimes introduced elements of market socialism in the 1970s and 1980s.

Markets are, of course, an ancient institution, present to some degree in nearly all human societies. Adam Smith (1970: 117) was certainly correct in regarding as universally human 'the propensity to truck, barter, and exchange one thing for another'. (He was also correct in seeing it as a distinctively human disposition, presupposing 'the faculties of reason and speech' and thus lacking in other animal species.) Markets, therefore, long antedate capitalism, as Marx recognized, although they are often equated with it in socialist or anti-capitalist discourse. Such major theorists of socialism as Marx, Lenin, Kautsky and Bukharin regarded socialism and markets as incompatible virtually by definition. More recently, Paul Sweezy (1971: 5) directly denied my previous statement in insisting that 'The very term "market socialism" is self-contradictory.' One is reminded of Robert Nozick's (1974: 163) brilliant *bon mot* that 'The socialist society would have to forbid capitalist acts between consenting adults.' Rejecting the market/ capitalism equation from the perspective of a historian, Braudel repeatedly deplored their conflation, maintaining that the market economy existed in the *longue durée* of history whereas capitalism is a relative newcomer. Not just markets but *free* markets in which the rate of exchange or price fluctuates (within limits) in response to perceived magnitudes of supply and demand are also, Braudel (1986: 227) pointed out, both ancient and widespread. Markets spring up spontaneously in a variety of different situations often in the face of attempts by powerful authorities to suppress them. Black markets subvert wartime rationing, underground market economies have flourished in all communist countries, covert markets in scarce or illegal goods and services quickly come into being in prisons and detention camps often improvising new media of exchange such as cigarettes.

Markets presuppose real competition between independent producers or traders. Alec Nove (1990) recently observed that, economically speaking, the opposite of competition is not co-operation but monopoly, including state monopolies. But the competing units need not be 'private' individuals or groups owning their own means of production. Nove (1983: 200–1) distinguishes five distinct types of unit that might exist in his model of feasible socialism: large state-owned and controlled enterprises, autonomous state or worker-owned enterprises, co-operatives, small private businesses, and self-employed individuals. The preponderance of the first three types justifies the socialist label given that private property is clearly a *sine qua non* of capitalism as conventionally understood. Nove's model is actually that of a mixed economy including different kinds of publicly and privately owned enterprises, combining some government planning with the market, and providing generous state welfare services.

From a pro-capitalist standpoint directly opposed to Paul Sweezy's socialist view, Peter Berger (1986: 187–9,226) joins Sweezy in denying the meaningfulness of 'market socialism'. He explicitly defends as a 'hypothetical proposition' — the forty-eighth of fifty that he formulates — that 'There can be no effective market economy without private ownership of the means of production' (Berger, 1986: 190). Berger is narrowly empiricist in equating socialism entirely with the Soviet model. He readily accepts the terms of conventional ideological controversy in treating capitalism and socialism as stark mutually exclusive alternatives. Although conceding that no pure case of either has ever existed, Berger (1986: 194–209) insists that an economy *must* be primarily one or the other without precisely specifying the meaning of 'primarily'. The whole notion of property and what it means to own it, and the relationship of legal ownership to control, raise exceedingly complex conceptual and substantive issues. Berger cogently disaggregates capitalism as an economy from modernity as such, but he accepts capitalism (and socialism, for that matter) as irreducible aggregates.

What of that old socialist saw favoring production for use over production for profit, or the Marxist goal of abolishing 'commodity production' and 'exchange value'? Production for profit presupposes that the product is useful; otherwise, the makers of pet rocks might be aspiring to enter the ranks of the *Fortune* 500. If exchange value were determined solely by the amount of labor required to produce a commodity plus the surplus labor appropriated as profit by the capitalist, there would be flourishing markets for immensely expensive pins with the Lord's Prayer hand carved on their heads and for ship models built inside narrow-necked bottles. Free markets indeed require that enterprises show a profit as a measure of their efficiency, but the profit need not end up lining the pockets of an individual owner. Both as a test of efficiency and as an incentive, profit can accrue to organizations as collective entities regardless of who, if anyone in any meaningful sense, owns them. Property relations, as Marxists like to call them, are just not of critical importance with respect to economic performance.

As for a free labor market, in practice labor has rarely if ever been treated as a 'mere' commodity offered for sale by its owners out of sheer necessity, not even in the era of the 'dark satanic mills' of early industrial England, as Marx and Engels themselves acknowledged. Denial of the status of labor as a marketed commodity like any other is the centerpiece of Lester Thurow's (1983: 173–215) critique in *Dangerous Currents* of the 'equilibrium price-auction' model of the market, as he calls it, that dominates neo-classical economics. Independent trade unions and protective labor legislation exist, though notoriously not to the same degree, in all democratic capitalist countries.

I note with satisfaction the increasing use of the term 'the market mechanism' to describe how contemporary mixed economies work. A mechanism is what it is and does what it does; it inspires neither love nor hate, incarnates neither good nor evil. It also suggests something operating within a larger established context that can be turned on or off, accelerated or decelerated, muffled or allowed free play. I think this is the way we ought to look at capitalism as an economic system, distinct from its historically contingent social and cultural supports, and capable of being disaggregated into its component economic elements.

Perhaps the very name 'capitalism' ought to be confined to the dynamically expanding market, creating unprecedented economic growth and social dislocation, that contributed so greatly to the modernization process, the great transformation, the breakthrough to modernity, or whatever one chooses to call it, that began in Western Europe just over two centuries ago. So used, it would, as distinct from the concept of a market economy, constitute a 'historical individual' in Weber's sense. I have considerable sympathy with Anthony Giddens's (1985: 289) rejection of the frequent substitution of 'industrial' for 'capitalist' on the grounds that 'industrialism first emerged within the institutional nexus of capitalism, whose competitive pressures served in substantial part to generate it'. Peter Berger, despite his effort to dissociate capitalism from modernity, notes his own past failure, as well as that of others, even to identify it as a causal factor in the modernization experience undergone by the West. 'Marxists,' he writes, 'have been obsessed by capitalism; "bourgeois sociologists" have at times failed to notice it' (Berger, 1986: 226).

The collapse of communism and the ongoing globalization of markets mark a historical divide. It is a good moment to divest the idea of capitalism of the penumbra from the past that still clings to it by treating it primarily as an economy and separating its various economic components. One would like to see sociologists and economists collaborate in this task.

Note

1. For a celebrant of capitalism who lauds the 'invention' of the market, see Michael Novak, *The Spirit of Democratic Capitalism*, (1982: 65, 76–7, 88, 116); for a detractor who regards Adam Smith as the eulogist of 'selfish' behavior and the virtual founding father not only of economics but of market capitalism itself, see Barry Schwartz, *The Battle for Human Nature* (1986: 57–68, 301, 308).

References

Abercrombie, N., S. Hill and B.S. Turner (1986) *Sovereign Individuals of Capitalism*. London: Allen & Unwin.

Berger. P. (1986) *The Capitalist Revolution: Fifty Propositions About Prosperity. Equality and Liberty*. New York: Basic Books.

Braudel, F. (1986) *The Wheels of Commerce: Civilization and Capitalism 1500-1800, Volume II*. New York: Harper & Row.

Gellner, E. (1974) *Contemporary Thought and Politics*. London: Routledge.

Giddens, A. (1985) *The Nation-State and Violence*. Oxford: Polity Press.

Novak, M. (1982) *The Spirit of Democratic Capitalism*. New York: Simon & Schuster.

Nove, A. (1983) *The Economics of Feasible Socialism*. London: Allen & Unwin.

Nove, A. (1990) Remark at a conference on 'Market Socialism' organized by *Dissent* Magazine, New School for Social Research, New York, 12 May.

Nozick, R. (1974) *Anarchy, State and Utopia*. New York: Basic Books.

Schwartz, B. (1986) *The Battle for Human Nature*. New York: W.W. Norton.

Smith, A. (1970) *The Wealth of Nations, Books I–III*. Harmondsworth: Penguin.

Stern, Fritz (1987) *Dreams and Delusions: The Drama of German History*. New York: Knopf.

Sweezy, P. and C. Bettelheim (1971) *On the Transition to Socialism*. New York: Monthly Review Press.

Thurow, L. (1983) *Dangerous Currents*. New York: Random House.

Weber, Max (1930) *The Protestant Ethic and the Spirit of Capitalism*. New York: Scribner's.

Dennis H. Wrong is Professor of Sociology at New York University and currently a Fellow at the Wilson Center in Washington. He is author of *Skeptical Sociology and Power: Its Forms, Bases and Uses*.

The Heroic Life and Everyday Life

Mike Featherstone

The modern hero is no hero; he acts heroes. (Benjamin, 1973: 97)

Perhaps it is precisely the petit-bourgeois who has the presentiment of the dawn of a new heroism, a heroism both enormous and collective, on the model of arts. (Musil, *The Man Without Qualities*, quoted in de Certeau, 1984: 1)

I do not like heroes, they make too much noise in the world. (Voltaire, quoted in Gouldner, 1975: 420)

To speak of the heroic life is to risk sounding a little dated. Intellectual and academic life have long sustained strong countercultural traditions which have favoured an anti-heroic ethos. Periodically these traditions have gained greater prominence such as in the 1960s. The most recent manifestation of this antinomian spirit, postmodernism, has little time for elevating artistic, intellectual and other cultural pursuits to the status of coherent lifestyles capable of making grand statements which will be generally illuminating and instructive. Conceptions such as the artist as hero with their associated notions of genius and a life-ordering sense of calling and mission have given way to a less elevated valuation of the popular and the detritus of everyday mass and consumer cultures. Postmodernism has also been associated with the positive evaluation of local and popular cultures, the minor traditions and the 'otherness' excluded by the universalistic pretension of the modern. This suggests an increasing sensitivity to the more complex levels of unity, to the syncretism, heterogeneity, and the common taken-for-granted, 'seen but unnoticed' aspects of everyday life. Of course, the sociology of everyday life cannot be reduced to an effect of postmodernism. Rather we should regard postmodernism as enhancing tendencies to transform the cultural sphere which gained a strong impetus from the 1960s. The rise of new social

Theory, Culture & Society (SAGE, London, Newbury Park and New Delhi), Vol. 9 (1992), 159–182

movements, feminism, ecology and the increasing significance of leisure and the quest for self-expression and self-realization not only pointed to the capacity to transform the institutions of public life, but also raised the profile of the life left behind. Everyday life, with its focus upon reproduction, maintenance, common routines, the sphere of women, receptivity and sociability has gained impetus with the problematization of the dominant legitimacy of the world of production with its emphasis upon instrumental rationality, transformation and sacrifice.

If everyday life is usually associated with the mundane, taken-for-granted, commonsense routines which sustain and maintain the fabric of our daily lives, then the heroic life points to the opposite qualities. Here we think of extraordinary deeds, virtuosity, courage, endurance and the capacity to attain distinction. If the very taken-for-grantedness of everyday life means the necessity of subjecting one's activities to practical knowledge and routines whose heterogeneity and lack of systemicity is rarely theorized, then the heroic life cuts a swathe through this dense facticity. It points to an ordered life fashioned by fate or will, in which the everyday is viewed as something to be tamed, resisted or denied, something to be subjugated in the pursuit of a higher purpose.

Everyday Life
More than most sociological concepts 'everyday life' has proved exceedingly difficult to define. This would seem to be the case because everyday life is the life-world which provides the ultimate ground from which spring all our conceptualizations, definitions and narratives. At the same time, from the perspective of constituted specialist forms of knowledge which have forgotten this, it appears to be a residual category into which can be jettisoned all the irritating bits and pieces which do not fit into orderly thought. Indeed, as commentators are quick to point out, to venture into this field is to explore an aspect of life whose central features apparently lack methodicalness and are particularly resistant to rational categorization (see Geertz, 1983; Heller, 1984; Sharrock and Anderson, 1986; Bovone, 1989; Maffesoli, 1989). Bearing in mind this inherent ambiguity and lack of consensus, we can outline the characteristics most frequently associated with everyday life. First, there is an emphasis upon what happens every day, the routine, repetitive taken-for-granted experiences, beliefs and practices; the mundane ordinary world, untouched by great events and

the extraordinary. Second, the everyday is regarded as the sphere of reproduction and maintenance, a pre-institutional zone in which the basic activities which sustain other worlds are performed, largely by women. Third, there is an emphasis upon the present which provides a non-reflexive sense of immersion in the immediacy of current experiences and activities. Fourth, there is a focus on the non-individual embodied sense of being together in spontaneous common activities outside, or in the interstices, of the institutional domains; an emphasis upon common sensuality, being with others in frivolous, playful sociability. Fifth, there is an emphasis upon heterogeneous knowledge, the disorderly babble of many tongues; speech and 'the magic world of voices' are valued over the linearity of writing.

This aspect can be developed by referring to Agnes Heller's discussion of Plato's contrast between *doxa* (general opinion grounded in daily routines) and *episteme* (scientific knowledge which aims to provide more lasting truths). This can lead us to a relational view of everyday thought with its meaning defined in terms of its opposite modes of thought. Whereas everyday thought is heterogeneous and syncretic, scientific, philosophical and other formalized modes of thought are more systemic, reflexive and de-anthropomorphizing (Heller, 1984: 49ff). Such more formalized modes of thought themselves can be seen as striving for systemicity which increasingly separates them from their dependence on the prime symbolic media in which they are grounded. Alfred Schutz (1962) has referred to the everyday commonsense world as the 'paramount reality' which can be distinguished from a series of 'multiple realities' or 'finite provinces of meaning'. There are the 'worlds' of dreams, fantasies, day-dreams, play, fiction and the theatre as well as the more formalized worlds of science, philosophy and art. Each demands a different 'natural attitude', time sense and structure of relevance, and there are problems for individuals who do not observe them. Here it is possible to recall Schutz's (1964) description of the difficulties encountered by Cervantes's Don Quixote in mixing together fantasy and everyday life. There are, of course, some socially sanctioned occasions in which such intermixing is encouraged, where the world of fantasy becomes lived out in the midst of everyday life, such as festivals and the carnivalesque. Such liminal moments are usually well circumscribed, yet it can be argued that the syncretic and heterogeneous nature of everyday life means that the perceptions of the doubly-coded, the playful, desires and fantasies lurk within the interstices of everyday life and threaten to irrupt into it. As Schutz, Garfinkel and the ethnomethodologists remind us, it takes considerable taken-for-granted practical skill to negotiate these various worlds and the transitions between them. It can be added that the capacity to mobilize such a flexible generative structure capable of handling a wide variety and high degree of complexity of finite provinces of meaning cannot be understood as a historical constant. Indeed the nature and number of finite provinces of meaning and their relative separation or embeddedness in everyday life will vary historically. Hence it can be argued that a precise definition of everyday life cannot be given, rather we should seek to understand it as a process — and, as Nietzsche reminds us, that which has a history cannot be defined.

A number of theorists have sought to comprehend the historical processes which have led to the increasing differentiation and colonization of everyday life. The Frankfurt School (Held, 1980) and Lefebvre (1971) have, for example, focused on the commodification and instrumental rationalization of everyday life. Habermas (1981) has elaborated a distinction between system and life-world in which the instrumental rational action employed by the political-administrative and economic systems are seen to invade and erode the emancipatory communicative potential of the everyday life-world. Heller (1984), following Lukács, has drawn attention to the ways in which the heterogeneity of everyday life has been subjected to processes of homogenization. It is therefore possible to refer to an initial process of differentiation in which science, art, philosophy and other forms of theoretical knowledge originally embedded within everyday life become progressively separated and subjected to specialist development, followed by a further phase whereby this knowledge is fed back in order to rationalize, colonize and homogenize everyday life. The danger is to assume that this process has a self-propelling momentum and universalizing force which turns it into a logic of history beyond human intervention. Rather, it might be more useful to conceive of it in terms of the changing struggles and interdependencies between figurations of people bound together in particular historical situations in which they seek to mobilize various power resources, than to refer to a logic of history.[1] Elias (1987a) has discussed the process of differentiation whereby specialist functions previously carried out by the group as a whole become separated. Hence there is the emergence of specialists in violence control (warriors), knowledge specialists (priests) and eventually economic and political specialists. It is also possible to trace the emergence of other groups of specialists, such as cultural specialists who participate in the formation of a relatively autonomous cultural sphere in which scientific, philosophical and artistic symbolic media are developed. In addition in modern societies there is the whole array of experts such as those in the helping professions and mass media occupations which supply a variety of means of orientation and practical knowledge for everyday life. This should not be understood as an automatic and orderly process, the particular conditions of a society's state formation, and its relation to the other nation-states in which it is bound in a figuration, determine the actual type and degree of differentiation which may propel and maintain certain groups of specialists in positions of power. Under certain conditions priests may attain a dominant position within society and in other circumstances warriors may become dominant. The nature, extent and duration of their dominance will clearly have an impact upon everyday life. With the rise of Western modernity cultural specialists such as scientists, artists, intellectuals and academics have gained in relative power and have sought in various ways to advocate the transformation, domestication, civilization, repair and healing of what are considered the shortcomings of everyday life. Yet other cultural specialists have sought to promote and defend the intrinsic qualities of everyday life through the celebration of the integrity of popular cultures and traditions. For them everyday life is less regarded as raw material and 'otherness' ripe for formation and cultivation, rather they can be seen to advocate a reversal of the process of differentiation and a greater awareness of the equal validity, and in some cases even superior wisdom, of everyday knowledge and practices. Hence under certain conditions popular cultures are celebrated and the ordinary person's mundane life, the life of 'the man without qualities' heroicized. Such processes of de-differentiation, of re-heterogenization and re-immersion into the everyday have featured prominently in countercultural movements such as romanticism and postmodernism. It can also be argued that this can also be manifest in the critique of the heroic image of the cultural specialist, the scientist, artist or intellectual as hero, in favour of an emphasis upon everyday mundane practices which are regarded as equally capable of producing what some want to regard as extraordinary or elevated insights or objectifications.[2]

In this sense the positive or negative evaluation of everyday life can be seen to relate to the way in which its counter-concept is evaluated. For Habermas (1981) the system is the danger to the life-world and its intrusions must be controlled if the capacity for everyday life to open up its communicative potential is to be realized. Lefebvre (1971) also emphasizes the need to go beyond the commodification of contemporary everyday life in the 'bureaucratic society of controlled consumption' and release the festive aspects of everyday life. The positive evaluation of the qualities of everyday life are highlighted in Maffesoli's (1989) work in which he draws attention to the capacity of everyday life to resist the process of rationalization and preserve and foster sociality, a concern for the present, the frivolous, imaginative and Dionysiac forms of life which provide a sense of collective immersion, of giving up one's own individual being (*Einfuhlung*). In a similar way de Certeau (1984) affirms the ordinary practices of everyday life and its capacity to utilize modes of syncretism, the 'non-logical logics' of everyday life to oppose, transgress and subvert official dominant cultures and technical rationality.[3] Likewise Gouldner (1975: 421) seeks to draw attention to the critical potential of everyday life and the way in which it can function as a counter-concept:

> I have suggested repeatedly that EDL [everyday life] is a *counter*concept, that it gives expression to a *critique* of a certain kind of life, specifically, the heroic, achieving, performance-centred existence. The EDL established itself as real by contrasting itself with the heroic life and by reason of the crisis of the heroic life.

As we have suggested there are a range of counter-concepts against which everyday life can be defined; we will now turn to what can be considered the major one, the heroic life and the ways in which it becomes transformed and transfigured in other modes of life in the cultural sphere.

The Heroic Life

If everyday life revolves around the mundane, taken for granted and ordinary, then the heroic life points to its rejection of this order for the extraordinary life which threatens not only the possibility of returning to everyday routines, but entails the deliberate risking of life itself. The emphasis in the heroic life is on the courage to struggle and achieve extraordinary goals, the quest for virtue, glory and fame, which contrasts with the lesser everyday pursuit of wealth, property and earthly love. The everyday world is the one which the hero departs from, leaving behind the sphere of care and maintenance (women, children and the old), only to return to its acclaim should his tasks be completed successfully. A basic contrast then, is that the heroic life is the sphere of danger, violence and the courting of risk whereas everyday life is the sphere of women, reproduction and care. The heroic life is one in which the hero seeks to prove himself by displaying courage. Warriors were amongst the first heroes and as specialists in violence experienced the intense excitement of combat, an emotional force which needed to be controlled and subjected to the cunning of instrumental reason to ensure survival.[4] To achieve great deeds requires both luck, a sense of destiny, that one's particular quest and life are driven by forces outside oneself which offer extraordinary protection, and an inner sense of certainty that with circumspection, craft and compulsion one can overcome the greatest dangers and misfortunes, in effect that one can make one's own fate.

In many ways the heroic life shares the quality of an adventure, or series of adventures. Georg Simmel (1971a) in his essay on the adventure tells us that the adventure falls outside the usual continuity of everyday existence which is disregarded on principle. The adventurer has a different time sense which entails a strong sense of the present and disregard for the future. Simmel captures well the mixture of abandoning oneself to fate and making one's own fate we have spoken of. In the adventure we abandon ourselves to the 'powers and accidents of the world, which can delight us, but in the same breath can also destroy us' (Simmel, 1971a: 193). At the same time we forsake the careful calculation and accumulation of the world of work, for the capacity to act decisively in the world. Hence the adventurer 'has the gesture of the conqueror' who is quick to seize the opportunity and also 'treats the incalculable elements in life in the way we ordinarily treat only what we think by definition calculable' (Simmel, 1971a: 193). Furthermore the adventurer is capable of creating a sense of unity, a synthesis of activity and passivity, of chance and necessity. The adventurer makes a system out of his life's lack of system. It is this capacity to form life that points to the affinity between the adventurer and the artist, as well as the attraction of adventure for the artist. As Simmel (1971a: 189) remarks:

the essence of the work of art is, after all, that it cuts out a piece of the endless continuous sequences of perceived experience, detaching it from all connections with one side or the other, giving it a self-sufficient form as though defined and held together by an inner core. A part of existence, interwoven with the uninterruptedness of that existence, yet nevertheless felt as a whole, as an integrated unit — that is the form common to both the work of art and the adventure.

In some cases life as a whole may be perceived as an adventure and for this to happen 'one must sense above its totality a higher unity, a super-life, as it were' (Simmel, 1971a: 192). This capacity to order and unify life, to form it from within in terms of some higher purpose which gives life a sense of destiny, it can be argued, is central to the heroic life, especially those who are in Simmel's words 'adventurers of the spirit': intellectuals and artists. The way in which the adventure is lived from within like a narrative which has a beginning, middle and end points to the way life may seem to be like a work of art.[5]

In retrospect the adventure may appear to have a particularly compelling dreamlike quality in which accidental elements and inspired acts are woven together to give a strong sense of coherence. This capacity to retrospectively impose a narrative structure on the adventure should not be taken to imply that the original life 'beneath' the narrative was itself formless. Rather it is important to emphasize the potential to deliberately seek to live life as a unity from within and control and shape chance elements into a structure which seemingly serves some higher purpose, be it one's own glory, God's will, the survival of a nation or people. MacIntyre (1981: 191ff) emphasizes this point when he argues against the existentialism of Sartre and the sociological theories of Goffman and Dahrendorf who present the enactments of an individual life as a series of unconnected episodes. We find, for example, that Sartre's character Antoine Roquentin in *Nausea* argues that to present human life in the form of a narrative is always to falsify it (MacIntyre, 1981: 199). This approach is also evident in Merleau-Ponty's (1964) statement in the introduction to *Sense and Non-Sense* that we are for all intents and purposes separate persons at each stage of our lives which have happened to 'accidentally' inhabit the same body and whose various distinct selves become retrospectively woven together through a 'false' narrative which gives biographical unity. Indeed this 'liquidation of the self' into a set of separate situational role players also resonates with the emphasis in postmodern theories about the de-centring of the self and the presentation of the person as a bundle of loosely connected quasi-selves (see Featherstone, 1991b). For MacIntyre (1981: 197) this misses the point that human actions are enacted narratives; narratives are not imposed upon events which have no narrative order by novelists and dramatists. Rather he quotes Barbara Hardy who remarks that 'we dream in narrative, day-dream in narrative, remember, anticipate, hope, despair, believe, doubt, plan, revise, criticize, construct, gossip, learn, hate and love by narrative'. Yet it can be argued that the extent to which a larger narrative is employed and sustained to structure and unify a person's life as a whole can vary a great deal. We describe a person as displaying character or personality who achieves a high degree of consistency of conduct; in effect he seeks to impose a form on his life by seeking to follow some higher purpose rather than merely letting his life drift capriciously.

At this stage it might be useful to clarify the distinction between the hero, the heroic life and the heroic society. It is of course possible for anyone to become a hero, to perform a heroic deed without being a member of a heroic society or having a commitment to the heroic life. Hence in the popular media there is a constant celebration of ordinary heroes, those individuals who are thrust into a situation of extreme physical danger in which they show extraordinary courage such as risking or sacrificing their lives to save other people. It is this chance element, that fate might intervene and shatter the everyday order of the happy life and thrust any individual into a situation beyond his control which demands a response, which is fascinating to the public, who cannot but help wonder 'How would we respond to the test?' This can also be related to hero worship: the ways in which heroes are used as role models for people to identify with (see Klapp, 1969). In this case it is usually some strong person, politician, sportsman, explorer, adventurer, or those who increasingly represent these ways of life, the celebrities and stars of film, television and popular music, who becomes the object of various blends of fantasy and realistic identification.

This can be contrasted with heroic societies such as those described in the Homeric epics or the Icelandic and Irish sagas. Whatever the actual conditions of production of these heroic narratives and their relationship to particular social realities, they provide a picture of social orders in which a person's role and status and associated duties and privileges were well-defined within kinship and household structures. Such societies do not admit the possibility of a disjunction between motive and action, as MacIntyre comments (1981: 115): 'A man in heroic society is what he does.' Courage was a central quality necessary to sustain a household and a community, for the courageous person was one who could be relied upon, something which was an important element in friendship. For the Greeks the hero not only displayed courage, but sought to live up to the ideal of *aretē*,[6] a term which is often mistakenly translated as 'virtue', but is better rendered as 'excellence' (Kitto, 1951: 171ff). The heroic ideal was to attain excellence in all the ways in which a man can be excellent — physically, morally, intellectually, practically — without any privileging of the mind over the body. The individual who excelled in battle or contest was accorded the recognition of *kudos* or glory from his community (MacIntyre, 1981: 115). Yet while the hero is one who lives within a fragile world in which he is vulnerable to fate and death and can display courage in face of his destiny, he is effectively seeking to live up to an ideal of excellence which is a social role. Hence in heroic societies, the heroic person is one who excels at the performance of a necessary social role. What is interesting is the way in which the image of the hero is taken out of its context, and woven into a heroic life in which the social context becomes played down, or becomes one in which the hero distinguishes himself from and rises above the social. The influential reading of the Greek past in which a particular late nineteenth-century vision of distinction and individuality becomes blended together with elements from Greek heroic society became a particularly compelling image in the writings of Nietzsche, an image which MacIntyre (1981: 122) finds particularly misleading:

> What Nietzsche portrays is aristocratic *self*-assertion: what Homer and the sagas show are forms of assertion proper to and required by a certain *role*. The self becomes what it is in heroic societies only in and through its role; it is a social creation, not an individual one. Hence when Nietzsche projects back on to the archaic past his own nineteenth-century individualism, he reveals that what looked like an historical enquiry was actually an inventive literary construction. Nietzsche replaces the fictions of the Enlightenment individualism, of which he is so contemptuous, with a set of individualist fictions of his own.

MacIntyre's assertion that Nietzsche's particular version of the heroic life was a projection of nineteenth-century individualism might be more precisely formulated to highlight the tension between the higher person who displays genuine individuality and distinction (*Vornehmheit*) and the narrow *ressentiment* of the mass man. Furthermore Nietzsche's version of the heroic life did not merely remain as a set of individualist fictions, his particular fiction resonated strongly with notions of artistic and intellectual distinction which gained impetus from the life of Goethe and the Romantic Movement, to develop into a powerful cultural image, one which became influential in certain circles of turn of the century Germany and subjected to sociological investigation and theoretical formulation by Max Weber and Georg Simmel.[7]

Hero Ethics, Distinction and the Cultural Sphere

Max Weber's life and work have often been characterized as heroic. Manasse (1957: 287), for example, remarks that he was a 'type of man who was born in the world of Homer and of the Jewish prophets and has not yet disappeared with Nietzsche. Thus far he had his last great representative in Max Weber.' Manasse's statement was made in the context of a discussion of the impact of Weber on Karl Jaspers. For Jaspers Weber represented an extraordinary man, driven by a restless demonic force animated by a strong ethic of responsibility. This was manifest in Weber's honesty and consistency of purpose which was expressed in his work, the directness and lack of pretence in his life activities and dealings with other people and in his bodily gestures, bearing and demeanour. Jaspers regarded Weber as a representative of a new type of man and made him the model for his existential philosophy. This modern form of heroism is captured not only in the courage, consistency and unity of purpose Weber attained, but in a quality frequently associated with the heroic life: sacrifice. Without seeking immediate death this type of person 'lived as though they were dead' (Manasse, 1957: 389).

Such questions were, of course, addressed by Weber in his writings. In his discussion of charisma he refers to the capacity for sacrifice displayed by the charismatic leader and demanded of his followers. The charismatic hero's power does not lie in a legitimated social role, but in his extraordinary qualities as a person, the 'gift of grace' and the capacity to constantly subject it to demonstration and test. As Weber (1948a: 249) remarks 'If he wants to be a prophet, he must perform miracles; if he wants to be a war lord, he must perform heroic deeds.'[8] Such individuals intentionally organized their lives around an ultimate value and were therefore less dependent upon conventional modes of social approval and institutional authority. The injunction to follow some ideal or ultimate value, to form life into a deliberate unity whatever the personal cost, is also central to Weber's discussion of 'hero ethics'. He states

> One can divide all 'ethics', regardless of their material content into two major groups according to whether they make basic demands on a person to which he can generally *not* live up except for the great high points of his life, which point the way as guideposts in his *striving* in infinity ('hero ethics'), or whether they are modest enough to accept his everyday 'nature' as a maximal require-ment ('average ethics'). It seems to me that only the first category, the 'hero ethics', can be called 'idealism' . . . (Weber's comments on an essay by Otto Gross, quoted in Marianne Weber, 1975: 378)

Weber was later to qualify this strict dichotomy between 'hero ethics' and 'average ethics' to admit a more nuanced gradation. As Marianne Weber (1975: 388) tells us, his new insight was that 'there is a scale of the ethical. If the ethically highest is unattain-able in a concrete case, an attempt must be made to attain the second or third best.' This can be related to the discussion of the various modern life orders which had replaced the possibility of an ethical totality and unified personality which were associated with Puritanism. The process of differentiation has resulted in separate economic, political, aesthetic, erotic, intellectual and academic life orders (Weber, 1948b). Yet despite his heroic defence of science as a vocation and the ethic of responsibility as valid ways of living in the modern world, there is no sense for Weber that, in a cultural context of value pluralism, they could provide a sense of certainty and solutions to the problems of coherent mean-ing. The same could be said for the ways of life offered by the other life orders in the cultural sphere: the aesthetic, intellectual and erotic. For Weber the general process of rationalization signi-fied the decline in the possibility of developing into a genuine person, a unified personality who displays consistency of conduct and who can attain distinction which is captured in the Protestant idea of *Personlichkeit*, an ideal which Weber sought to uphold throughout his life.[9] Weber gives qualified acknowledgement that the artist, intellectual and erotic life orders could develop person-alities, albeit 'lesser' ones, and with progressive difficulty. In this sense it would be legitimate to investigate the artist as hero and examine, for example, the extent to which particular artists in specific social figurations (figures such as Goethe, Beethoven, Berlioz, Flaubert, van Gogh) were sustained by lifestyles and prestige economies which favoured the development of 'hero ethics'. In a similar way one could investigate the notion of the intellectual as hero and examine, for example, figures such as Marx, Zola, Sartre. Further categories suggest themselves in terms of the erotic life in social forms such as bohemias and countercultures (Otto Gross), and the turning of life itself into a work of art in dandyism and other modes (Beau Brummell, Huysmans's des Esseintes, Oscar Wilde, Stefan George, Salvador Dali, etc.). From Weber's perspective all these various manifestations of the heroic life within the cultural sphere tended to create an 'unbrotherly aristocracy' independent of personal ethical qualities, yet such a cultural aristocracy would best be sustained within a relatively independent cultural sphere. At one point Weber speaks of an intellectual aristocracy of independent rentiers, yet the specific conditions which had developed to favour this with the formation of the cultural sphere could be equally threatened with the deformation of the cultural sphere and the loss of the relative autonomy of cultural producers. On the one hand, this process could be related to the processes of rationalization, bureaucratization and commodification which changed the conditions of production and relation to their various publics of artists, intellectuals, academics and other cultural vocations. On the other hand, it could be described in terms of a perceived process of engulfment from below, the rise of the masses and their culture (Theweleit, 1987). The latter viewpoint finds one of its clearest expressions in the writings of Max Scheler who fretted about the ressentiment of the common man, who is poisoned by the repressed emotions of envy, spite, hatred and revenge and seeks to dissemble the social hierarchy between him and his betters and destroy those noble values that he does not possess (see Staude, 1967). Scheler sought a return to aristocratic values, some new 'spiritual aristocracy' for the modern age to re-establish noble and heroic models of life through the youth movements. Like Weber, Simmel and many of the generation which dominated German academic life around the turn of the century, Scheler was strongly influenced by Nietzsche's work. Yet of the three, Simmel was the only one who did not take up some form of nostalgic reaction to modernity and the prospective eclipse of the heroic life. Simmel's sociology of modernity pointed to the opposite outcome: it provided a completely new modern ideal of distinction (*Vornehmheit*) which for our purposes deserves examination for it suggests the persistence of a form of the heroic life.

It has often been remarked that whereas Simmel favoured the aesthetic way of being, Weber favoured the ethical (see for example Green, 1988). Both pointed to the differentiation and fragmentation of modern life, yet Simmel (1978) developed a more positive appreciation of the possibilities for an aestheticization of life released by the very capitalist money economy which many held was destructive for art and culture. While it is possible to point to a general aestheticization of everyday life in the large cities of the late nineteenth century (see Featherstone, 1991a: Ch. 5), the effects of the money economy on the development of personality have usually been regarded as negative. Simmel refers to the capacity of money to turn everything which has a specific quality into quantity, prostitution being a good example of this process of commodification, which points to the deformation of the person. It is however one of the merits of his *Wechselwirkung* approach, which points to the dense network of reciprocal interactions which make up the social world, that it provides unusual insights into how things usually held apart influence each other (e.g. culture on the economy, not just the economy on culture). Hence the processes of the levelling of distinct differences and the quantification of everyday life through the expansion of the money economy is presented as capable of provoking an opposite reaction, the determination to preserve and develop one's essential quality as a person which Simmel (1978: 389ff) referred to as *Vornehmheitsideal*, the ideal of distinction. Liebersohn (1988: 141) remarks that 'Simmel argued that the modern ideal of distinction was an absolutely new value brought into existence by the challenge to personal values of the money economy.' According to Liebersohn, Simmel took the ideal of distinction from Nietzsche's *Beyond Good and Evil* in which he argues that the distinctive type of man has developed in aristocratic societies with their rigid social hierarchy and well-defined differences which can supply the 'pathos of distance' whereby the ruling caste can look down on, and keep its distance from the rest.[10] For Simmel (1986: 168–9) this 'social aristocraticism' and 'morality of nobility' advocated by Nietzsche meant the employment of discipline and a sense of duty, a severity and 'selfishness in the preservation of the highest personal values'.

Yet self-responsibility should not be confused with egoism and hedonism, for in the ideal of distinction or personalism: 'Egoism aspires to have something, personalism to be something.'

Liebersohn (1988: 143) captures well the characteristics of the modern form of distinction when he states

> The person of distinction was possessed by a sense of the absolute worth of his soul without regard for the world and was ready to sacrifice everything to remain true to himself. His distinction supposedly asserts his independence from society. Yet paradoxically it shared modern society's impersonality. If impersonality signified the shifting effects of institutions and conventions on individual idiosyncrasies, *Vornehmheit's* inner law, too, eradicated every spontaneous impulse in the name of an artificial order. Absolute personal autonomy offset the social order only by internalizing its logic, creating, to be sure, a style setting the bearer apart, but doing so only through a pattern of radical repression. This was the price one paid for turning the modern fate into a personal destiny.

There are clear resemblances here with Weber's Protestant and Kantian ideal of *Personlichkeit*, which suggest that the ethical and aesthetic ideals are not so easily separated as some would like. Yet Weber held that *Personlichkeit* which had its origins in traditional Christianity, was increasingly becoming less tenable in the modern age, whereas Simmel's concept of *Vornehmheit* which depended upon social differentiation, could never have existed in a traditional community.[11]

Women, Consumer Culture and the Critique of the Heroic Life

The critique of everyday life is not a new phenomenon. As Gouldner (1975: 419) informs us, the critique of everyday life was evident in the literature of the Ancient Greeks. Euripides, for example, stood on the side of the common people, the world of women, children, old people and slaves. He called for the rejection of power, fame, ambition, physical courage and virtue, the essential features of the heroic life. The growth in the power potential of outsider groups such as women, the young, the elderly and ethnic and regional minorities has been part of a long-term process within Western modernity — something which some want to refer to as postmodernism and characterize as a significant cultural shift — has led to an assault on the heroic life. A key element in the current critique of the viability of the heroic life in the modern age has been provided by feminism, which regarded the heroic life as extolling the essentially masculine virtues of sacrifice, distinction, discipline, dignity, self-denial, self-restraint and commitment to a cause. In her extensive critique of Max Weber's commitment to the heroic life, Roslyn Bologh (1990: 17) remarks

> If I had to encapsulate all of these ideas into an image it would be that of the strong, stoic, resolutely independent, self-disciplined individual who holds himself erect with self-control, proud of his capacity to distance himself from his body, from personal longings, personal possessions and personal relationships, to resist and renounce the temptations of pleasure in order to serve some impersonal cause — a masculine, ascetic image. The image of devotion to some impersonal cause can be interpreted as rationalizing and justifying self-repression while channeling the aggressive, competitive, jealous, angry feelings that accompany such repression.

Against this masculine ideal of manliness and aggressive will to power, Bologh presents a feminine image of passivity and the acceptance of powerlessness. This lack of power is accompanied by a sense of vulnerability and desire for attachment, to be loved by others. The masculine heroic image requires the suppression of vanity, in effect recognition and glory should only be expected with the ultimate resolution of the quest. Hence the individual who follows the heroic life should be indifferent to hero worship, recognition and the love of others. The feminine ethic operates on the basis of a more prosaic desire for reciprocity in the love of the other, it accepts the emotional bonding with the other, identification and empathy. It assumes that erotic love can be maintained within everyday life, that it is possible to move to and fro from attachment to separation, from communion to differentiation within the same relationship. Bologh (1990: 213ff) therefore advocates an ethic of sociability against hero ethics which is less elevated, and more open to an egalitarian exploration of playfulness and pleasure with the other, to the immersion and loss of the self rather than the preservation and elevation of the self.

Sociability was, of course, one of the characteristic features of everyday life which we discussed earlier. To speak of sociability is immediately to recall the work of Georg Simmel and his influential essay on the topic. Sociability — 'the *play-form of association*' (Simmel, 1971b: 130) — entailed the setting aside of the normal status and objective qualities of the personality and is essentially a form of interaction between equals, without any obvious purpose or set content, in which talk and light playfulness becomes an end in itself. It is a further example of Simmel's *Wechselwirkung* approach, with its capacity to tease out unusual insights from seemingly contradictory perceptions, that in discussing the responses to the contradictions of modern culture, he not only pointed to the possibility of *Vornehmheit*, aesthetic responses and the detachment of turning life into a work of art, but pointed to an opposite response through the immersion in playful sociability. A further response which Simmel developed in the face of the tremendous expansion of objective culture and the oppressive weight of cultural forms was the affirmation of life itself. Life, the formless form, provided a sense of immersion and loss of self in the immediacy of experiences, it also proved to be a central preoccupation within cultural modernism with its fascination with the prosaic, the ordinary and the everyday (e.g. surrealism) which favoured an anti-heroic ethos and heroization of the mundane which sharply contrasts with the heroic life (Featherstone, 1991c).

The twentieth-century consumer cultures which developed in Western societies, with their expanded means of technical production of goods and reproduction of images and information, constantly play back these possibilities. Consumer culture does not put forward a unitary message. The heroic life is still an important image in this culture, and as long as there still exists interpersonal violence and warfare between states there is a firm basis for the preservation of this image, as the risking of life, self-sacrifice and commitment to a cause are still important themes sustained within male culture. Here one thinks of the discussion of the heroic military culture of extraordinary men who became involved in the development of the space programme of the United States described by Tom Wolfe (1989) in *The Right Stuff*. At the same time consumer culture puts out mythical hero images of the Superman and Rambo type, as well as pastiches and parodies of the whole heroic tradition such as the *Monty Python and the Holy Grail* film and various blends of both such as are found in the Indiana Jones films. The twentieth century, however, has seen the development of a strong anti-heroic ethos fostered by cultural modernism's antinomian movement away from notions of artistic and intellectual genius[12] and the retreat from life into art, to favour a blurring of the boundaries between art and everyday life which has been enhanced by surrealism, dada and postmodernism.[13] At the same time consumer culture has also enhanced this aestheticization of everyday life through the development of advertising, imagery and publicity which saturate the fabric of the lived environment and everyday encounters.

The decline of hero ethics also suggests a feminization of culture. Not that patriarchy and male supremacy have been eclipsed — far from it. But there has been a long-term swing of the balance of power between the sexes (Elias, 1987b) which has become more marked over the last century and has seen a rise in the power potential of women, one symptom of which has been their increased prominence and ability to raise questions in the public sphere about male domination, domestic violence and child abuse, issues which formerly could not be admitted. In the cultural sphere one manifestation of this relative shift in the balance of power has been the movement to accord greater legitimacy to everyday culture, the cultural pursuits of women such as popular romance and soap operas. These areas of popular and mass culture and the whole area of women's everyday culture which revolves around the production and management of consumption, areas which were previously seen as peripheral in contrast to the perceived centrality of production and stratification, are being subjected to more intense study by social scientists and students of the humanities, and hence are gaining in legitimacy. Yet if this provides an alternative set of mass cultural images to those of the heroic life, to what extent does it suggest possibilities for new heroes and heroines? How far do Hollywood and media stars and celebrities provide extensions of Simmel's model of distinction or Weber's notions of *Personlichkeit* and charisma? Is it possible to discuss these issues in a relatively detached way without making the judgement that they can only achieve the status of regressions, pale imitations of the heroic life?

It has been remarked that mass culture has often been associated with women and real authentic culture with men (Huyssen, 1986: 47). Certainly in Nietzsche's view the masses, the herd, are perceived as feminine, in contrast to the artist or philosopher as hero who displays masculine characteristics. As Huyssen (1986: 52) remarks an examination of European magazines and newspapers of the late nineteenth century would show that

> the proletarian and petit-bourgeois were persistently described in terms of a feminine threat. Images of the raving mob as hysterical, of the engulfing floods of revolt and revolution, of the swamp of big city life, of the spreading ooze of massification, of the figure of the red whore at the barricades — all of these pervade the writings of the mainstream of the media . . . [14]

Nietzsche provides a further indication of the association of femininity and mass culture in his hostility towards theatricality, shown, for example, in his writings on the Wagner cult. In the *Gay Science* he also writes that 'It is impossible to dissociate the questions of art, style and truth from the question of women' (quoted in Sayre, 1989: 145). For Nietzsche and, following him, for Weber and Simmel the genuine heroic person was characterized not by what they do, but by what they are — the qualities are within the person and hence genuine personality is a matter of fate. Weber, for example, held in contempt the development of the modern notion of personality which is associated with mask-wearing and celebrity. Yet within the consumer culture which developed in the twentieth century, the new popular heroes were less likely to be warriors, statesmen, explorers, inventors, scientists and more likely to be celebrities, albeit that some of the celebrities would be film stars who would play the role of these former heroes. Lowenthal (1961: 116) reminds us that whereas in the past heroes were 'idols of production', now they are 'idols of consumption'. The characteristic demanded of celebrities is to have *personality*, to possess the actor's skills of presenting a colourful self, to maintain allure, fascination and mystery. These are seen to replace the more traditional virtues of *character*, which emphasized moral consistency, sincerity and unity of purpose. Kasson (1990) has detected a shift in etiquette books in late nineteenth-century America from proclaiming the virtues of moral character to acting as guides for individuals who must learn to read and portray techniques of self-presentation in a complex urban environment with the ever present possibility of deception. The perception of the self as a series of dramatic effects, of learned techniques as opposed to inherent good moral characteristics, leads to a problematization and fragmentation of the self. Today's stars in the motion picture, television and popular music industries (Dyer, 1979; Frith and Horne, 1987; Gledhill, 1991) would therefore appear to be a long way from the heroic life. But need this be the whole story? Does not this judgement show a nostalgia for a particular formulation of the heroic life, one which penalizes women and mass culture in allowing men to achieve heroism through high cultural pursuits? To answer this question we would need to investigate more closely the formation of consumer culture stars and celebrities in particular contexts. It might be, for example, that the position of monopolization achieved by the Hollywood studio system in the 1930s was able to support particular lifestyles akin to those of the artist as hero, or artists of life. Moreover, the major contemporary 'superstar' Madonna has been instrumental in developing a different type of femininity which is more self-confident and assertive as well as attempting to redefine her performances as art rather than popular music. Such crossovers (Walker, 1987) may suggest that while the end of art, the end of the intellectuals and the avant-garde have been proclaimed, interesting new possibilities could have been developing in the twentieth century which present new variations on the heroic life — that is, if one still accepts that we do not yet live in a post-modern 'retro' or playback culture and that the long-term processes of cultural formation, deformation and reformation can still be sustained.

Notes

An earlier version of this paper was presented at the Nordplan Conference on Everyday Life, Stockholm, January 1991. I would like to thank all who attended for their helpful comments. I have also benefited from discussions and suggestions for revision from: Zygmunt Bauman, Eric Corijn, Mike Hepworth, Harry McL. Currie, Hans Mommaas, Roland Robertson, John Staude, Bryan S. Turner and Cas Wouters.

1. Here we think for example of Heller's (1978) study of the ways in which art, philosophy and science were separated from everyday life and used to criticize it. At the same time she points to the ways in which science percolated down into everybody's daily life and the way in which there were moves to humanize and aestheticize everyday life. Elias's (1978, 1982) investigation of the 'civilizing process' in Western Europe points to the complex interplay between the production of expert knowledge (e.g. manners books) and its utilization and dissemination by various groups of people bound together through the dynamic of state formation processes, to alter the nature of everyday practices.

2. For discussion of the everyday routines of science and the way they operate to produce various notions of 'truth' and 'results' see Knorr-Cetina (1981) and Latour (1987).

3. Traces of this positive evaluation of everyday life by Maffesoli and de Certeau can be found in the writings of Baudrillard. In particular there is his affirmation of the cynical and 'mirror-like' capacity of the masses to resist absorption and manipulation by the mass media (see Baudrillard, 1983).

4. See on this Horkheimer and Adorno's (1971) discussion of the development of enlightened reason in Homer's Odysseus, the Greek hero who risks his life in the pursuit of glory and who eventually survives to return home to the little pleasures of the settled and ordered everyday life. Odysseus is presented as the prototype of the bourgeois individual.

5. Those individuals who deliberately seek to make of their own life and persona a work of art and aestheticize life (e.g. the dandy) will be discussed below.

6. The assumption that *aretê* was a quality of the body and bodily activities as well as those of the mind implied a unity of the aesthetic, the moral and the practical. For the Greeks *aretê* entailed an aesthetic dimension, activities or lives which displayed excellence were assumed to be beautiful and as a corollary those which were base or disgraceful were ugly (Kitto, 1951: 170; see also Bauman, 1973: 10–17 for an illuminating discussion of the Greek notion of culture). Despite the much remarked upon Western mind–body dualism, the sense of the way they are practically conjoined and the beautiful body goes along with a beautiful soul is an important aspect of our tradition as well. Wittgenstein for example, remarks 'The human body is the best picture of the human soul', an assumption of unity which has a dynamic life-course aspect as Orwell's statement that 'At 50 everyone has the face he deserves' reminds us (quoted in MacIntyre, 1981: 176).

7. The impact of the First World War is particularly interesting in this context with the interplay of technology, traditional military heroics and various artistic impulses and movements. In addition there was the overall tension between the heroic public imagery and the 'everyday' experience of trench warfare as filth, degradation and terror (see Wohl, 1980; Fussell, 1982; Eckstein, 1990). The various shifts in Simmel's attitude towards the war are discussed in Watier (1991).

8. There is not the space here to go into the relationship between the emotional basis of charisma and the heroic life. For discussions see Wasielewski (1985) and Lindholm (1990). Needless to say there has been a good deal of controversy about the extent to which Weber himself admired the charismatic hero (in some cases with the qualifier 'despite himself'). Hence Lindholm's (1990: 27) statement that 'Thus Weber, the most sophisticated and disenchanted of rational thinkers, fell prey in the last analysis, and very much despite himself, to a desperate worship of the charismatic hero' is hardly uncontentious.

9. Weber's pessimism about the fate of *Personlichkeit* in the modern age and concern about the newly emerging human type to replace the Protestant type was by no means unqualified. This is apparent in his discussions of the working class. At some points he argues that with the decline of religion, non-elites will find meaning through identification with their communities, through the multiplicity of communal groups with bonds of varying intensity, the most important of which is the nation. Hence 'ethnic honour' with its exclusivity and egalitarianism could provide a sense of identity for the masses, while elites strive adequately to follow a professional vocation or some diluted notion of *Personlichkeit* (see Portis, 1973: 117). On the other hand he was intrigued by the results of Gohre's study of the working class which suggested that they had discovered a primitive *Personlichkeit* manifest in a longing for freedom from residual feudal bonds. This provided a motivation for Weber's proposed study of the press and the question of the effect of the mass media on habitus formation (see Liebersohn, 1988).

10. This is not of course the only ideal Nietzsche presents and in recent years, under the influence of poststructuralism and postmodernism, the Dionysian loss of self and immersion in life as mentioned in *The Birth of Tragedy* has gained favour (see Stauth and Turner, 1988).

11. For Simmel, Stefan George embodied the modern distinction ideal. Max Weber, on the other hand, was concerned about the folly of trying to reintroduce charisma in modern societies. Liebersohn (1988: 151) tells us that George was one of the first cultural heroes of the twentieth century and was accorded the adulation later to be experienced by film stars and politicians.

12. Postmodern theory has little time for notions such as genius and originality. Rosalind Krauss (1984), for example, argues that modernism and the avant-garde work within a 'discourse of originality' which wrongly suppresses the right of the copy and repetition. For a critique arguing that she herself inadvertently reiterates the discourse of originality see Gooding-Williams (1987). Scheff (1990) has developed an acute sociological theory of the development of genius. For a discussion of the various historical forms of the idea of genius see Moore (1989) and Battersby (1989). The latter provides an important discussion of the ways in which women have been excluded from the idea of genius.

13. This is not to say that the anti-hero cannot himself be sustained by and develop within a form of the heroic life which is particularly compelling and exemplary for a wide following. Jean-Paul Sartre's life is a major example of this (see Brombert, 1960; Bourdieu, 1980).

14 Huyssen (1986: 59) regards the positive evaluation of the masses and the popular and everyday life by postmodernism as associated with the emergence of feminism and women as a major power in the arts which has led to the admittance and re-evaluation of formerly excluded genres (soap operas, popular romance, the decorative arts and crafts, etc.).

References

Battersby, C. (1989) *Gender and Genius*. London: Women's Press.

Bauman, Z. (1973) *Culture as Praxis*. London: Routledge.

Baudrillard, J. (1983) *In the Shadow of the Silent Majorities*. New York: Semiotext(e).

Benjamin, W. (1973) *Charles Baudelaire: A Lyric Poet in The Era of High Capitalism*. London: New Left Books.

Bologh, R. (1990) *Love or Greatness. Max Weber and Masculine Thinking — a Feminist Inquiry*. London: Unwin Hyman.

Bourdieu, P. (1980) 'Sartre, or the Invention of the Total Intellectual', *London Review of Books* 2 (22), 20 Nov–3 Dec.

Bovone, L. (1989) 'Theories of Everyday Life: A Search for Meaning or a Negation of Meaning', *Current Sociology* 37(1).

Brombert, V. (1960) *The Intellectual Hero: Studies in the French Novel 1880–1955*. London: Faber & Faber.

de Certeau, M. (1984) *The Practice of Everyday Life*. Berkeley: California University Press.

Dyer, R. (1979) *Stars*. London: British Film Institute.

Eckstein, M. (1990) *The Rites of Spring. The Great War and the Birth of the Modern Age*. New York: Doubleday.

Elias, N. (1978) *The Civilizing Process Volume 1*. Oxford: Blackwell.

Elias, N. (1982) *The Civilizing Process Volume 2*. Oxford: Blackwell.

Elias, N. (1987a) 'The Retreat of Sociologists into the Present', *Theory, Culture & Society* 4(2–3).

Elias, N. (1987b) 'The Changing Balance of Power Between the Sexes', *Theory, Culture & Society* 4(2–3).

Featherstone, M. (1991a) *Consumer Culture and Postmodernism*. London: Sage.

Featherstone, M. (1991b) 'Personality, Unity and the Ordered Life', in H. Martins (ed.), *Essays for John Rex*. Forthcoming.

Featherstone, M. (1991c) 'Georg Simmel: An Introduction', *Theory, Culture & Society* 8(3): 1–16.

Frith, S. and H. Horne (1987) *Art into Pop*. London: Methuen.

Fussell, P. (1982) *The Great War and Modern Memory*. Oxford: Oxford University Press.

Geertz, C. (1983) *Local Knowledge*. New York: Harper.

Gledhill, C. (1991) *Stardom: Industry of Desire*. London: Routledge.

Gooding-Williams, R. (1987) 'Nietzsche's Pursuit of Modernism', *New German Critique* 41.

Gouldner, A. (1975) 'Sociology and the Everyday Life', in L. Coser (ed.), *The Idea of Social Science*. New York.

Green, B.S. (1988) *Literary Methods and Sociological Theory: Case Studies of Simmel and Weber*. Chicago: Chicago University Press.

Habermas, J. (1981) *The Theory of Communicative Action Volume 1*. London: Heinemann.

Held, D. (1980) *Introduction to Critical Theory*. London: Hutchinson.

Heller, A. (1978) *Renaissance Man*. London: Routledge.

Heller, A. (1984) *Everyday Life*. London: Routledge.

Horkheimer, M. and T. Adorno (1971) *Dialectic of Enlightenment*. New York: Herder & Herder.

Huyssen, A. (1986) 'Mass Culture as Women: Modernism's Other' in A. Huyssen, *After the Great Divide*. Bloomington: Indiana University Press.

Kasson, J.F. (1990) *Rudeness and Civility*. New York: Hill & Wang.

Kitto, H.D.F. (1951) *The Greeks*. Harmondsworth: Penguin.

Klapp, O.E. (1969) *The Collective Search for Identity*. New York: Holt, Rinehart & Winston.

Knorr-Cetina, K. (1981) *The Manufacture of Knowledge. An Essay on the Constructivist and Contextual Nature of Science*. Oxford: Pergamon.

Krauss, R. (1984) 'The Originality of the Avant-Garde: A Postmodern Repetition', in B. Wallis (ed.), *Art After Modernism*. New York: Museum of Contemporary Art.

Latour, B. (1987) *Science in Action*. Milton Keynes: Open University Press.

Lefebvre, H. (1971) *Everyday Life in the Modern World*. Harmondsworth: Allen Lane.

Liebersohn, H. (1988) *Fate and Utopia in German Sociology 1870–1923*. Cambridge: MIT Press.

Lindholm, C. (1990) *Charisma*. Oxford: Blackwell.

Lowenthal, L. (1961) *Literature, Popular Culture and Society*. Palo Alto: Pacific Books.

MacIntyre, A. (1981) *After Virtue*. London: Duckworth.

Maffesoli, M. (1989) 'The Sociology of Everyday Life (Epistemological Elements)', *Current Sociology* 37(1).

Manasse, E.M. (1957) 'Jaspers' Relation to Weber' in P.A. Schlipp (ed.), *The Philosophy of Karl Jaspers*. New York: Tudor Publishing Co.

Merleau-Ponty, M. (1964) *Sense and Non-Sense*. Evanston: Northwestern University Press.

Moore, P. (ed.) (1989) *Genius: The History of an Idea*. Oxford: Blackwell.

Portis, E.B. (1973) 'Max Weber's Theory of Personality', *Sociological Inquiry* 48(2).

Sayre, H.M. (1989) *The Object of Performance: The American Avant-Garde Since 1970*. Chicago: Chicago University Press.

Scheff, T.J. (1990) 'Language Acquisition versus Formal Education: A Theory of Genius', in T.J. Scheff, *Microsociology: Discourse, Emotion and Social Structure*. Chicago: Chicago University Press.

Schutz, A. (1962) 'On Multiple Realities', in *Collected Papers Volume 1*. The Hague: Nijhoff.

Schutz, A. (1964) 'Don Quixote and the Problem of Reality', in *Collected Papers, Volume 3*. The Hague: Nijhoff.

Sharrock. W. and B. Anderson (1986) *The Ethnomethodologists*. London: Tavistock.

Simmel, G. (1971a) 'The Adventurer' in D. Levine (ed.), *Georg Simmel on Individuality and Social Forms*. Chicago: Chicago University Press.

Simmel, G. (1971b) 'Sociability', in D.L. Levine (ed.), *Georg Simmel on Individuality and Social Forms*. Chicago: Chicago University Press.

Simmel, G. (1978) *The Philosophy of Money*. London: Routledge.

Simmel, G. (1986) *Schopenhauer and Nietzsche*. Amherst: Massachusetts University Press.

Staude, J. (1967) *Max Scheler: An Intellectual Portrait 1874–1928*. New York: Free Press.

Stauth, G. and B.S. Turner (1988) *Nietzsche's Dance*. Oxford: Blackwell.

Theweleit, K. (1987) *Male Fantasies Volume 1: Women, Floods, Bodies, History*. Oxford: Polity Press.

Walker, J.A. (1987) *Crossovers: Art into Pop/Pop into Art*. London: Methuen.

Wasielewski, P.L. (1985) 'The Emotional Basis of Charisma', *Symbolic Interaction* 8(2).

Watier, P. (1991) 'The War Writings of Georg Simmel', *Theory, Culture & Society* 8(3).

Weber, Marianne (1975) *Max Weber: A Biography*. New York: Wiley.

Weber, Max (1948a) 'The Sociology of Charismatic Authority' in H.H. Gerth and C. Wright Mills (eds), *From Max Weber*. London: Routledge.

Weber, Max (1948b) 'Religious Rejections of the World and their Directions', in H.H. Gerth and C. Wright Mills (eds), *From Max Weber*. London: Routledge.

Wolfe, T. (1989) *The Right Stuff*. London: Black Swan.

Wohl, R. (1980) *The Generation of 1914*. London: Weidenfeld & Nicholson.

Mike Featherstone teaches Sociology at Teesside Polytechnic.

Ideology and Utopia in the Formation of an Intelligentsia: Reflections on the English Cultural Conduit

Bryan S. Turner

> But we can't stop desiring utopia even if rationally we know that it will never come. (Terry Eagleton)

Introduction: nostalgia

English[1] intellectuals have a peculiar relationship to global culture. As native speakers of English, they have an automatic and privileged access to the world market of intellectual production. For example, they can anticipate that their texts will reach a world market without the inconvenience of translation. By contrast, many of their European colleagues, especially Danish, Dutch or Swedish intellectuals, are either forced to cope with relatively small, local markets, or they will be faced with the expense of translation. In addition to this language advantage, English intellectuals, partly as a result of British imperial history, have also enjoyed until recently a privileged access to university positions in the United States and the Commonwealth. The oddity is that this global access has been combined with a remarkably complacent parochialism and insularity. English intellectuals, precisely because of the strategic importance of English as a global means of communication, are not noted for their language abilities.

English intellectuals have rarely been at the forefront or core of global intellectual developments; their main function has been rather as a global conduit of cultural exchange. If England has been a nation of shopkeepers, then its own intellectuals have been passive traders between the old and new world. They have been interpreters and purveyors of 'foreign' ideas, especially French and German ideas. Various versions of Marxism have been an

Theory, Culture & Society (SAGE, London, Newbury Park and New Delhi), Vol. 9 (1992), 183–210

essential ingredient of this foreign impact. Apart from the possible and dubious exceptions of anthropology and economics, they have been uncommonly uncreative. In political terms, English intellectuals who are dissatisfied with their own society have always had the option of simply leaving. They have been individual migrants and so their critical frustration has been somewhat dispersed and unfocused. Whereas other migrant intellectuals have tended to form communities, English intellectuals have merged (superficially) with their 'host' populations. They do not form a diaspora because the advantages of language and colour have meant that the English have rarely been the targets of an exclusionary process. English intellectuals simply disappear. What they leave behind is a highly fragmented intellectual deposit.

In the last decade, even this parasitic role has been threatened by a significant discharge of English academics into North American, Australian and New Zealand universities and by a further erosion of public support for the traditional independence of the university sector. Thus, the peculiarity of the English has been their high profile in the global intellectual scene by virtue of their native language ability and access to major London-based publishers, and their resilient attachment to cultural philistinism and localism. In the past, of course, English intellectual life depended heavily on a 'white migration' of (mainly Jewish) intellectuals from the continent — Ernest Gellner, Norbert Elias, Morris Ginsburg, Ilya Neustadt, Karl Mannheim, Alfred Sohn-Rethel, Ludwig Wittgenstein, Zygmunt Bauman, Ralf Dahrendorf, John Westergaard and Bronisław Malinowski. However, with the approach of European unification and the restructuring of higher education in Eastern Europe, many existing insular practices of British universities are being called into question. English intellectuals, rather like Westminster, will have to find a new global niche. We can expect that academic tensions between the North Atlantic and continental Europe will increase as recent reviews (Denzin, 1991; Vidich, 1991) of Jean Baudrillard's *America* (1988) and *Cool Memories* (1990) would appear to indicate.

It is a good time for taking stock and settling accounts. With the approach of the end of the century, there is a strong smell of diagnosis, introspection and nostalgia in the air. For some writers, the approaching end of the century has a strong apocalyptic quality, encouraging Baudrillard (1987) to declare that the new era of 2000 has already arrived. The *fin-de-siècle* combination of the end of organized capitalism, post-Fordism, postmodernity and cynical reason (Sloterdijk, 1988) has suggested to other observers that we are entering a panic period (Kroker et al., 1989). One crucial question on the agenda is whether any form of Marxist social theory will survive into the next century, or whether the collapse of organized communism in Eastern Europe has no relationship to the intellectual problems of Marxist thought. Professional sociological celebrations of the end of the century are likely to be more sober and modest, but nevertheless nostalgic. If we define the decades of 'classical sociology' as broadly the period 1890–1930 (Hughes, 1959), then there are good reasons for comparing the 1890s with the 1990s. Classical sociology was born out of a sense of crisis (essentially the transition from *gemeinschaft* to *gesellschaft*) which generated a parcel of concepts (anomie, alienation, community and disenchantment) by which twentieth-century social theorists have attempted to understand our times (Frisby, 1983; Liebersohn, 1988). Whether or not this story is true may not be terribly interesting; the point is that sociologists *see* the intellectual history of their discipline within these parameters. In this respect we can analyse sociology as a primarily nostalgic discourse which recounts how authentic communities were destroyed by the ineluctable advance of industrial capitalism across urban space, leaving behind it the debris of egoistic individualism, other-directed personalities, anomic cultures and homeless minds.

The role of intellectuals in relation to this crisis has been the fascination of intellectuals over the last century. However, there are now a number of new ingredients, chiefly the relationship of intellectuals to the tension between mass and popular cultures (as potentially oppositional forces) and high culture (as the embodiment of discipline and distinction). More precisely the current fascination with intellectuals, as manifested in Zygmunt Bauman's *Legislators and Interpreters* (1987), Russell Jacoby's *The Last Intellectuals* (1987), Alain Finkielkraut's *La Défaite de la pensée* (1987), Pierre Bourdieu's *Homo Academicus* (1988) and Andrew Ross's *No Respect* (1989), is a product of changing relations between the state, intellectuals and popular culture. The debate about postmodernity in this context of cultural struggle can be read as an attempt to discover a new social role for intellectuals in a post-literate society.

These issues which hinge upon the historical relationship of the intellectuals to high culture in the context of either state or court patronage can be illustrated through the whole field of 'cultural studies'. Although there have been a number of important contributions to the theoretical analysis of culture in Britain and North America — Robert Wuthnow's *Meaning and Moral Order* (1987), Patrick Brantlinger's *Crusoe's Footprints* (1990), Margaret Archer's *Culture and Agency* (1988), Mike Featherstone's *Consumer Culture and Postmodernism* (1991) and Jeff Alexander's *Durkheimian Sociology: Cultural Studies* (1988) — the subject has yet to find an appropriate niche within the interdisciplinary exchange between humanities and social sciences. The problem for sociology is that a sociology of culture is not an adequate answer to the issue of cultural sociology.

Intellectuals in General
There are two interrelated aspects to my argument concerning intellectual communities. First, following Max Weber's epistemological views on the relationship between sociology and history, I start with a truism: there is a tension between the theoretical drive in sociology towards very general concepts and, if possible, general explanations, and the fact that all social phenomena are historically grounded, and thereby characterized by their own specificity. We want to define 'intellectual' in a very general way to permit historical comparisons which in turn would allow us to arrive at a 'theory' of the origins and social role of the intelligentsia as a social group, but we are invariably confronted by particular histories of particular intellectual strata operating under specific historical conjunctures. I take Russell Jacoby's *The Last Intellectuals* (1987) to be a case in point. It is a superb account of the erosion of the public intellectual as a consequence of the rise of the professional academic in the context of university expansion. The book provokes numerous comparisons with similar processes in Great Britain, Holland, Germany and Australia, but we should also be aware that Jacoby's study is profound, precisely because it *is* a detailed and specific study of the urban transformation of the Village and the cultural accommodation of the New York Jewish intelligentsia. The intellectual value of the study is, therefore, exactly this specificity and not its generality. However, it may be that no general conclusions about intellectual life as such can be drawn from Jacoby's account, because this concatenation of historical concreteness has been produced nowhere else.

Second, it now seems impossible to discuss the intelligentsia without some reference to the legacy of Mannheim's *Ideology and Utopia* — hence the title of this article. Mannheim's views on intellectuals are very widely cited in general in discussions of the conditions for intellectuality; the controversy which surrounded his sociology of knowledge in the 1930s is still with us (Meja and Stehr, 1990). More importantly, Mannheim raised questions, at least in his early work, about the role of utopian aspiration in all intellectual and political life. His *Essays on the Sociology of Culture* (1956) contains one of the few serious attempts to understand the democratization of culture in modern societies with the decline or erosion of the aristocratic ethic. Thus, there are three important features of Mannheim's position. Following Alfred Weber, he attempted to locate some sociological conditions which would guarantee intellectual autonomy or at least free intellectuals from the problem of conceptual relativism — this was the famous solution of the free-floating intellectuals, and the distinction between relativism and relationalism. The second part of the legacy is the contrast between ideology as a system of belief which requires a vision of stability and permanence, and the notion of utopia which rules out any sense of the legitimacy of the status quo. Revolutionary world-views, millenarianism and socialism are examples of utopia, but the deeper meaning is closer to Weber's distinction between charisma and tradition. Like charisma, utopia is a threat to established or routinized procedures of a social order. In Mannheim's sociology, utopia had originally a spiritual significance, namely that human beings cannot live meaningful lives without a utopia. Without a vision of the future, the present is meaningless. The third aspect of Mannheim's sociology of knowledge was developed during his life in England, namely a sense of the importance of planning in the democratic restructuring of society. In his contribution to British reformism, Mannheim came to give a special emphasis to educational modernization as a preparation of the population for democratic social change and to the university as the cradle of the planner-intellectual.

For a study of intellectuals, this Mannheimian legacy leaves us with three broad questions: (1) what is the relationship of intellectuals as a social group to the macro social structure of the society in which they live, specifically the relationship to patrons and audiences, (2) what is the relationship of intellectuals to utopia or, in modern parlance, to progressive social forces, and (3) what is the relationship of intellectuals to the state and to the question of social reconstruction through planning and legislation? Is planning merely the routinization of utopia, namely ideology? The idea of the intellectual as the heroic leader of the revolutionary vanguard of the masses is, of course, scarcely credible as an image of the contemporary role of the intellectual in relationship to politics. To some extent, this more modest self-image has been described and legitimized by Michel Foucault in the idea of the 'specific intellectual' as opposed to the 'general intellectual'. The specific intellectual has to examine the specificity of power in order to problematize taken-for-granted knowledge, because 'the role of an intellectual is not to tell others what they have to do' (Foucault, 1988: 265). The problem of the intellectual in our time cannot be separated from the issue of democracy.

Now the legacy of Mannheim is a very general legacy; it has generated a broad tradition of sociological inquiry about the recruitment of intellectuals, the social role of intellectuals and questions about whether intellectuals can actually direct social change. However, what we have perhaps ignored is once more the very specificity of the historical circumstances which produced Mannheim's theory. Mannheim inherited initially a particular tradition of Jewish intellectual life from Budapest. There were two images of the intellectual in the Habsburg empire. There was the revolutionary agitator who sought to transform society by a violent struggle which could be either nationalist or working class. It was this romantic-chiliastic vision of the intellectual as apocalyptic leader of violent masses which Georg Lukács embraced during the Hungarian Soviet Republic (Kadarkay, 1991). There was an alternative legacy, that of the *Bildungsbürgertum*, namely the educated planner of a civilized transformation. In his lifetime, Mannheim experienced both. He was closely involved with Soviet Republic of Bela Kun, with the radical ideas of Georg Lukács and the cultural ambitions of the free University of Budapest. In Britain, Mannheim switched to the idea of the intellectual as the educated state official who, guided by rationality, attempts to redesign society without revolutionary struggle. Here we see both the tensions between the general and the specific, and between utopia and ideology. It is probably no accident that Ivan Szelenyi, himself a refugee intellectual and product of the Budapest elite, should see the role of the intellectual as the rational and teleological manager of social change, whose power base is located inside the state (Konrad and Szelenyi, 1979).

There are two ways of expressing this idea of the progressive intellectual. We can either argue that intellectuals produce abstract and universal thought (Nettl, 1969) because they are not attached to a *particular* social group or social class, or we can say that intellectuals are progressive because they stand outside society, and therefore do not serve a specific set of social interests. The classic idea of the free-floating intellectual is in fact a version of Georg Simmel's 'The Stranger' (1971), and the epitome of the Simmelian stranger is the free-floating urban Jew. It is a matter of common observation that sociology and socialism were almost entirely produced by Jews — from Marx to Durkheim, from Mannheim to the Frankfurt School and, in our own period, the so-called New York intellectuals, the Budapest Circle in Australia and Norbert Elias. These intellectuals had very diverse institutional backgrounds and sources of patronage. The contrasts between Daniel Bell as a Harvard professor, Alfred Sohn-Rethel as a Birmingham school teacher, and Alfred Schutz as a banker are stark and obvious, but representative: is it possible that their Jewishness alone explains their alienation and distance from Gentile society? The idea here is that distance (whether free-floating or outside) produces the sociological conditions that generate radical and/or universalistic thought. Detachment itself is often seen as 'the platform of sociological observation' (Shils, 1980: 1).

Any reference to 'progressive intellectuals' in the conventional sociological literature typically means 'socialist intellectuals', but we should not forget that Mannheim's most sustained study of the intelligentsia was in his essay on *Conservatism* (Mannheim, 1986). Where conservatism was a romantic critique of capitalism, then conservatism functioned as a utopia, not as an ideology. Indeed Mannheim went out of his way to correct the assumption that an anti-capitalist utopia would be a socialist utopia. The origins of the anti-capitalist movement lay not with proletarian socialism but religious and aristocratic conservatism. We can think of many illustrations of this romantic critique of capitalism by conservative intellectuals: the English conservative intellectuals such as the (American) T.S. Eliot in *The Waste Land*, the protests against capitalist inauthenticity by the poet Rilke, the romantic philosophical anthropology of Arnold Gehlen, or the Stefan George Circle at Heidelberg. Perhaps Mannheim himself was a romantic critic, in the sense that planning was to restore order to the conflictual system of egoistic, anarchic capitalism. Finally, if we accept the arguments of Robert Nisbet (1967) in *The Sociological Tradition*, then the whole sociological movement of the late nineteenth century (including Durkheim, Simmel and Toennies) was deeply influenced by the conservative reaction against capitalism. In the contemporary controversy surrounding Martin Heidegger's relationship to national socialism, there is a very clear illustration of this point. Victor Farias (1989) has shown all too clearly Heidegger's deep involvement in the fascist movement, especially within the German university system, and how this involvement was also part of a legacy of Catholic conservatism in South Germany which goes back to the violently anti-semitic ideas of Abraham a Sancta Clara. The principal enemies of his Swabian fatherland were American materialism and communist atheism. Whether or not Heidegger's political views during his rectorate were merely contingently related to his abstract philosophy is much disputed (Wolin, 1990). What is remarkable, however, is how Heidegger's philosophy has been embraced, with the collapse of Marxism, by many sectors of the French left (Ferry and Renaut, 1990). Any simple notion that being an intellectual means being a left-progressive intellectual is clearly fraught with difficulties. Similar issues have to be faced in the case of the politics of Paul de Man (Pels, 1991).

Intellectuals perhaps should be defined not by reference to their relationship to 'Progress' but in terms of their attitudes towards modernization. I put the question in this framework as a pretext for employing an argument by Ron Eyerman (1990) on intellectuals and progress to sketch out various approaches to the historical relationship between intellectuals and the processes of modernization. Eyerman points out that the very notion of an intellectual is a product of the Enlightenment response to modernization in the seventeenth and eighteenth centuries. The Enlightenment intellectuals, who were Mannheimian free-floating critics par excellence, produced the basic framework of modern analysis: social contract theory, individualism, scepticism, empiricism and secularity. Eyerman begins to define the intellectuals, therefore, as any group which challenges the existing order in the name of progress; in Mannheimian terms, they are utopians.

There are two versions of this notion of the intellectual as a progressive. The Marxist version is that intellectuals are a segment of the bourgeoisie which breaks away from its class roots to give an articulate expression to the class interests of the proletariat.

The specific function of the intellectual is to universalize the particularistic character of working-class trade unionism; the intellectual transforms the local struggle of workers into a historic feature of the global process of revolution. However, as Eyerman points out, there is an ambiguity in Marxism. While in Marxist theory the intellectual must somehow depart from his/her bourgeois origins in order to provide a radical articulation of proletarian interests, there is also an anti-intellectualism in Marxism-Leninism which distrusts the intellectuals precisely because they are *declassé*. The second approach to the intellectual as agent of change came from a liberal tradition which sought to protect or to create a public arena in which radical ideas could be discussed and exchanged. The role of the intellectual is seen to be educative. The liberal intellectual attempts to educate and lead public opinion towards a more refined, sophisticated and informed position. The classic liberals in this tradition were, in England, J.S. Mill, Herbert Spencer and to some extent Mannheim himself. This is the intellectual as educator. Their role is both to create and respond to public opinion. Marxist and liberal accounts eventually converged around the importance of democracy against authoritarianism as the political context in which a free exchange of ideas can take place.

The main problem with this aspect of Eyerman's account is that he fails to identify a third response to modernization, namely the so-called conservative and romantic response to modernization (in England for example from Edmund Burke through Shelley and Wordsworth to poets like T.S. Eliot and J.R.R. Tolkien). I assume he wants to exclude these on the grounds that they are not progressive, but I think this is a mistake. The Romantics were critical of existing conventions and customs; what they wanted to restore was a romanticized utopia of a lost world. The Romantics sought a rural arcadia and a modern version of the Land of Cokaygne. Their response to modernization was nostalgic and nationalistic, but it was no less critical or radical. Again it is dangerous to generalize about 'Romanticism' as such. In England, the Lake poets were oppositional in working outside the court; their framework was the 'country', that is, a rural idyll and the nation (Butler, 1988).

This great European tradition of the intellectuals was, according to Eyerman, eventually challenged by the entry of the state into the twentieth-century welfare system. With the emergence of a welfare consensus in the capitalist democracies, intellectuals were domesticated. They were no longer an external force outside the political system; they became professional academics as a consequence of the educational revolution of the 1950s; they became managers of an academic empire; or they were co-opted into the great army of social workers, welfare analysts and educational bureaucrats. In this regard, Eyerman adopts part of Jacoby's argument in *The Last Intellectuals*, although his own perception of the demise of the intellectuals is based on his analysis of the Swedish welfare system (Eyerman, 1985).

Eyerman, however, wants to suggest an alternative future scenario. He argues that, while between the 1940s and 1950s intellectuals were incorporated into the system of agents of rational planning, the growth of alternative new social movements in the 1970s and 1980s (the women's movement, peace movements and the Greens) has created a new social role for the 'movement intellectual'. However, the nature of this intellectual movement is rather different. The new social movements are, if anything, anti-progressive in the sense that they have questioned the value of unimpeded industrialization by developing alternative enterprises, and they have questioned the desirability of unification, universalism and globalism by defending localism. In fact, their response to modernity is, in the literal sense, reactionary, because new social movements are anti-progress. The 'movement intellectuals', according to Eyerman, operate outside the university complex and they are not members of a new middle-class intelligentsia.

This argument is clearly important. It provides an alternative to Jacoby's view that the intellectual died with the creation of the new university boom of the post-war period. It also takes account of the new interests of movement intellectuals: gender divisions, peace, alternative economies and ecology. His argument is underdeveloped, however, in at least three related areas. First, he fails to notice that the reaction against progressive industrialization, mass democracy and universalism was also the agenda of romantic conservatives. Tolkien's mythologies were also condemnations of a world with street lighting, automobiles and industrial development just as Ludwig Klages of the Heidelberg George Circle (about whom Mannheim was very critical) wanted to return to more natural rhythms of pre-industrial societies in his notion of cosmic love. Heidegger's critical views (1977) on technology and Arnold Gehlen's critique (1980) of the processes of deinstitutionalization in the age of technology can also be regarded as radical conservative criticisms of industrial capitalism. In the Weimar period and in the Third Reich, there was a general and persistent intellectual relationship between the critique of technology and a conservative cultural reaction, which Herf (1984) calls 'reactionary modernism' as a reworking of the romantic tradition. The question is: how are the movement intellectuals of the 1990s different from the romantic critics of rational capitalism in the nineteenth century?

In passing, we can note that much of this debate was anticipated in the controversy surrounding Weber's 'Science as a Vocation' (Gerth and Mills, 1991), namely if rationality is self-defeating because it robs the world of the moral legitimation which makes rational inquiry purposeful, what options are still open? Weber of course tried to rule out mysticism and romanticism, which he thought was represented in his own day by the prophets around Stefan George. The ethic of responsibility, which calls intellectuals to face up to their times without the false supports of psychotherapy, religion, bohemianism or hedonism, was meant to provide a realistic, if minimalist, answer to the nihilistic implications of instrumental rationalism.

Second, Eyerman fails to consider the possible parallels between a romantic critique of industrialization and a postmodern critique of modernization. If postmodernism challenges modernism by bringing into question the possibility of a unified rationality, then there may be some intriguing possibilities in linking romanticism and postmodernism. For some writers (Lash, 1990), there are strong connections between the classical humanism of the Renaissance and postmodern critiques of the anti-humanism of modernity. While postmodernism is often identified with anti-political cynicism, it may be possible to identify a political or moral programme hidden inside postmodernity. This possibility further complicates the definition of 'progressive' as a basis for identifying oppositional intellectuals.

Third, there is a weakness in Eyerman's position, because he is, in fact, attempting to analyse the experience of the Swedish intelligentsia but he wants to suggest that the incorporation of the intelligentsia in the middle of the twentieth century was a common, global experience. There is at least one important difference between the Swedish and other cases. Eyerman wants to argue that in the nineteenth century intellectuals were a diverse social group of marginalized, *declassé* radicals, workers, poets and private intellectuals, but the great expansion of the welfare state in the twentieth century produced the state intellectual, regardless of whether he or she worked in a university, the civil service administration or wherever. One obvious problem with this generalization is that the history of the welfare state is extremely different as between, for example, Sweden, Britain and the United States. In the middle-class social democracies (Scandinavia) and the corporatist systems (Germany), state involvement is high, personal taxes are high and welfare is not confined to stigmatized social groups. In the liberal welfare states of Great Britain and the United States, the welfare system is residual, personal taxation is low and welfare benefits are for target groups, such as the elderly and the sick. In the liberal welfare states, intellectuals can and do have a critical role to play, because they emerge as the advocates of the principle of egalitarian redistribution and the idea of citizenship social rights as necessary and universal. In short, what we might call the Welfare Intellectual is not necessarily a co-opted agent of the state. The more important point is that the role and place of universities in these diverse welfare systems are also very different, and so the context of intellectual work must be different. The theoretical point I am trying to make is that Eyerman treats a specific case history — intellectuals in the context of the growth of Swedish social democracy — as if it could without qualification be generalized.

Although we can have some view on the global nature of the *fin de siècle* and on the general functions of the intellectuals, we also need some understanding of local circumstances and in particular of the indigenous circumstances determining the role of intellectuals within national cultures. Although sociology, for example, has often aspired to be a science of 'Man' (Hennis, 1988), it typically reflects national problems and values (Turner, 1990a). In order to develop the notion of a 'specific intellectual', we require a more elaborate understanding of the local conditions which produce intellectuals.

Intellectuals in Particular: The English Case
Drawing extensively on the arguments of Perry Anderson (1964), it is clear that without an English revolutionary transformation the English intelligentsia never evolved to assume a critical and decisive social position within English cultural life. The English intelligentsia, for these historical and structural reasons, has been

unable to fulfil any national function in relation to, for example, the defence of the national language, the Church or the national culture. The English intellectuals have never successfully secured a structural location with a social class or other social stratum, for which it could act as guardian and defender. They have not formed an integrated or truly coherent social group. Although it is clear that Oxford and Cambridge have had a pivotal role in the reproduction of the dominant class, the universities in general have not provided a reliable or valid platform for the support of a national intelligentsia. English intellectuals in this respect have been distinctive by comparison with Irish and Scottish intellectuals, who have been an influential group in the development of a national culture.

If it is the case that England is characterized by an absent intelligentsia (Turner, 1990b), it is not at all surprising that there is, in the educated English middle class, a deep embarrassment about the very notion of the intellectual, let alone an intelligentsia. Max Beloff (1985: 402) has noted that 'few Englishmen would have wished or would now wish to be called intellectuals'. English culture has been dominated by empiricism and pragmatism and, as a result, abstract or general theory does not flourish in English institutions. Utilitarianism has penetrated the universities, reinforcing and encouraging the native hostility to abstract thought, especially when undertaken by 'foreigners'. Hostility to abstraction and outsiders has been nicely illustrated in a recent special issue on British sociology in the *British Journal of Sociology* (Halsey, 1989).

The enthusiasm for the study of intellectuals which is characteristic of North America, France and the Netherlands is largely absent in Britain. Indeed it is hard to imagine that volumes like Alvin Gouldner's *The Future of Intellectuals and the Rise of the New Class* (1979) or Arthur Kroker's *Technology and the Canadian Mind* (1984) could be written in England. Equally, Konrad and Szelenyi's *The Intellectuals on the Road to Class Power* (1979), with its notion of the teleological role of the intellectual, could only make sense in a society in which the intellectual stands in some opposition to the party bureaucracy within a politically regulated system. Mannheim's aspirations about the intellectual as planner in a democratically reorganized post-war Europe probably had a similar cultural origin. The relationship between state and intellectual in England has had a very different character. The absence of a public role for the intellectual is related to the fact that historically the connection between the state and intellectuals in England has been distant and weak. The liberal tradition of the nightwatchman state, the late intervention of the state into higher education, the continuity of the celebration of amateurism, the ethic of the gentleman as scholar and the marginal role of the universities in the training of professionals have not created a public space for the intellectual as a significant figure in the making of public opinion.

A radical intelligentsia is typically the product of the cultural crisis which results from major structural transformations of a national society. These structural transformations are likely to be the consequence of massive class conflict, military takeover, economic collapse or a major natural disaster resulting in chronic epidemics and famine. These catastrophic events, when they pose a major threat to the continuity of a national culture, call forth and constitute a national intelligentsia. Under such crisis conditions, an intellectual stratum may become a self-conscious, committed and coherent intelligentsia. The classical illustrations of this thesis are the Russian and Hungarian intelligentsia. However, if we add to this account of crisis the consequences of large-scale migration and alienation, then further examples might include the Frankfurt School but also the Palestinian intelligentsia.

Within this framework, it is the relative gradualism of English political history, the failure of any conquest after 1066 and the relative success of the state in imposing a national culture, which explains the absence of a radical, organized intelligentsia. Here again this account of British history depends heavily on the work of Perry Anderson (1974), Barrington Moore (1968) and Michael Mann (1986). After the political conflicts of the seventeenth century, England made the transition from a traditional argrarian feudal society to capitalism without a successful revolutionary conflict between social classes. The 1688 settlement created some of the preconditions for a parliamentary system, which evolved by gradual steps through the eighteenth and nineteenth centuries. Because the English Civil War had curtailed the development of absolutism, the English state did not acquire a massive repressive apparatus; in the development of the state, the navy rather than a standing army had been the crucial issue. In short, the English upper classes had been demilitarized relatively early and English capitalist society assumed a number of specific features, namely a laissez-faire economy, class compromise, a common law tradition, individualism and a liberal political system.

The empiricism of English social thought, the rejection of idealism and grand theory meant that a general theory of (English) society did not develop, because English intellectuals were not called upon to theorize an alternative social system, or to provide a defence of liberal bourgeois democracy against a proletarian revolution or a fascist takeover. Intellectual life was dominated by the utilitarianism of Bentham and Mill, the empiricism of David Hume, the political philosophy of Locke and, later, by the middle-class idealism of T.H. Green. Although the Halèvy thesis cannot be swallowed in its entirety, it is the case that Methodist principles probably did more to shape the everyday world of the nineteenth-century working class than either socialism or liberalism. Neither Hegelian nor Marxist grand theory acquired a significant following among the intellectuals.

Intellectual life in England was, and to some degree remains, divided into two separate and distinctive sectors. There is the tradition of the Oxbridge gentleman-academic, who is a person of 'independent means' and for whom the university functioned as a special club within which one could undertake scholarly research and professional engagements. Within this traditional setting, the gentleman-scholar was typically a writer of essays and articles rather than of systematic treatises, because the essay is more compatible with and symbolic of leisure and the cult of the amateur. The general essay avoids any hint of scientific specialization. The gentleman is independent, seeking no patronage from the state. Occasionally the gentleman-scholar might combine these activities with an ecclesiastical living. This habitus produced the concept of a 'fine mind', that is, an intellectual for whom brilliance comes naturally without effort, and whose talents might find expression simultaneously in almost any field from patristic theology to nuclear physics.

By contrast, there was the dissenting scientist of the provinces, whose academic interests were often adjacent to employment in business or industry. They were often associated with provincial scientific societies. These independent academies had often been created by dissenting religious groups (Baptists, Methodists and Quakers). There was an important cultural division between these provincial academies and the traditional elites in the Anglican Church and the ancient universities. To some extent, the origins of English sociology were in the dissenting, provincial milieu of the Midlands and northern England. Herbert Spencer, nonconformist, railway engineer and amateur scientist, was a typical example.

I have employed the idea of an 'absent' intelligentsia to characterize the English intellectual experience. Now the word 'absent' has a number of functions. It refers to the migrant English academics who have in waves left England to work in the United States and what used to be the Commonwealth. It indicates the absence of a cultural centre of the English social system. It refers to the absence of an English core to the global academic field, despite the dominance of English as an international language. It notes the absence of a genuine English model of the intelligentsia which is partly a function of English empiricism and its traditional hostility to universalistic, abstract thought. It points to the cultural ambivalence which surrounds describing oneself in English life as 'an intellectual'. It signifies the absence in England of any debate about intellectuals. Whereas in America there has been a great outpouring of self-critical analysis — *The Last Intellectuals* (Jacoby, 1987); *The Winding Passage* (Bell, 1980); *The Liberal Mind in a Conservative Age* (Pells, 1985); *The New York Intellectuals* (Wald, 1986); *The Closing of the American Mind* (Bloom, 1987) and *Prodigal Sons* (Bloom, 1986) — there has been little or no discussion of 'the intellectuals' in British life which could compare.

The explanation for this absence has to be sought in a number of macro, long-term features of English social structure and history. The underlying assumption has been that a collection of anomic and anonymous intellectuals are forged into a coherent intelligentsia as a consequence of some massive cultural, social, moral or military threat. Let me highlight the important aspects of this claim. Much of the intellectual excitement of so-called white-settler societies (especially Australia, New Zealand and Canada), especially in the post-war period, has been generated by the cultural confrontation which has been produced by the question 'what is the national character?' as a consequence of the impact of multi-culturalism on a traditional Wasp host system. England by contrast had Englishness imposed on it by a powerful state from at least the sixteenth century. The state exercised a powerful orchestration and articulation of a moral view of English identity. Of course, this cultural reach did not successfully include the Celtic fringe, but it is only in the last two decades that this cultural hegemony in England has begun to collapse. Tom Nairn's book *The Break-Up of Britain* (1977) signalled that the traditional consensus was under siege (especially from the Celtic fringe, and more recently from Islam).

There is clearly a major issue relating to social class in England in relation to intellectuals. Historically, the great majority of English intellectuals (whether socialist, liberal or conservative) were recruited from the landed upper classes, they were trained within the London–Oxbridge axis, and they were often oppositional to bourgeois-industrial-provincial culture. The expansion of universities in the 1960s created a new stratum of university-trained social critics who were drawn from the middle and lower middle classes and who were educated (often in the social sciences) at provincial universities. Historically, intellectual adoption of Marxism, especially in a discipline like sociology which was largely confined to and contained within a group of provincial universities such as Leicester, Leeds and Hull, signified one's ideological separation from the traditional academic establishment.[2] This social group of 'up-starts' is genuinely detached and *declassé*, but it has little political or social influence in the system. Those radical academics who are recruited into the university establishment, such as Eagleton, are self-defined outsiders, but they also retain an ambiguous relationship to working-class politics. They could neither connect with the trade-union leadership of the working class in the traditional Labour Party nor expand in any significant numbers into the radical circles of the old university elite. They are also absent. Radical English intellectuals have had an ambiguous relationship, therefore, to their working-class constituency, because their very success in academic terms necessarily cuts them off from their roots. The humorous aspects of these paradoxical social relationships have often been captured successfully in novels such as *The History Man*. In fact, much of the genuine social criticism which has existed in Britain in the post-war period was dominated by British humour. *The Goon Show* created a new form of humour which, as a radio programme, depended on linguistic absurdity. Although *The Goon Show* provided a radical critique of the class structure in such figures as Major Bloodnock, it also celebrated English parochialism in its racist stereotyping. More recently, *Monty Python's Flying Circus* is a form of humour which was originally a public-schoolboy protest against the cultural stupidity of the English class system.

The absent English intelligentsia should be contrasted with the radical place of poets, artists and academics as a marginalized intelligentsia in Scotland, Ireland and Wales. The dominance of the cultural revival to Celtic identity — often led by the arts faculties of the Scottish and Welsh universities — was taken to be further support for my argument. Nevertheless, the English case remains something of an enigma. To take one example, between approximately 1945 and 1965, Great Britain witnessed the loss of one of the largest empires in human history, partly under military pressure and partly as a consequence of pragmatic politics and economic realism. Almost no trace of that loss can be found overtly in the intellectual culture of Britain.

The New Left

The notion that the English intelligentsia has been absent is not to suggest that England has no intellects — far from it. As a counterweight to my own ironic view of intellectual life in England, I want briefly to discuss Perry Anderson's 'A Culture in Contraflow' (1990), which is primarily concerned with the nature of British intellectual life as it is expressed in the social sciences. I have argued that an intelligentsia arises in response to some major catastrophe or national crisis; for Anderson, the English catastrophe is to some extent Thatcherism. The very success of Thatcherism as a form of authoritarian populism has put left-wing, radical intellectuals to the test. The result, for Anderson, despite the failure and irrelevance of organized socialism, has been a remarkable cultural effervescence. He argues that out of that trial emerged 'the liveliest republic of letters in European socialism' (Anderson, 1990: 44). As evidence of this cultural renaissance, he lists *Iron Britannia, Zero Option, Towards 2000, The Road to Wigan Pier Revisited, For a Socialist Pluralism, The Enchanted Glass, The Hard Road to Renewal, Politics for a Rational Left* and *Theatres of Memory*. He also draws our attention to a flurry of new journals which came into existence in the 1970s and 1980s which were typically not dependent on traditional cultural centres and covered the entire range of disciplines. The list includes *Marxism Today, Screen* (1969), *Radical Philosophy* (1972), *Economy and Society* (1972), *Critique* (1973), *Oxford Literary Review* (1974), *Critique of Anthropology* (1974), *History Workshop* (1976), *Social History* (1976), *Capital and Class* (1977), *Cambridge Journal of Economics* (1977), *Feminist Review* (1979) and *Theory, Culture & Society* (1982). He also provides a detailed study of four academic figures whom he regards as major contributors to a significant re-evaluation of historical materialism, namely Michael Mann, Anthony Giddens, Ernest Gellner and W.G. Runciman (Hall, 1989). In Anderson's view, these intellectual developments constitute a rebirth of British social thought and something approaching a late English intelligentsia.

There are obviously problems with Anderson's enthusiastic celebration of the British republic of letters. As he recognizes (Anderson, 1990: 50), most of the best British academics work wholly or partly abroad — MacIntyre, McCabe, Lukes, Heritage, Mann and Anderson. Gellner is part of the white migration and Runciman is an example of the classic industrialist-scholar. For Anderson, also, the essential feature of British sociology is the development of 'large-scale theories of history' which in one way or another have engaged with the critique of Marxist historical materialism, but this judgement ignores some of the achievements and limitations of what many refer to as 'British cultural studies' (G. Turner, 1990).

The Field of Cultural Studies
The study of culture in Britain has had a number of distinctive features, but perhaps the central issue has been a concern

> not so much with the relationship between socially shaped interests and knowledge (the German focus) or between the social structure and modes of thought (the dominant French perspective) but with the *natural intimacy* of culture and social relationships and structures — culture as the *way of life* of a people. (Robertson, 1988: 13)

To be more precise, cultural studies in Britain has been the study of the way of life of social class. The great classic studies which laid the foundations for subsequent cultural studies were Richard Hoggart's *The Uses of Literacy* (1957)[3] and Raymond Williams's *Culture and Society 1780–1950* (1958). While Hoggart's study of the impact of the media and commercialization on working-class culture in northern England was a nostalgic recreation of the idea of cultural wholeness, Williams's approach attempted, partly within the literary tradition of F.R. Leavis, to identify patterns of culture and structures of feeling which could be studied as cultural wholes. Another highly influential study from this period was of course E.P. Thompson's *The Making of the English Working Class* (1963), which had an important impact on the development of cultural studies, especially in terms of debates about agency/structure and the base/superstructure metaphor in Marx. These three studies established the paradigm of British cultural studies in its first wave:

the notion of the serious academic as politically committed; middle-range theorizing with an antipathy to abstract thought; the merging of historical and anthropological techniques and assumptions about the pattern of cultural life; the privileging of the working class as the principal historical agent, and thus some notion of the working class as a community or *gemeinschaft*; a nostalgic view of pre-industrial society as more authentic than urban industrial society; and, finally, a covert but resolute commitment to the study of English culture.

Recent historical studies of the development of cultural studies have seen the emergence of British cultural studies as highly discontinuous. Following Terry Eagleton's early criticisms in his *Criticism and Ideology* (1978) of the legacy of Williams, subsequent writers have noticed a decisive turn towards more abstract theory under the impact of Althusserian structuralism, a stronger preoccupation with the problems of ideological analysis, especially the Gramscian notion of 'hegemony', a greater openness to other theoretical traditions such as discourse analysis, and a subtle but important shift from the singular notion of culture to the plural view of cultures. These developments were in particular associated with the Birmingham Centre for Contemporary Cultural Studies, which had been established in 1964 under the directorship of Hoggart who was succeeded by Stuart Hall (in 1969), Richard Johnson (in 1979) and recently by Jorge Larrain. The work of the CCCS has obviously changed over time; the early emphasis on the mass media gave way to the analysis of subcultures; and subsequently new interests emerged around the analysis of texts, subjectivities and ideology.

There are three crucial aspects of British cultural studies which appear to be continuous, underlying assumptions of research on culture. First, they have been obsessed with questions of class and ideology, and both have been approached within the paradigm which is heavily influenced by Althusser, Poulantzas and Gramsci. The main theoretical thrust of these approaches has been to break out of the legacy of the base/superstructure notion and the idea of a dominant ideology thesis (Abercrombie et al., 1980). Although there have been important and valuable developments in this area, the general problematic of neo-Marxism remains. Research in Britain has focused predominantly on the idea of popular culture as part of the ideological system which, in the last instance, can only be understood by reference to dominant and dominated classes. Thus, 'hegemony' may be a more complex notion than 'dominant ideology' but they still come out of the same stable. For example, David Morley's very important audience studies (1980), which did much to improve our ideas of reception theory, have not gone beyond the original paradigm of ideology. The main addition to the original Althusserian paradigm has been to reject the idea of the passive audience which is interpellated by ideology in favour of the idea of resistance (Hall and Jefferson, 1976). Morley's version of reception theory shows that the way audiences receive messages is more active and more complex than orthodox Althusserian versions of ideology allow. The interest in Michel de Certeau's *The Practice of Everyday Life* (1984) is centred on the idea that in everyday life people appropriate space, technologies and utilities which they adapt to their own needs. Thus, while there has been much theoretical elaboration and empirical illustration, the dominant intellectual paradigm has focused on the production of culture and its ideological effects; 'In many accounts of the role of culture, there is a reluctance to face up to the fact that people derive pleasure from their cultural pursuits and that this pleasure requires explanation' (Abercrombie, 1990: 199). This theoretical 'reluctance' is connected to the fact that the sociology of consumption in general is a neglected area of sociology. The absence of such a theory makes it very difficult for sociologists (not to mention economists) adequately to understand the *meaning* of consumption for social actors. Perhaps the only important contributions to this problem in recent years have been Colin Campbell's *The Romantic Ethic and the Spirit of Modern Consumerism* (1987), Nicholas Xenos's *Scarcity and Modernity* (1989) and Mary Douglas and Baron Isherwood's *The World of Goods* (1980).

The second feature is the continuing dependence on continental European social theory as the principal source of analytical inspiration. Of course, the strength of the Frankfurt School is still obvious in the notion of 'the culture industry' (Bernstein, 1991), although Walter Benjamin's critique of those assumptions in his 'The Work of Art in the Age of Mechanical Reproduction' in *Illuminations* (1973) has probably been the most influential single article in cultural studies. In recent years the influence of Althusser, Poulantzas and Gramsci has been partly replaced by that of Pierre Bourdieu, especially through his work on cultural capital (Bourdieu and Passeron, 1990) and distinction (Bourdieu, 1984). Here again

Bourdieu has been acceptable within a British tradition because, in some respects, his idea of 'cultural capital' supplements existing class-theoretical approaches to culture. Thus continental influences have partly overshadowed the legacy of Williams and Hoggart. Indeed although Williams is normally referred to in fairly reverential terms it is not clear how the Williams legacy will survive, because there is no distinctively Williams School. The dominance of the class–ideology paradigm has meant that important contributions from alternative paradigms have been somewhat marginalized. For example, Bernice Martin's *A Sociology of Contemporary Cultural Change* (1981) did not receive the attention which it so clearly deserved. From a different perspective, the bleak anti-Parsonian and anti-Bell sentiment of post-war British social theory meant that many important American contributions were precluded. Few British sociologists were willing to admit that Daniel Bell's *The Cultural Contradictions of Capitalism* (1976) remains one of the most important and innovative analyses of the relationship between economics, politics and culture of our period (Turner, 1990c), or that in his work on values, norms and culture Talcott Parsons had placed cultural sociology at the top of his own research agenda. British theoreticism was both parasitic (on predominantly contintental engagements with the ghost of Marx) and totally sectarian.

Third, English social theory acted as an intellectual conduit, whereby these limited selections from Marxist and post-Marxist authors in Paris and Frankfurt could be re-exported, along with the migration of English academics themselves, to Auckland, Brisbane, Hong Kong, Adelaide, Toronto, Pittsburgh and California. The scale of this migration in the 1970s and 1980s has yet to be fully appreciated, but it has meant that the British version of cultural studies was successfully exported to a global audience, while the cultural homeland of this global phenomenon was slowly but surely stifled by the decay of British higher education under Thatcherism. It is a global diaspora without a 'homeland' and without any self-consciousness of itself as a displaced social movement. Hence the impact of the British translation of European social theory is influential but highly dispersed and fragmented.

Conclusion

In this critical discussion of English intellectual life, I have tried to show that, within the context of the sociology of Mannheim, there is no national intelligentsia, that English intellectual life has been in many ways parasitic on contintental European thought, that the legacy of Marxism and the sociology of knowledge have been dominant paradigms for understanding knowledge, ideology and culture and, finally, that this paradigm has been selective and sectarian. For example, while Bourdieu's notion of 'cultural capital' has been embraced by English sociologists (especially in the field of educational sociology), his more interesting notions about practice, habitus and field have received relatively little attention. British cultural studies have been primarily engaged with debates which grew out of a Marxist legacy — that of Althusser, Gramsci, Poulantzas — and with attacks on that legacy —Foucault, Barthes, Baudrillard. In this respect, the English intellectual scene has operated as a conduit between Europe and the global English-speaking community, but this role of intellectual mediation has been combined with a pronounced involvement with and focus on national English questions: primarily the historical transformation of working-class culture and the rise of mass culture. Despite changing theoretical paradigms and vocabulary, it has been centrally concerned with the transformation of a *gemeinschaftlich* working-class culture by commodification and commercialization. Soaps, series and films such as *Coronation Street, East Enders, Z-Cars, Educating Rita* and *Boys from the Black Stuff* have provided cultural sociologists with a rich documentation of these processes. In this respect, English intellectuals have seen themselves, at least implicitly and covertly, as Mannheimian intellectuals whose function is to expose the ideological facade of inauthentic culture in pursuit of a utopian alternative of organic class culture. While radical intelligentsia in Russia, the Middle East and France have been constituted by national struggles especially against external colonialization and military destruction, English intellectuals have been more typically mobilized around the defence of class. It is probably for this reason that English sociologists have embraced a *gemeinschaftlich* conception of the working class (Holton and Turner, 1989: 160–96) as a combative community, and hence the notion of culture as a way of life which can be understood through the tools of literary analysis. Hoggart's celebrated chapter on the division between 'Them' and 'Us' is a classic illustration of this claim.

It could be objected that, while many of these claims were true, they are now hopelessly out of date. The impact of feminism, film theory, discourse analysis, postmodernism and deconstructive techniques has been either to demolish the traditional Marxist and neo-Marxist paradigms or at least to marginalize them. The defence of my argument would point to the fact that a number of recent general evaluations of 'culture' and 'cultural studies' (Brantlinger, 1990; G. Turner, 1990) have seen the specifically British contribution in terms of the couple incorporation/resistance and falsification/authenticity. To assume that Marxist paradigms are dead and buried is to underestimate the long-term impact of Thompson, Hoggart, Williams and the CCCS on British approaches to the field of culture. It is also to underestimate the central impact of literary theory, especially Eagleton (1978) and Macherey (1978) on both the social sciences and humanities. In this respect, Robert Young (1990: 21) strikes exactly the right note when he observed that 'For much of this century Marxist literary criticism monopolized the realm of literary theory, for the simple reason that only Marxists consistently believed in its value and strategic necessity.' However, precisely because these influences have been so powerful, the study of culture has not yet been successfully released from a set of narrow and national concerns about ideology and knowledge.

Notes

A version of this article was first given as a public lecture at a conference on Intellectuals and Political Commitment in the Netherlands. I am grateful to Jan Rupp and Russell Jacoby for critical comments on my argument about radical politics, conservatism and intellectuals.

1. Throughout this discussion, I have used the term 'English' specifically to distinguish the experience of English intellectuals from that of Scottish and Welsh intellectuals. The role of the intellectual within the nationalist movements of the Celtic fringe has been quite different from that of English intellectuals.

2. As an undergraduate student of sociology at the University of Leeds in the 1960s, Marxist theory was part of the taken-for-granted reality of sociology courses. I well remember a Marxist member of staff recommending that in the final analysis the only way to destroy capitalist power was by arming the miners. As I recall, no one took much notice of this call to action, including the authorities.

3. Again the undergraduate sociology programme at the University of Leeds was highly dependent on a number of key texts such as Hoggart's *The Uses of Literacy*, Dennis et al.'s *Coal is Our Life* (1956) and Willmott and Young's *Family and Kinship in East London* (1957). I completed my undergraduate degree believing that cultural studies were equivalent to community studies, which were basically concerned with the (male) leisure activities, such as pigeon racing, of a depressed working class. Hoggart, who had been born in Leeds and educated at the city's university, was affectionately seen in Leeds University circles as a 'local lad'.

References

Abercrombie, N. (1990) 'Popular Culture and Ideological Effects', pp. 199–228 in N. Abercrombie, S. Hill and B.S. Turner (eds), *Dominant Ideologies*. London: Unwin Hyman.

Abercrombie, N., S. Hill and B.S. Turner (1980) *The Dominant Ideology Thesis*. London: Allen & Unwin.

Alexander, J.C. (ed.) (1988) *Durkheimian Sociology: Cultural Studies*. Cambridge: Cambridge University Press.

Anderson, P. (1964) 'The Origins of the Present Crisis', *New Left Review* 23: 26–53.

Anderson, P. (1974) *Lineages of the Absolutist State*. London: New Left Books.

Anderson, P. (1990) 'A Culture in Contraflow', *New Left Review* 180: 41–57.

Archer, M.S. (1988) *Culture and Agency: The Place of Culture in Social Theory*. Cambridge: Cambridge University Press.

Baudrillard, J. (1987) 'The Year 2000 has Already Happened', pp. 35–44 in A. Kroker and M. Kroker (eds), *Body Invaders*. London: Macmillan.

Baudrillard, J. (1988) *America*. London: Verso.

Baudrillard, J. (1990) *Cool Memories*. London: Verso.

Bauman, Z. (1987) *Legislators and Interpreters: On Modernity, Post-modernity and Intellectuals*. Cambridge: Polity Press.

Bell, D. (1976) *The Cultural Contradictions of Capitalism*. New York: Basic Books.

Bell, D. (1980) *The Winding Passage: Essays and Sociological Journeys 1960–1980*. New York: Basic Books.

Beloff, M. (1985) 'Intellectuals', pp. 401–3 in A. Kuper and J. Kuper (eds), *The Social Science Encyclopedia*. London: Routledge & Kegan Paul.

Benjamin, W. (1973) *Illuminations*. London: Fontana.

Bernstein, J.M. (1991) 'Introduction' to Theodor W. Adorno, *The Culture Industry: Selected Essays on Mass Culture*. London: Routledge.

Bloom, A. (1986) *Prodigal Sons: The New York Intellectuals and Their World*. New York and Oxford: Oxford University Press.

Bloom, A. (1987) *The Closing of the American Mind*. New York: Simon & Schuster.

Bourdieu, P. (1984) *Distinction: A Social Critique of the Judgement of Taste*. London: Routledge & Kegan Paul.

Bourdieu, P. (1988) *Homo Academicus*. Cambridge: Polity Press.

Bourdieu, P. and J.-C. Passeron (1990) *Reproduction in Education, Society and Culture*. London: Sage.

Brantlinger, P. (1990) *Crusoe's Footprints: Cultural Studies in Britain and America*. New York: Routledge.

Butler, M. (1988) 'Romanticism in England', pp. 37–67 in R. Porter and M. Teich (eds), *Romanticism in National Context*. Cambridge: Cambridge University Press.

Campbell, C. (1987) *The Romantic Ethic and the Spirit of Modern Consumerism*. Oxford: Basil Blackwell.

Dennis, N., F. Henriques and C. Slaughter (1956) *Coal is Our Life*. London: Eyre & Spottiswoode.

de Certeau, M. (1984) *The Practice of Everyday Life*. Berkeley: University of California Press.

Denzin, N.K. (1991) 'Paris, Texas and Baudrillard on *America*', *Theory, Culture & Society* 8(2): 121–33.

Douglas, M. and B. Isherwood (1980) *The World of Goods*. Harmondsworth: Penguin.

Eagleton, T. (1978) *Criticism and Ideology*. London: Verso.

Eyerman, R. (1985) 'Rationalizing Intellectuals', *Theory and Society* 14: 777-807.

Eyerman, R. (1990) 'Intellectuals and Progress: The Origins, Decline and Revival of a Critical Group', pp. 91-105 in J.C. Alexander and P. Sztompka (eds), *Rethinking Progress: Movements, Forces and Ideas at the End of the 20th Century*. Boston: Unwin Hyman.

Farias, V. (1989) *Heidegger and Nazism*. Philadelphia: Temple University Press.

Featherstone, M. (1991) *Consumer Culture and Postmodernism*. London: Sage.

Ferry, L. and A. Renaut (1990) *Heidegger and Modernity*. Chicago and London: University of Chicago Press.

Finkielkraut, A. (1987) *La Défaite de la pensée*. Paris: Gallimard.

Foucault, M. (1988) *Politics, Philosophy, Culture: Interviews and Other Writings 1977-1984*. London: Routledge.

Frisby, D. (1983) *The Alienated Mind: The Sociology of Knowledge in Germany 1918-1933*. London: Heineman Educational Books.

Gehlen, A. (1980) *Man in the Age of Technology*. New York: Columbia University Press.

Gerth, H.H. and C. Wright Mills (eds) (1991) *From Max Weber, Essays in Sociology*. London: Routledge.

Gouldner, A.W. (1979) *The Future of Intellectuals and the Rise of the New Class*. New York and London: Oxford University Press.

Hall, J.A. (1989) 'They Do Things Differently Here, or, The Contribution of British Historical Sociology', *British Journal of Sociology* 40(4): 544-64.

Hall, S. and T. Jefferson (eds) (1976) *Resistance through Rituals*. London: Hutchinson.

Halsey, A.H. (1989) 'A Turning of the Tide? The Prospects for Sociology in Britain', *British Journal of Sociology* 40(3): 353-73.

Heidegger, M. (1977) *The Question Concerning Technology and Other Essays*. New York: Harper & Row.

Hennis, W. (1988) *Max Weber: Essays in Reconstruction*. London: Allen & Unwin.

Herf, J. (1984) *Reactionary Modernism, Technology, Culture and Politics in Weimar and the Third Reich*. Cambridge: Cambridge University Press.

Hoggart, R. (1957) *The Uses of Literacy*. London: Chatto & Windus.

Holton, R.J. and B.S. Turner (1989) *Max Weber on Economy and Society*. London: Routledge.

Hughes, H.S. (1959) *Consciousness and Society, The Reorientation of European Social Thought 1890-1930*. London: MacGibbon & Kee.

Jacoby, R. (1987) *The Last Intellectuals: American Culture in the Age of Academe*. New York: Noonday Press.

Kadarkay, A. (1991) *Georg Lukács: Life, Thought and Politics*. Oxford: Basil Blackwell.

Konrad, G. and I. Szeleyni (1979) *Intellectuals on the Road to Class Power*. New York: Harcourt Brace Jovanovich.

Kroker, A. (1984) *Technology and the Canadian Mind: Innis/McLuhan/Grant*. Montreal: New World Perspectives.

Kroker, A., M. Kroker and D. Cook (1989) *Panic Encyclopedia*. London: Macmillan.

Lash, S. (1990) 'Postmodernism as Humanism? Urban Space and Social Theory', pp. 62–74 in B.S. Turner (ed.), *Theories of Modernity and Postmodernity*. London: Sage.

Liebersohn, H. (1988) *Fate and Utopia in German Sociology, 1870–1923*. Cambridge: MIT Press.

Macherey, P. (1978) *A Theory of Literary Production*. London: Routledge & Kegan Paul.

Mann, M. (1986) *The Social Sources of Power, Volume 1, A History of Power from the Beginning to A.D. 1760*. Cambridge: Cambridge University Press.

Mannheim, K. (1956) *Essays on the Sociology of Culture*. London: Routledge & Kegan Paul.

Mannheim, K. (1986) *Conservatism*. London: Routledge & Kegan Paul.

Mannheim, K. (1991) *Ideology and Utopia*. London: Routledge.

Martin, B. (1981) *A Sociology of Contemporary Cultural Change*. Oxford: Basil Blackwell.

Meja, V. and N. Stehr (1990) *Knowledge and Politics, The Sociology of Knowledge Dispute*. London: Routledge.

Moore Jr, B. (1968) *The Social Origins of Dictatorship and Democracy*. Harmondsworth: Penguin Books.

Morley, D. (1980) *The 'Nationwide' Audience*. London: BFI.

Nairn, T. (1977) *The Break-Up of Britain*. London: New Left Books.

Nettl, J.P. (1969) 'Ideas, Intellectuals and Structures of Dissent', pp. 53–124 in P. Rieff (ed.), *On Intellectuals Theoretical Studies. Case Studies*. New York: Doubleday

Nisbet, R.A. (1967) *The Sociological Tradition*. London: Heinemann Educational Books.

Pells, R. (1985) *The Liberal Mind in a Conservative Age: American Intellectuals in the 1940s and 1950s*. New York: Harper & Row.

Pels, D. (1991) 'Treason of the Intellectuals: Paul de Man and Hendrik de Man', *Theory, Culture & Society* 8(1): 21–56.

Robertson, R. (1988) 'The Sociological Significance of Culture', *Theory, Culture & Society* 5(1): 3–23.

Ross, A. (1989) *No Respect: Intellectuals and Popular Culture*. New York and London: Routledge.

Shils, E. (1980) *The Calling of Sociology and Other Essays on the Pursuit of Learning*. Chicago and London: University of Chicago Press.

Simmel, G. (1971) 'The Stranger' pp. 141–9 in D.N. Levine (ed.), *Georg Simmel on Individuality and Social Forms*. Chicago and London: University of Chicago Press.

Sloterdijk, P. (1988) *Critique of Cynical Reason*. London: Verso.

Thompson, E.P. (1963) *The Making of the English Working Class*. New York: Vintage.

Turner, B.S. (1990a) 'The Two Faces of Sociology: Global or National?' *Theory, Culture & Society* 7: 343–58.

Turner, B.S. (1990b) 'The Absent English Intelligentsia', *Comenius* 38: 138–51.

Turner, B.S. (ed.) (1990c) *Theories of Modernity and Postmodernity*. London: Sage.

Turner, G. (1990) *British Cultural Studies. An Introduction*. London: Unwin Hyman.

Vidich, A.J. (1991) 'Baudrillard's *America*', *Theory, Culture & Society* 8(2): 135–44.

Wald, A. (1986) *The New York Intellectuals: The Rise and Fall of the Anti-Stalinist*

Left. Chapel Hill: University of North Carolina Press.

Wernick, A. (1991) *Promotional Culture*. London: Sage.

Williams, R. (1958) *Culture and Society, 1780–1950*. New York: Harper & Row.

Willmott, P. and M. Young (1957) *Family and Kinship in East London*. London: Routledge & Kegan Paul.

Wolin, R. (1990) *The Politics of Being: The Political Thought of Martin Heidegger*. New York: Columbia University Press.

Wuthnow, R. (1987) *Meaning and Moral Order: Explorations in Cultural Analysis*. Berkeley: University of California Press.

Young, R. (1990) *White Mythologies, Writing History and the West*. London: Routledge.

Xenos, N. (1989) *Scarcity and Modernity*. London and New York: Routledge.

Bryan S. Turner is Professor of Sociology at the University of Essex.

'Civilization' and the Civilizing Process: Elias, Globalization and Analytic Synthesis

Roland Robertson

Humanity is simply another word for the totality of human societies, for the ongoing process of the figuration which all the various survival units form with each other . . . In former days, the term humanity often served as a symbol of a far-fetched ideal beyond the reach of social science inquiries. It is far-fetched no longer nor is it an ideal. At a time when all the different tribes, all states of the world, are drawn together more closely, humanity increasingly represents a purely factual frame of reference of sociological inquiries into past no less than present phases of social development. (Norbert Elias, 1987: 244)

In this discussion I consider the general relevance of Norbert Elias's work to the current concern with globalization. Specifically, I consider the degree to which Elias's work is relevant to *world*, as relatively distinct from *state*, formation. Although I concentrate here upon inter-state relations I certainly do not think the conception of the world is by any means exhausted by those relations. In my discussion I draw considerably upon Gong's (1984) analysis of 'the standard of "civilization" ' and to a lesser degree on Cuddihy's (1987) work on civility, as well as Parsons's (1977) concepts of differentiation, normative upgrading, inclusion and value generalization.

Elias and Globalization

Few of Elias's interpreters or critics have attended directly to the relevance of his work to the theme of globalization, Mennell (1990) being a significant exception.[1] Mennell in fact discusses what he calls Elias's theory of globalization. This, however, is somewhat misleading, insofar as Mennell does not suggest what Elias might have made of that concept nor what he himself precisely means by it. Nor does he specifically link Elias's work to any of the current literature on that theme. It is nonetheless certainly necessary

Theory, Culture & Society (SAGE, London, Newbury Park and New Delhi), Vol. 9 (1992), 211–227

to attend to his interesting arguments. Haferkamp (1987a) has also focused briefly, in a review essay, on Elias's ideas concerning inter-state relationships, arguing that around 1980 Elias became so much concerned with inter-state 'civilization' that post-1980 work constituted a new phase, virtually a new Elias. Haferkamp (1987a: 546) argued that

> the 'new' Elias set inter-state–societal processes in the centre of the stage, that these processes were no longer a starting mechanism for a new level of civilization as they had been earlier. Certainly they *may* have this effect but they *could* just as well be a completion process, leading to the downfall and destruction of civilization.

Haferkamp went on to argue that Elias underestimated the effects of intra-societal civilizing processes on inter-state–societal processes and that Elias reified 'hegemonical regularities' (Haferkamp, 1987a: 555). Arguing against what he saw as undue pessimism and/ or lack of insight on Elias's part, Haferkamp (1987a: 555) asks 'how Elias would explain the widespread acceptance of human rights, the international rejection of slavery, the codifying of the crime of genocide'. These are, I believe, important criticisms, although Haferkamp himself inevitably had to situate his critique within the bipolar-superpower world of the 1980s. His assessment was also, in my judgement, insufficiently adventurous.

On the other hand, Mennell (1987) has argued that there was no 'new Elias', that Haferkamp set up 'a false polarity between intra-state and inter-state processes, which have always been two sides of the same coin in Elias's thinking' (Mennell, 1987: 559). Elias simply paid more attention to inter-state processes in his later years. In fact, Mennell points out that in *The Civilizing Process* (Elias, 1978, 1982) 'inter-state processes are discussed in considerable detail', the leading argument being that the reduction of intra-societal violence went hand in hand with 'the relatively unbridled persistence in violence between states' (Mennell, 1987: 559); although, as Haferkamp (1987b) pointed out, there is an aspect of Elias's work which points to the ways in which the area of 'civilization' is *enlarged* by inter-state conflict. In a separate paper, the one in which he talks more directly about Elias's ideas on globalization, Mennell (1990: 369), agrees that 'Elias's own writing about the globalization of human society had centred mainly on the chances of nuclear war', but that there is much in Elias's work, 'in his underlying theoretical strategy', which will be of great help to those now analyzing 'other aspects of global society'. Mennell (1990: 369) provides as an example Elias's early work on manners, asking about 'the prospects for the globalization of manners'. That is indeed a significant topic, to which I will return. But for the moment I want to deal with a much more general issue.

The present paper is part of a larger project in which I am attempting to connect important and influential ideas within a number of sociological traditions to the contemporary discussion of globalization. Elias's work obviously has to be considered in any such exercise. His long interest in what he called the civilizing process and his figurational sociology generally were clearly based on a profound concern with and for what I myself have called the global-human condition (Robertson, 1989). My opening quotation draws sharp attention to that concern. In that connection it may be worth saying that, from time to time, Elias has been characterized, pejoratively of course, as being a 'Comtean'. While I am not directly interested here in either the substance or the academic politics of that charge, it is worth saying that the 'global' perspectives of Comte, as well as those of Saint-Simon, appear in a new and somewhat more appreciable light as the debate about globalization gains momentum (Albrow, 1990; Turner, 1990). One of the things which the present discussion aims for is the modification of Elias's alleged evolutionism or developmentalism by a more epigenetic and global perspective, which allows for the emergence of increasingly global constraints *on* the affairs of 'survival units' — although, it does seem that Elias recognized that increasingly through historical time it is the *world,* or 'humanity' as a whole, which becomes the primary, in a sense perhaps the only, survival unit. In any case my main concern is to add to, modify and connect Elias's work to relevant others.

It is thus not my purpose here to present a general assessment of Elias's theory of the civilizing process nor certainly of his figurational sociology as a whole. Rather, as I have indicated, I want to consider strengths and weaknesses in particular reference to the rapidly increasing interest in globalization. In general I consider that Elias's ideas concerning the contingent internalization of restraint within societies — or, survival units — to be equally applicable to inter-societal systems, indeed to *the* contemporary globe-wide inter-societal system. As Mennell implies, Elias himself more than hinted at that in the second volume of *The Civilizing Process*, but he did not, in my view, make enough of it even in his phase of direct concern with Cold War inter-state relations. Indeed, Mennell (1990: 368) says that Elias remained skeptical of ideas that appear to flow from what he had to say about inter-state relations in his early work. Bentham van den Burgh (1983, 1989) has, according to Mennell (1990: 367), perceived an analogy between Elias's basically intra-societal civilizing processes, on the one hand, and the function of nuclear weapons as '*an external constraint towards self-restraint* in international relations' (Mennell, 1990: 367, italics in original). Thus the 'principle' of mutually assured destruction could have come to acquire what Mennell (1990: 367), calls 'a civilizing function in international politics'. Citing Goudsblom, Mennell invokes the notion of 'mutually expected self-restraint'. Apparently Elias was not convinced by this line of thinking.

To some extent these considerations have been relativized by the severe attenuation of the Communist presence — more specifically Soviet strength — in the contemporary world since 1989. In Elias's phrase, 'the hegemonical fevers' are not what they used to be. Nonetheless the general problem of thermonuclear destruction has by no means disappeared, as the circumstances surrounding and raised by the Gulf War have well demonstrated. Speaking in reference to nuclear tension centered on USA–USSR conflict Elias argued, again according to Mennell (1990: 368), that humanity appeared to stand at a saddle point: 'the possibility of global pacification on the one side, and on the other the chances of destruction through nuclear holocaust or ecological disaster — both produced by the globalization of human interdependence'. However, in the changed inter-state situation of the 1990s a different prospect emerges (leaving the ecological issue on one side). While always present since the acquisition of nuclear weapons by the People's Republic of China and India, even by France, there now veers more clearly into view the problem of the global 'democratization' of nuclear, as well as biological and chemical weaponry. In some respects, as many have noted, this is a more dangerous circumstance, certainly less controllable and predictable, than the old Cold War centered global situation. From one, somewhat perverse, perspective the Cold War circumstance came, in a neo-duopolistic way, to resemble Elias's hope for 'a single central political institution and thus for the pacification of the earth' (quoted in Mennell, 1990: 364). (In the McLuhanite way of thinking 'the Cold War bomb' performed the function of God.) Elias, clearly, would have resisted this idea. But I would still insist that the world 'learned' something about what has been called 'mutually expected self-restraint' during the Cold War period.

In the world of the 1990s — the world in which there emerges the so-called problem of 'the new world order' — the situation has changed, perhaps drastically. Regardless of the residual possibility of the USSR reasserting itself in a Cold War posture there has arisen as an object of very direct concern the problem of 'rights' with respect to the manufacture of and threat to use nuclear and other weapons of mass destruction. Whereas previously it was taken for granted that 'the great powers' had such weapons and that there was a problem of deciding whether or not to enter 'the nuclear club', the problem has now become much more delicately balanced. In spite, in a sense because of, almost world-wide prognoses to the contrary, the USA has emerged unambiguously — at least for the time being — as the strongest power. Its attempt, after many years of being more-or-less anti-UN, to fuse the future of the United Nations with American self-interest has resulted in a situation in which the world is now on a rather different saddle point. The USA now has the problem of legitimizing its position as the guarantor of 'world peace' — of increasingly denying to every other nation the right to overwhelming 'warlike' nuclear and 'post-nuclear' power. For the moment, and it may only be a brief world-historical moment, the USA — in part via the United Nations — bears some resemblance (not that he would have liked it) to Elias's hope for 'a single central political institution and thus [?] for the pacification of the earth'.

But where does all of this leave the civilizing process, self-restraint, and so on? Mennell (1990: 368) is almost certainly right in claiming that the dominant motif in Elias's work was 'the long-term integration of humanity and the obstacles it encounters'. And he is correct in emphasizing that 'interdependence is Elias's central category' (Mennell, 1990: 369). Yet there are a number of lacunae in the Eliasian program. One of these has to do with the relative autonomy of inter-state and trans-state norms and practices. Without denying for a moment the horrors of the history of inter-state warfare and genocide, particularly during the twentieth century, we should not forget that there is, to take a major aspect of the problem, a remarkably complex body of international law. As Lechner (1991: 268) has written:

> By analogy with normative order within societies we can say that international law provided for many centuries and even before the official 'start'

of the Wallersteinian world system, the pre-conflictual elements in international conflict and the pre-contractural elements in trans-societal contracts.

Lechner notes that apart from the hundreds of international governmental and non-governmental organizations there are also more than twenty thousand treaties and conventions. Citing Berman (1982) Lechner (1991: 266–7) also observes that commercial law has become 'an intricate, autonomous legal order on a transnational scale, developed over many centuries by participants in a truly international community'. Parallel comments could be made about other spheres, perhaps most notably science.

Whatever Elias may have written in conceptual detail about the problematic and uncertain move towards a unified humanity there can be no doubt that he did so without unpacking the idea of 'the pacification of the earth'. Rather like Comte, Elias seemed to hope for a final jump into 'peace', a utopian end to global *complexity*. This arises, in Elias's case, from his basically intra-societal, or at the most, intra-civilizational, way of thinking. He did indeed talk a lot about inter-societal, occasionally about inter-civilizational, relations, but he seems not to have had any realistic conception of the relative autonomy of the globalization process (Robertson, 1990). He didn't seem to appreciate that, insofar as the world moves toward unicity (Archer, 1990) it does so in significant part in 'its own' terms. While Eliasian theory may be able to accommodate Giddens's (1987) notion of 'self-reflexive monitoring' on the part of nation-states it is not equipped to deal with the proposition that, in part, globality preceded societality. More specifically, the relative autonomy, and the history of, the 'culture' of inter-state relations is ignored.[2] Elias (1987) demanded that we should not 'retreat into the present', but in spite of his cogent injunctions in that regard he failed to recognize that the world has become, or is becoming, 'one' along a somewhat more global, as opposed to societal, path than he, and many others, have acknowledged.[3]

Some aspects of the issue of globality can be expressed in terms of the relationship between the ideas of institutionalized individualism and institutionalized societalism. Whereas the Durkheimian–Parsonian idea of institutionalized individualism is compatible with — although not so rich as — Elias's idea of the civilizing process, there is nothing really in Elias's work which corresponds to institutionalized societalism. The problem of globally institutionalized societalism (Lechner, 1989; Robertson, 1991) has become particularly evident in the current phase of post-communism and post-colonialism and the ending of the 'old style' Cold War between the USSR and the USA. Rapidly increasing global interdependence, on the one hand, and the fluidity and multipolarity of international relations, on the other, increase the 'necessity' for widespread societal self-restraint – a restraint which was in a sense not so 'necessary' *across the globe* in the classic phase of the Cold War. As I have suggested, Elias wrote virtually all of what he had to say about inter-state relationships in embryonic or actual Cold War circumstances and that, I believe, somewhat blinded him to long-term trends; although he was most certainly not uninterested in the matter of self-restraint at the inter-state level. At the same time Elias had only a limited conception of what has come to be called the globalization process, in which he is certainly not alone. In spite of being much more aware than most contributors to the debate about globalization (e.g. Giddens, 1990) that globalization has been 'a very long-term social process' (Mennell, 1990), Elias appears not to have appreciated that globalization has, at least in recent centuries, acquired a specific, if malleable, *form* (Robertson, 1990) which is certainly not reducible to his particular conception of the civilizing process.

In any case, by broadening the scope of the idea of the civilizing process, I believe that it can be made central to the discourse of globalization. It is in that respect that Gong's work on 'the standard of civilization' (1984) becomes relevant. At precisely the same time that the notion of civilization was acquiring critical social-scientific status, particularly in Germanic contexts, it was also rapidly becoming a normative, indeed a legal, concept in international relations and diplomacy. It should be noted, however, that the uses of 'civility' and 'civilization' can be traced in terms of definite *English* usage to the second half of the eighteenth century.[4] In any case, traditional inattention to international law on the part of sociologists can be alleviated by consideration of Gong's work on 'the standard of "civilization" '.

The Standard of 'Civilization'
Gong (1984) notes that there was quite a significant pre-history to the systematic employment of the standard of civilization but that it was during the early years of the twentieth century that it became central to international relations. While the standard was often imposed coercively upon non-European countries by

major European powers, it is also the case that the leaders of a number of non-European countries aspired to meet it. They, and here one thinks of Japan in particular, came to regard some kind of conformity to it as an entry ticket to Eurocentric 'international society' (Bull and Watson, 1984). To take two other examples, in the early weeks of 1918 Lenin proclaimed that the newly created Soviet Union would not be taken seriously as a member of civilized international society if it did not adopt the Gregorian calendar (Zerubavel, 1981: 99); while in 1912, on the day that the Republic of China was formally announced, its leader Sun Yat-sen proclaimed that his provisional government would 'try [its] best to carry out the duties of a civilized nation so as to obtain the rights of a civilized nation' (quoted in Gong, 1984: 158). I could provide a number of other examples, but the main point is simple. Elias's important ideas on the civilizing process take insufficient account of the respects in which 'civility' became a regulative principle in inter-state relations and indeed, that 'the civilizing process' operated as an *external*, politico-cultural constraint on nation states. Elias uses the concept of 'civilizing process' mainly in reference to a pattern of objectively discernible trends in the direction of self- as opposed to external constraint, thus largely ignoring the ways in which the process of civili*zation* came to take on a global 'life of its own'.

The standard of 'civilization' reached its zenith during the 1920s with respect to its being essentially a regulative principle concerning inter-state relations. However, two things need to be said immediately about its demise. First, it appears to have been modified into the principle of national self-determination, strongly (and problematically) advocated by Woodrow Wilson at the Paris Conference following World War I — and then generalized to what became known as the Third World after the Second World War. Second, the emergence of the relatively autonomous legal principles of humanity, human rights and so on, can be traced to the period when the standard of civilization was in its most explicit phase in the early years of this century. The latter point is particularly relevant to such themes in Elias's work as his own frequently expressed concern for 'humanity' and the accusation that his was but a version of a discredited Comte-like sociology of and for humanity.

It is necessary at this point to say something about Elias's general orientation to long-term encompassing change. Elias has often been accused of undue optimism, indeed utopianism and naiveté (in spite of pessimism about superpower confrontation). Ironically Elias's *betê noire*, Talcott Parsons, has often been similarly characterized. Unfortunately a number of Elias's students and *aficionados* have added fuel to the fire by contrasting, in *ad hominem* ways, Parsons's alleged privileges with Elias's struggles to achieve academic recognition. The irony as far as the latter is concerned is that while Parsons certainly did not, unlike Elias, experience at first, agonizing hand the inhumanity of German fascism, he did spend much of his formative intellectual period in fighting fascism from the Eastern shore of America (Nielsen, 1991). In any case it is worth recording that Parsons and Elias have often been attacked for the same 'sins'. They have both been charged with a naive unilinear evolutionism, while Parsons's voluntarism has been subjected to critiques which bear a strong resemblance to attacks on Elias's insistence on the universal tendency towards increasing self-restraint. Both were subjected to attacks on their 'multidimensionality' — their resistance to single-factor accounts of human society — at least until 'multidimensionality' became the current fashion through the writings of Luhmann, Alexander and, as a recent convert, Giddens (1990). Both Parsons and Elias were convinced that the interpretation and/or explanation of social life was impossible without an understanding of death and the significance of the body. One could go on to talk about other points of positive and negative convergence, not the least of which would be the similarities between their four-dimensional (dare one say four-*functional*?) conception of 'survival units' (Elias, 1987).

Let us return, however, to the standard of civilization. The standard of 'civilization' arose during the nineteenth century when Asia and Africa 'were brought within the compass of the expanding European-centered international system' (Bull, 1984: vii). From the European point of view a major issue was that of the conditions under which European states 'would or would not admit non-European political communities to membership of the international society they formed among themselves' (Bull, 1984: vii). That issue was resolved in principle by the establishment of the standard of civilization. Asian or African 'communities' had to meet that standard if they were to be accepted into 'international society' (Bull, 1984: vii). On the other hand, the idea of 'civilization' certainly acquired a bad name. Even in the nineteenth century, people from such ancient cultures as China and Persia expressed their deep indignation about European arrogance and presumptuousness when the standard was presented to them, particularly when application of it was seen to involve a privileged legal status for Europeans in the form of the right of 'extraterritorial jurisdiction'. By the post-Second World War period the standard of civilization was, at least in international law, completely dead and, as Bull (1984: viii) remarked 'now appears to us part and parcel of an unjust system of domination and exploitation against which the peoples of Asia and Africa have rightly revolted'. Indeed it has by now become a forbidden term in certain circles, a good example of which is the rule that authors of papers presented at meetings of or published in journals sponsored by the British Sociological Association may not use it without heavy qualification. In that connection it is, however, of considerable interest in the present context to note that the BSA makes a special exemption in respect of the use of 'civilization' and terms of family resemblance. When the term 'civilizing process' is used within the tradition established by Norbert Elias it is considered permissible by the BSA to enter what we may call the discourse of civilization. One of my points is to show that things are not as simple as that.

Bull argued, in summary of Gong, that the view that the standard of civilization laid down by Europeans in the late nineteenth and early twentieth centuries was a central component of 'an unjust system of domination and exploitation' is without doubt true, but that 'the truth is more complex than that' (Bull, 1984: viii). For a start, the requirement that

> governments aspiring to membership of international society should be able to meet standards of performance . . . similar to those which European states expected of each other rested not upon ideas of superior right but on a need for reciprocity in dealing between European and non-European powers, which the latter were either not able to nor willing to meet. (Bull, 1984: viii)

While we may well have reservations about Bull's dismissal of the idea of the European presumption of superiority his point about reciprocity is important — for without adherence to such norms as protection of the rights of citizens, capacity to adhere to rules of international law and diplomatic relations, avoidance of slavery and so on, reciprocity was not attainable. Thus even though there was much unjust treatment (and not a little racism) it is difficult to deny Bull's (1984: ix) main point:

> [T]he demand of Asian and African peoples for equality of rights in international law was one that the latter did not put forward until they had first absorbed ideas

of equal rights of states to sovereignty, of peoples to self-determination, and of persons of different races to individual rights, which before their contact with Europe played little or no part in their experience.

Gong adopts a politico-cultural approach to international relations. Moreover he belongs to that school of international relations specialists who subscribe to the notion of international society. As defined by Bull and Watson (1985: 1) an international society is

a group of states (or, more generally, a group of independent political communities) which not merely form a system . . . but also have established by dialogue and consent common rules and institutions for the conduct of their relations, and recognize their common interests in maintaining these arrangements.

Gong's discussion of the standard of civilization is geared considerably to the problematic of the making of contemporary 'international society'. Thus even though much of his book addresses the question of the admission of non-European political communities to Eurocentric 'society', he also insists that that standard of civilization was largely an outcome of *encounters between civilizations*.[5] Even though a basically European standard came to prevail, that standard 'was central to the changes *within* the European international society and within those non-European countries which sought to enter it' (Gong, 1984: 238; emphasis added). Moreover these changes were 'aspects of the greater global transformation which paralleled the expansion of the previously European international society into a global "civilized" society' (Gong, 1984: 238).

Gong is critical of the argument of Alexandrowicz (1967: 1973) for being unsophisticated in its conceptions of 'the Family of Nations'. Gong argues against the natural law tendencies of many writers on international law after Vitoria and Grotius on the grounds that it was not the rise of positive legal doctrines which brought about either the increasing specificity of international law nor the exclusion of non-European countries from the Family of Nations. The classic, natural law perspective was simply an idealized 'conceptual creation of international theorists rather than the product of universally-sustained international relations' (Gong, 1984: 239). This argument, in effect against both natural and positive interpretation of the history of international law, is important. He points out that to argue that 'international law discriminated against non-European countries simply because it originated in Europe is a non sequitur' (Gong, 1984: 45). On the other hand to consider how 'the social and intellectual assumptions inherent in European society influenced' the emergence of the standard of civilization 'is something else' (Gong, 1984: 45). (One might add, however, that the natural law tradition has played a significant part in developing ideas as to a shared global-human condition.)

Civility, Inter-ethnic Relations and Modernity

Let us now turn much more briefly to Cuddihy, whose major contribution to the relevant theme is primarily addressed to what he has called 'the Jewish struggle with modernity' and deals particularly with the writings of Freud, Marx and Lévi-Strauss. His *The Ordeal of Civility* was criticized in some quarters when it first appeared in 1974 on the grounds that that it leaned in an anti-Jewish direction, although it must be emphasized that that was not by any means the dominant view. One reviewer wrote: 'The book's greatest value lies in its heuristic *chutzpah*, its "rude" stirring of the sediment of conventional thinking.' While I think that Cuddihy's book is valuable for more substantive reasons than that, that reviewer's opinion does address the issue of Cuddihy's 'rudeness' very effectively. Cuddihy argues that it was 'the failure of civility [which] came to define "the Jewish problem" as this problem reconstituted itself in the era of social modernity' (Cuddihy, 1987: 3). He goes on to argue that 'this ordeal, this problem of the ritually unconsummated social courtship of Gentile and Jew . . . is formative for the labors of the secular intelligentsia of the nineteenth and twentieth centuries' (Cuddihy, 1987: 3–4). According to Cuddihy (1987: 4) the problem derives from what he calls 'a disabling inability of Judaism to legitimate culturally the differentiation of culture and society', a point which is well captured in the following paragraph:

> Thus, Jewish emancipation, assimilation, and modernization constitute a single, total phenomenon. The secularizing Jewish intellectual, as the avant-garde of his decolonized people, suffered in his own person the trauma of this culture shock. Unable to turn back, unable completely to acculturate, caught between 'his own' whom he had left behind and the Gentile 'host culture' where he felt ill at ease and alienated, intellectual Jews and Jewish intellectuals experienced cultural shame and awkwardness, guilt and the 'guilt of shame'. (Cuddihy, 1987: 4)

I shall not address here the details of Cuddihy's interpretation of Freud, Marx and Lévi-Strauss, except to say that for him Marxist, Freudian and closely related ideologies are both hermeneutical and practical. They seek to reinterpret and to change. Speaking specifically of Marx and Freud he argues that in each case the problem began with 'the public delict of Jewish behavior — the scene it was making in the public places of the Diaspora' and which led to the advocacy of change (collective, revolutionary change for Marx and incremental, individual change for Freud).

Cuddihy (1987: 9) describes his as 'a study in subculture-boundedness'. His most general concern in this respect is with orientations to modernity, the argument being that 'with perhaps unpardonable oversimplification' the modern intelligentsia, since at least the beginning of the nineteenth century, have been opposing modernity. Modernity and thus, at least loosely, modernization was — according to Cuddihy (1987: 9) — best captured by Parsons, specifically in his 'differentiation model' of modernity and modernization. 'Parsons . . . displayed . . . an all but sovereign indifference to the high cost of [the] "passing of traditional society" . . .' As Cuddihy (1987: 9) further writes, 'members of the Protestant core-culture like Parsons, theorize from within the eye of the hurricane of modernization, where all is calm and intelligible. But for the underclass below, as for the ethnic outside, modernization is a trauma.' Cuddihy's central concept of civility, is presented as 'the very medium of Western social interaction'; and it presupposes the differentiated structures of a modernizing 'civil society'. Civility is not merely regulative of social behavior; it is an order of ' "appearance" constitutive of that behavior' (Cuddihy, 1987: 14). Civility, argues Cuddihy, minimally requires differentiation between private affect and public demeanor.

The most important part of Cuddihy's analysis for present purposes is his attempt to generalize beyond his discussions of particular Jewish intellectuals to brief comparisons of the Jews and the Irish, as peoples rather than nations, who were latecomers to modernity; and of the experiences of Jewish emancipation and the new nations which sought global acceptance after the Second World War. It is of course in the latter respect that Cuddihy's interest converges most clearly with that of Gong. Neither Gong nor Cuddihy refer to each other. There is one rather vague reference to Elias by Cuddihy; none, as far as I know, by Elias to Cuddihy. And neither Gong nor Elias refer to each other. Taken together, Gong and Cuddihy provide different but complementary additions to and revisions of Elias's work on the civilizing process and on inter-state relations. Gong supplies much with respect to the internationally and interculturally negotiated dimensions of 'civilization' and the ways in which the standard of 'civilization' was at one crucial historical moment a definite external constraint, not just on 'uncivilized' and 'semi-civilized' but *also* on 'civilized' societies. On the other hand, Cuddihy provides much in respect of the 'sub-cultural' aspects of civility and its negotiation.

At the same time it can be seen that Parsons's concepts of *differentiation*, *normative upgrading*, *inclusion* and *value-generalization* are both enriched and consolidated by such considerations. Gong's work tells us a lot about inclusion, normative upgrading and value generalization at the global level, Cuddihy's book informs us particularly about 'subcultural' inclusion; but it also has something to say about differentiation, as well as inclusion in inter-societal terms.

Conclusion

Towards the end of his paper on Elias's theory of 'globalization', Mennell (1990: 369) contends that even though Elias's writing about 'the globalization' of human society was centered on the possibility of nuclear war, there is much in his 'underlying theoretical strategy' which can be of assistance in our efforts to study the world as a whole. After observing that Elias began his work on European civilizing processes by noting 'that the notion of civilization represented the self-satisfaction of Europeans in a colonialist age', Mennell asks: 'What are the implications now for a world-wide civilizing process, considered as changes in ways of demanding and showing respect, when Europe and Europe-over-the-ocean no longer occupy the hegemonic position?' (Wisely Mennell adds the question 'Or do they?')

Perhaps the main point of this paper has been that these are precisely the kinds of questions which have been and continue to be tackled by theorists of globalization. Although not cast specifically in the language of globalization, Gong's work, as well as that of Bull and others, has been directly concerned with the ramifications of European 'self-satisfaction'. Gong has traced in some detail the ways in which the European standard of 'civilization' was developed, extended, modified and upgraded. From a different perspective, and with specific reference to some of the work which immediately preceded the current interest in globalization (Lagos, 1963; Nettl and Robertson, 1968), Cuddihy has directly addressed the issue of civility in terms of the dynamics of inclusion and exclusion (which certainly has some overlap with Elias's interest in the insider–outsider phenomenon) in a way that is clearly comple-mentary to Parsons's work on long-term, increasingly large-scale change.

Consideration of the work of Elias, Gong, Cuddihy and Parsons in connection with the civilization process, civility and the standard of 'civilization' assists in the consolidation of a theoretically and empirically rich perspective on globalization.

Notes

An earlier version of this paper was presented at the Conference on the Frontiers of European Culture, University of Aberdeen, Scotland, July, 1991 (and thus prior to the events of August 1991 in the USSR).

1. In addition to those specified in the text mention should also be made of Arnason (1987), who has in various papers discussed the relationship between Elias's work and some of the themes of the present paper. I have been unable to trace a paper in which Arnason apparently considers Elias's theory of civilization in even more direct relationship to the concerns of this discussion (Arnason, 1987: 454).

2. See Arnason (1987) for discussion of Elias's neglect of culture. Arnason (1987: 450) specifically remarks upon Elias's 'emphasis on the continuity of Euro-pean history and the postponement of any detailed comparison with other civilizations'.

3. Various strands of world-system theory have, of course, talked much of the global *economic* path. Sociologists and anthropologists influenced by the world history approach have also, more diffusely, done much to broaden the sociological perspective.

4. For discussion of the different senses of 'civilization' as process, the outcome of a process and as a condition, see Gong (1984: 45–53).

5. The concept of inter-civilizational encounter was central to the work of Benjamin Nelson (1981). This is as good a place as any to mention the important con-tributions to 'civilization analysis' of Kavolis (1986, 1987).

References

Albrow, Martin (1990) 'Globalization, Knowledge and Society: Introduction', in Martin Albrow and Elizabeth King (eds), *Globalization, Knowledge and Society*. London: Sage.

Alexandrowicz, C.H. (1967) *An Introduction to the History of the Law of Nations in the East Indies*. Oxford: Oxford University Press.

Alexandrowicz, C.H. (1973) *The European–African Confrontation*. Leiden: Sijthoff.

Archer, Margaret (1990) 'Foreword', in Martin Albrow and Elizabeth King (eds), *Globalization, Knowledge and Society*. London: Sage.

Arnason, Johann (1987) 'Figurational Sociology as a Counter-Paradigm', *Theory, Culture & Society* 4(2–3): 429–56.

Bentham van den Bergh, Godfried van (1983) 'Two Scorpions in a Bottle: The Unintended Benefits of Nuclear Weapons', in William Page (ed.), *The Future of Politics*. London: Francis Pinter.

Bentham van den Bergh, Godfried van (1990) *The Taming of the Great Powers*. Aldershot: Gower.

Berman, Harold J. (1982) 'The Law of International Commercial Transactions', in W.S. Surrey and D. Wallace (eds) *International Business Transactions* Part III.

Bull, Hedley (1984) 'Foreword', in Gerritt W. Gong, *The Standard of 'Civilization' in International Society*. Oxford: Clarendon Press.

Bull, Hedley and Adam Watson (1984) 'Introduction', in Hedley Bull and Adam Watson (eds), *The Expansion of International Society*. Oxford: Clarendon Press.

Cuddihy, John Murray (1987) *The Ordeal of Civility: Freud, Marx, Lévi-Strauss and the Jewish Struggle with Modernity*. Boston: Beacon Press (second edn).

Elias, Norbert (1978) *The Civilizing Process Volume I: The History of Manners*. New York: Pantheon Books.

Elias, Norbert (1982) *The Civilizing Process Volume II: State Formation and Civilization*. Oxford: Basil Blackwell.

Elias, Norbert (1987) 'The Retreat of Sociologists into the Present', *Theory, Culture & Society* 4(2–3): 223–48.

Featherstone, Mike (1987) 'Norbert Elias and Figurational Sociology: Some Prefatory Remarks', *Theory, Culture & Society* 4(2–3): 197–211.

Giddens, Anthony (1987) *The Nation-State and Violence*. Berkeley: University of California Press.

Giddens, Anthony (1990) *The Consequences of Modernity*. Stanford: Stanford University Press.

Gong, Gerritt W. (1984) *The Standard of 'Civilization' in International Society*. Oxford: Clarendon Press.

Haferkamp, Hans (1987a) 'From the Intra-State to the Inter-State Civilizing Process', *Theory, Culture & Society* 4(2–3): 545–58.

Haferkamp, Hans (1987b) 'Reply to Stephen Mennell', *Theory, Culture & Society* 4(2–3): 562.

Kavolis, Vytautas (1986) 'Civilizational Paradigms in Current Sociology: Dumont vs. Eisenstadt', *Current Perspectives in Social Theory* 7: 125–40.

Kavolis, Vytautas (1987) 'History of Consciousness and Civilization Analysis', *Comparative Civilizations Review* 17 (Fall): 1–19.

Lagos, Gustavo (1963) *International Stratification and Underdeveloped Countries*. Chapel Hill: University of North Carolina Press.

Lechner, Frank J. (1989) 'Cultural Aspects of the Modern World-System', in William H. Swatos Jr (ed.), *Religious Politics in Global and Comparative Perspective*. New York: Greenwood Press.

Lechner, Frank J. (1991) 'Religion, Law, and Global Order', in Roland Robertson and William R. Garrett (eds), *Religion and Global Order*. New York: Paragon House.

Mennell, Stephen (1987) 'Comment on Haferkamp', *Theory, Culture & Society* 4(2–3): 559–61.

Mennell, Stephen (1990) 'The Globalization of Human Society as a Very Long-Term Social Process: Elias's Theory', in Mike Featherstone (ed.), *Global Culture: Nationalism, Globalization and Modernity*. London: Sage.

Nelson, Benjamin (1981) *On the Roads to Modernity: Conscience, Science and*

Civilizations (ed. Toby E. Huff). Totowa: Rowman & Littlefield.

Nettl, J.P. and Roland Robertson (1968) *International Systems and the Modernization of Societies: The Formation of National Goals and Attitudes*. New York: Basic Books.

Nielsen, Jens Kaalhauge (1991) 'The Political Orientation of Talcott Parsons: The Second World War and its Aftermath', in Roland Robertson and Bryan S. Turner (eds), *Talcott Parsons: Theorist of Modernity*. London: Sage.

Parsons, Talcott (1977) *The Evolution of Societies* (ed. Jackson Toby). Englewood Cliffs: Prentice-Hall.

Robertson, Roland (1989) 'A New Perspective on Religion and Secularization in the Global Context', in Jeffrey K. Hadden and Anson Shupe (eds), *Secularization and Fundamentalism*. New York: Paragon House.

Robertson, Roland (1990) 'Mapping the Global Condition: Globalization as the Central Concept', in Mike Featherstone (ed.), *Global Culture: Nationalism, Globalization and Modernity*. London: Sage.

Robertson, Roland (1991a) 'Globalization, Modernization and Postmodernization: The Ambiguous Position of Religion', in Roland Robertson and William R. Garrett (eds), *Religion and Global Order*. New York: Paragon House.

Robertson, Roland (1991b) 'Social Theory, Cultural Relativity and the Problem of Globality', in Anthony D. King (ed.), *Culture, Globalization and the World-System: Contemporary Conditions for the Representation of Identity*. London: Macmillan.

Turner, Bryan S. (1990) 'The Two Faces of Sociology: Global or National?', in Mike Featherstone (ed.), *Global Culture: Nationalism, Globalization and Modernity*. London: Sage.

Zerubavel, Eviatar (1981) *Hidden Rhythms: Schedules and Calendars in Social Life*. Chicago: University of Chicago Press.

Roland Robertson is Professor of Sociology at the University of Pittsburgh. He is the author of the forthcoming *Globalization* (Sage).

On Status Competition and Emotion Management: The Study of Emotions as a New Field

Cas Wouters

During the Gulf War fighter pilots, interviewed for TV in their planes before taking off, admitted to being afraid. They did this in a matter of fact way. This would have been almost unthinkable in the Second World War, when such behaviour would have been equated almost automatically with being fear-ridden, a condition in which it was thought to be impossible to perform well. The dominant response at that time, in answer to the problem of how to prevent soldiers from giving in to fear may be summarized in a quotation from a 1943 manual for American officers: it is the soldier's 'desire to retain the good opinion of his friends and associates . . . his pride smothers his fear' (Stearns and Haggerty, 1991). Precisely the same pride kept soldiers from admitting they were afraid, especially before an operation. At the time of the Gulf War, all this had obviously changed. Today, admitting one is afraid no longer means that one has automatically to act upon the emotion. It has become quite common to admit feeling this or that, and yet to act differently. This is an example of a change in the codes of behaviour and emotion management in the direction of an 'emancipation of emotions'; an example of the long-term process of *informalization*, in which behavioural, emotional and moral codes have relaxed and differentiated (Wouters, 1986, 1987, 1989). This same process may help to explain why the study of emotions has emerged and is expanding in all the disciplines of the social sciences, including history.

From the mid-1970s onwards, interest in this subject has found expression in rapidly increasing numbers of psychological, sociological and historical studies, and in the formation of study groups

Theory, Culture & Society (SAGE, London, Newbury Park and New Delhi), Vol. 9 (1992), 229–252.

within official academic associations. In the 1980s, the American and the British Sociological Associations both established 'sociology of emotions' study groups. Theodore Kemper, editor of a reader in the sociology of emotions, refers to 1975 as the watershed year (Kemper, 1990). In that year, Arlie Hochschild published an influential article on emotions, Thomas Scheff organized the first session on emotions at the American Sociological Association meetings, and Randall Collins theorized a central place for emotions in his book *Conflict Sociology*. At present, the study of emotions is booming.

This paper seeks to explain the rise and the rising importance of the study of emotions from the perspective of figurational or process sociology. The search for an explanation mainly consists of an attempt at connecting this rise to the social process of intensified status competition within increasingly dense networks of interdependency. From this perspective, a first clue is to be found in the fact that focusing on emotions and emotion management seems to have spread predominantly in Western societies, where increasing numbers of people have experienced rising degrees of physical safety and material security, in the course of which the dangers of violence and poverty have become less topical. In these parts of the world, one's *individual* style of emotion management has gained importance in the struggle for status and power, as a criterion in the process of ranking, whereas in most countries of the Third World, status criteria like 'birth' and wealth — referring to *groups* and their proximity to the centres controlling the dangers of violence and poverty — strongly dominate over other criteria. In the West, these dangers have diminished as political, economic and cultural networks of interdependency expanded and became more dense. Correspondingly, the more traditional status criteria like 'birth' and wealth have lost some weight, without becoming unimportant, whereas ranking criteria like *individual* merit and achievement, lifestyle and style of emotion management have gained in importance.[1] In the same broad process, a wide range of emancipation movements have been established and ideals of equality have spread. Succeeding waves of democratization and the redistribution of economic surpluses according to welfare-state principles have resulted in the depletion or disappearance of the groups at either end of the social ladder, with a sharp increase of the jostling and status struggle in the middle. As hierarchical differences between individuals and groups diminished and bonds of co-operation as well as competition between increasing numbers of people expanded and intensified, all have increasingly exerted pressure upon each other to take more of each other into account more often. In this way, the sensitivity for each other's emotional life has increased, allowing for a wider social acceptance of all kinds of emotions, with the exception of feelings of superiority and inferiority. These emotions had to be increasingly curbed, as these movements and ideals have limited power to express social distance and distinction.

At the beginning of this century, in a still strongly hierarchical society like Wilhelminian Germany, status differences and related feelings of superiority and inferiority were still expressed directly and plainly:

> Anyone who displayed any weakness counted for a nullity. Here, people were fundamentally trained to strike hard whenever they knew they were confronted with a weaker person, to demonstrate immediately and unmistakably their own superiority and to rub in the other's inferiority. Not to do that was weakness, and weakness was something contemptible. (Elias, 1989: 144)

According to the dominant code of the more egalitarian and democratic societies of today, such a plain display of superiority is no longer *bon ton*. On the contrary, it would bring a loss of status and face. Gestures and feelings of superiority have become more repugnant and are more easily met with moral indignation. This represents an advance in the threshold of shame and repugnance or embarrassment in the make-up of Western people, the development of a particular kind of drives/control balance (Elias, 1978, 1982).[2] Not only transgressions like outbursts of physical — and sexual — violence, but also other ways of inflicting humiliation have increasingly come to be seen as intolerable displays of arrogance or self-aggrandizement, especially if based on biologically or socially inherited possessions and positions. They meet with stronger individual and collective repugnance and moral indignation. As subordinate social groups were emancipated, references to 'better' and 'inferior' kinds of people, to hierarchical group differences, were increasingly tabooed.[3] But exactly because displaying these feelings has become such a strong threat to one's status and self-esteem, the insight that feelings of superiority and inferiority are inherently provoked by any status competition is often lost — covered by status fears. The same goes for the insight that part of any encounter or gathering is a 'trial of strength', a power and status competition.

One of the difficulties in realizing these insights stems from the fact that in the same process of social equalization and democratization, the wish to defy this pressure — that is, the wish and the ideal of being able to articulate and distinguish oneself as an authentic individual, not just a group specimen, has simultaneously been stimulated and strengthened. To distinguish oneself from others gives value and meaning to one's *own* life, although it can only be done if one at the same time avoids any trace of feelings of superiority and inferiority, of violence, aggrandizement or other forms of humiliation. Ideally, avoidance of these traits should come 'naturally' or as the product of 'second nature', which means that it is done either unconsciously and automatically, or secretly. The complexity of this ideal may explain why references to feelings of superiority and inferiority, to the 'secret' part of emotion management, are soon felt to discredit the credibility or authenticity of individuals — and therefore their status, and why 'exposures' offer a view into the cauldron of emotion management that is often experienced as 'treacherous'. As Tom Wolfe observed: 'We are in an age when people will sooner confess their sexual secrets — much sooner in many cases — than their status secrets, whether in the sense of longings and triumphs or humiliations and defeats' (Wolfe, 1976: 189). In Western societies of our time, discussing the importance of status for someone's identity has indeed become increasingly embarrassing and difficult. However, no matter how people try to keep their status secrets, even to intimates, a trained ear detects expressions of inferiority and superiority every day, whether in guarded terms or

> in indirect and seemingly colourless terms which lacked the emotional directness with which people of higher status in less democratic ages spoke of their own superior status, but which, nevertheless, was quite unambiguous.
>
> The [status] yardsticks are almost always implied as part of an axiomatic communal belief system and the ranking is usually expressed by means of simple value terms which have the character of communal code words, such as 'better' or 'not quite nice', 'all right' or 'okay'.
>
> No individual grows up without this anchorage of his personal identity in the identification with a group or groups even though it may remain tenuous and may be forgotten in later life, and without some knowledge of the terms of praise and abuse, of the praise gossip and blame gossip, of the group superiority and group inferiority which go with it. (Elias and Scotson, 1965: 29, 41, 105)

Thus, on the one hand, *contrasts* in emotion management have diminished in contexts where feelings and displays of superiority and inferiority, inherently provoked by any competition, have become tabooed, repressed and denied, while on the other hand *varieties* in ways of managing emotions have increased in contexts where creating a particular impression, 'styling' or 'image building' within these borderlines has gained importance — and it has gained considerable importance. Impression management (see Goffman, 1959)[4] has even become a speciality, the job of an increasing number of emotional labour specialists (see Hochschild, 1983) working in advertising bureaux, departments of public relations and in an enormously expanding service industry. Particularly with regard to styles of emotion management, status competition has intensified. The rising importance of emotion management has in turn stimulated an awareness of this management as well as curiosity about what exactly is managed, how it is done and why.

Thus, the development towards intensified status competition within increasingly dense interdependency networks has exerted seemingly opposing pressures, conceptualized by Norbert Elias as diminishing contrasts and increasing varieties in behaviour and emotion management (Elias, 1982 II: 251–7; Mennell, 1985: 317–32). On the one hand, there is the pressure to repress feelings of superiority and inferiority, in which process they are often put behind some social and individual scene or 'cover'. This curbing of displays of superiority and inferiority represents a diminishing of contrasts in behaviour and emotion management. On the other hand, there is a pressure to 'discover', to gain greater awareness, and more curiosity. To experiment with new, and new combinations of, alternatives and lifestyles has become more important as one of the ways in which individuals are able to distinguish themselves from others — taste and style have gained importance as beacons.[5] Attempts in this direction have created pressures towards an increase in socially accepted emotional and behavioural alternatives, towards informalization. This represents an increase in varieties in behaviour and emotion management.

In an attempt to show that the rising popularity of the study of emotions is part of this trend of diminishing contrasts and increasing varieties in behaviour and emotion management, I will first elaborate upon this trend by presenting some familiar examples from the history of violence and money, freedom and welfare.

Changing Regimes of Power and Emotions: Violence and Money
The main contrasts that have been diminishing are those in displays
of superiority and inferiority as expressed in the use of physical and
sexual violence. Expression of emotions and impulses that could
possibly provoke the danger of outbursts of physical and sexual
violence has been increasingly excluded from the spectrum of
socially acceptable behaviour.

In the long period of peace and prosperity after the Second World
War, political emancipation and the presence of nuclear weapons
have created a situation *between* states that has been summed up as
Mutually Assured Destruction (MAD), in which states have exerted
pressure on each other towards higher levels of Mutually Expected
Self-restraints (MES). Particularly *within* industrialized Western
states the use of violence has become increasingly tabooed and
constraints on violent impulses and emotions have expanded to all
walks of life (see Stearns, 1989). Even where until recently men as
'heads of the family' could let themselves go and behave in relatively
passionate and unrestrained ways towards their 'own' wife and
children, they have now come to be both morally and legally constrained to curb their violent and sexual impulses. The recent wave
of collective moral indignation and embarrassment about sexual
harrassment, rape in marriage, incest or other forms of lack of
control in this context reinforces this constraint.

Also outside the family, on the streets, changes have taken place
in the same direction. Street fighting, the most basic expression of
ongoing struggles between families, neighbourhoods or classes, has
become relatively rarer (Dunning et al., 1987). At present, the stage
at which children and adults lose control, are overwhelmed by
violent impulses and *have* to give in to them, has receded. In
Western societies of the seventeenth and eighteenth century, the
emphasis in anger control still rested on obedience, on social control
rather than on individual control of emotions:

> This meant . . . that outside the hierarchical relations within which the control
> of obedience was meant to operate, there were no real standards for anger
> restraint . . . anger was not specifically reproved save when its expression
> contravened hierarchy. (Stearns and Stearns, 1986: 23)

In the course of centuries, these standards have developed. In this
process, status anxiety — the fear of loss of face and status —
particularly functioned as a motor toward repressing and denying
the emotions that could lead to violence. Among growing parts of

the population, people pressured each other to restrain themselves in more drastic and more automatic ways: Mutually Expected Self-control of violent emotions and impulses increased. But, as fairly large groups remained poorly integrated into these nation-states, upper- and middle-class people for a long time continued to be afraid of this danger and to avoid as much as possible 'contaminating contact with the spiritually inferior and the repugnant' (Van Zutphen van Dedem, 1928: 162) — an example of status anxiety. Through emancipation movements the possibilities for this avoidance-behaviour decreased as social integration and equalization increased.[6] Together with growing pressures toward closer and more alert observation of oneself and others, the fear of each other had to be brought under firmer control. Thus, a further rise in the level of Mutually Expected Self-control came about which, in turn, as a necessary condition, allowed for a less rigid social regulation and for a less rigid and more varied self-regulation, for informalization. In other words, this rising level of Mutually Expected Self-restraints has allowed an 'emancipation of emotions' that destroyed the old conviction incorporated in the traditional mode of emotion management that being open to such emotions would almost inevitably be followed by acting upon them. Violent impulses and emotions even came to be more and more recognized as regular and normal aspects of emotional life. They not only became accepted as conversation topics but more and more people also took the liberty to vent these feelings, accepting that they 'come up for air' every now and then. In this movement, cursing, calling each other all sorts of names, and making allusions to violence all seem to have spread (see Stearns and Stearns, 1986: 229). In this way people provoke and test their own and each other's emotion management. This kind of behaviour signifies an experimenting with emotions and impulses that until recently were more rigidly denied and repressed. In this development, increasing numbers of people have become aware of emotions and temptations in circumstances where fears and dangers had been dominant before — the temptations of 'sex, drugs and rock and roll', of tax evasion, shoplifting, swearing, etc. This provocative and experimenting attitude can be understood as the direct counterpart of what has been called the 'equanimity of the welfare state' (Stolk and Wouters, 1987). This equanimity refers to the decline in the fear of poverty resulting from the welfare state system. In the long period of peace and prosperity after the Second World War, physical safety and also, through the spreading of wealth according to the principles of the welfare state, material security have become much less problematic. A change in the structure of the state was mirrored in a change in the structure of fears and anxieties: 'social security' generated a greater personal security.[7] This 'peace' in material respects functioned as a breeding ground in which much relational unrest took root: men found themselves in a sense competing with the state, as the welfare system weakened the traditional dependence of women on men. But this 'equanimity of the welfare state' was also soon accompanied by an increasingly intense competition in emotion management, as expressed in displays of confidence and in a 'quest for risks'.

At this point, Tom Wolfe's comparison of some changes in the 1960s and 1970s with those in the upper classes in London during the Regency period (roughly, 1800 to 1830), is illuminating. At that time, he writes,

> Both young men and women of the upper classes were swept by *nostalgie de la boue* — a longing to recapture the raw and elemental vitality of the lower orders . . . The middle classes had so much new money they threw traditional social lines into great confusion in London . . . Wealth was no longer a buffer between the classes; but the old aristocratic manner of *confidence* was. The middle classes had money but lacked the confidence to be anything but ever more ornately respectable. (Wolfe, 1968b: 169)[8]

In recent decades wealth has spread almost explosively to many more classes than during the Regency period, the importance of emotion management (of confidence) has increased, and the spectrum of socially accepted modes of expression has become much more colourful and varied.

Not only violent impulses, but also sexual impulses and emotions have been collectively brought under firmer individual control, and in this process the fear of sexual passions has diminished. How intense this anxiety has been may be inferred from the reactions of established groups in the 1920s, when the old tradition of chaperonage came to an end in the historical novelty of 'free' social intercourse between the sexes, particularly in dance halls and cinemas. The government of the Netherlands, for example, was worried enough to establish a government committee with the task of investigating the 'problem of dancing'. One of the recommendations in the committee's report (*Rapport*, 1931) was a mandatory appointment of 'dancing masters' in charge of surveillance in dance halls. The emphasis in sexual control still rested on obedience, on social control rather than on individual control of emotions. The report displayed hardly any confidence in the 'self-surveillance' of both sexes and was written on the implicit assumption that both men and women would give in to their sexual desires if social control was lacking:

> In the modern dances, the danger of sexual titillation has reached a degree that was absent before . . . And thus, every young girl that visits a public dancing hall runs the risk of being 'led' in a reprehensible way, unnoticed by the public, and against which she practically cannot defend herself. And then we still assume the favourable condition, that the will to defend herself is present. But how many . . . do not maintain the moral endurance, here required, and end up with the rendez-vous. (*Rapport*, 1931: 31)

The lack of any confidence in self-control is also clearly demonstrated in exclamations from that period such as 'if the bridle is removed, sexuality gallops' (Ritter, 1933: 152). In contrast, the current collectively expected mode of emotion management implies that even when 'surveillance' (this social constraint) is absent, self-constraint will be strong enough to prevent sexual impulses from giving way to sexual violence. Stronger control over these impulses and emotions, along with the fear of losing this control and of losing face, function as a basic condition for enabling people to experiment with their impulses and emotions more frankly, provided this experimenting is done with mutual consent. This means that, by analogy with contests in which allusion is made to violence, in sexual encounters too, increasing numbers of people are sooner and more frequently able to provoke and challenge, while avoiding humiliation. To challenge, provoke, conquer fears and search for limits has become a popular kind of sport. This 'sport' is expressed not only in all sorts of social relationships, but also in ways of dressing: the warlike punk outfit and 'hot pants', for example, demonstrate provocative fantasies. And it is particularly prevalent in the realm of imagination and amusement: both sexual and violent emotions and impulses are more or less expressed in a wide variety of pornography — Tom Wolfe speaks of 'pornoviolence':

> Violence is the simple, ultimate solution for problems of status competition, just as gambling is the simple, ultimate solution for economic competition. The old pornography was the fantasy of easy sexual delights in a world where sex was kept unavailable. The new pornography is the fantasy of easy triumph in a world where status competition has become so complicated and frustrating. (Wolfe, 1976: 162)

The search for the limits of emotion management in mutual contests and provocations, and the pleasure of sniffing the dangers on the other side of the tracks, may satisfy the yearning for risks and the quest for excitement in welfare-state societies (see Elias and Dunning, 1986). This 'sniffing of dangers' can be taken quite literally sometimes, as is demonstrated by the words of 23-year-old cocaine user: 'The first time you try some coke you're afraid because you don't know what it is. But you want to conquer that fear' (van Hunnik, 1989: 505). This 'quest for risks and excitement' seems to have become just as typical of welfare-state societies as their equanimity.

In displays of confidence and in the 'quest for risks' too, people have pressured each other to greater awareness and knowledge of emotions and emotion management. This knowledge has created the feeling of a distance from these emotions themselves. This has intensified the quest for behaviour that is experienced as 'natural', 'relaxed', 'spontaneous', 'authentic' and 'informal', and it has also created a nostalgic yearning for the experience of (non-violent) emotions of an intensity that completely takes up the self and consciousness.[9] This may explain why the longing for gratifying emotional and sexual bonds seems to have grown stronger, and why losing oneself in making love and in orgasm, called the 'little death' for this reason (Bataille, 1971), seems to have become more highly valued the more this form of status competition has intensified. It has become more strongly experienced as a road to uncomplicated and unreflected existence, the sublime romance of naturalness. The same goes for other arts and sports, and this may partly explain why in this century these activities have gained considerable mass following.

The now dominant mode of emotion management has apparently reached a strength and scope that enables people to admit violent and/or sexual emotions and impulses to themselves and each other, without provoking the fear of losing control and of having to give in to them. Only when the level of Mutually Expected Self-restraints has risen to this level, do experiments in loosening restraints stand a chance of becoming successful. Otherwise, the 'decontrolling of emotional controls' is not sufficiently 'controlled' and is thus too risky. That is precisely the tenor of the story about a kindergarten where children were allowed to take their 'weaponry' along. The arms race and fights did not reach the saturation point that the parents had hoped and waited for. Paul Kapteyn concludes:

> The increased tolerance and flexibility of adults towards the children's violence, this violation of a taboo, could only be understood and followed by the children when they had first become quite familiar with the taboo — when they had first learned what they later to some extent could unlearn. (Kapteyn, 1980: 179)

In this example, one may recognize a sequence that Piaget and Kohlberg incorporated in their models on intellectual and moral development, that is, the sequence in which children at first are preoccupied with their own emotions and cling to the social routines of what they perceive as 'the done thing'. From the age of 11 or 12 onwards, role-taking and the balancing of their own feelings and the feelings of others become more generally possible. From then on, they may learn to individualize and improvise, that is, to choose their *own* strategy or procedure for *this* situation and in relation to *that* person. Thus, in this respect, in individual civilizing processes a similar structure can be discerned as in the civilizing processes of societies, in which the long-term process of informalization was preceded by a long-term process of formalization.

Changing Regimes of Power and Emotions: Irritation and Nostalgia

As rising numbers of people have been integrated into increasingly dense and democratized networks of interdependency, not only have demands on emotion management and awareness of it increased, but at the same time ambivalences and insecurities in emotion management and identity-formation have intensified. When more and more people were drawn into increasingly dense interdependency networks, people who earlier had avoided each other came at a later state to have to (and also to wish to) relate to each other. In this process, the groups about which individuals had learned to say 'we' — we-groups — went through changes that forced them to adjust their we-identities and we-feelings. This kind of change, in many respects similar to the changes inherent to the process of growing up, affects different layers of personality and often creates an ambivalence, sometimes conceptualized as 'estrangement'. Entangled in these changes, many people have been drawn into a tug-of-war between old and new we-feelings. This pendulum sometimes swings heavily towards romanticizing old feelings and memories, even towards inventing them (see *The Invention of Tradition*, Hobsbawm and Ranger, 1983). If this ambivalence finds expression in the romantic way, the changes in groups and in society at large are easily interpreted as predominantly oppressive, and irritation dominates. In these cases, the changes seem to have robbed individuals of their we-feelings or identification with some cohesive we-group. In their nostalgia, that 'melancholy yearning for a sense of belonging which is often seen as being in the past' (Bailey, 1988: 31), the emphasis is on the loss of we-feelings and on the oppression of a particular kind of intense I-feelings, while the other side of the coin, namely increasing possibilities of expressing I-feelings of another kind — more managed ones, but still relaxed and informal — is neglected. When we-groups have lost their cohesion and grip on individuals, directly exerted group pressures and group constraints have diminished. This has opened new possibilities for individual initiative and for asserting oneself as an individual — that is, to claim the right to be evaluated on the basis of individual achievement and personality. 'Pessimists of the mind' tend to underestimate the fact that in this century, chances for I-feelings to find expression have increased, while related dangers — like being expelled from the old we-group and having to suffer their they-feelings and punitive sanctions — have diminished.

Nevertheless, these chances may not be experienced as such. They may be experienced as demands, and with some justification: as extreme expressions of social and psychological distance were banned and gradually vanished, and as contrasts in behaviour and feeling diminished, respect and self-respect indeed demanded a more individual articulation and profiling, including a demand for what is generally experienced as an inner authenticity and an authentic profundity. Increased sensitivity in these matters makes for a presentation of self that is soon experienced as artificial and superficial, as just the mask of an 'inner-directed Macho' or an 'inner-directed Amazon'. At the same time, people have found themselves more often in situations where they feel obliged to create and to endure differences, even contradictions between their emotions and their emotion management. As hierarchical differences have diminished, people have increasingly forced each other toward striking a more subtle and harmonious balance between all kinds of opposing motives and behaviour, like directness and tactfulness, simplicity and sophistication, compelling and being compelled, attracting and repelling, being charming and being daunting. Simultaneously, the art of producing and maintaining a gratifying and harmonious balance, one that to a certain extent surpasses or sublimates[10] these tensions, has become more demanding.[11] In addition to a widening range of alternatives for behaviour and the expression of emotions, the process of informalization at the same time entails an increasing demand to manage emotions in more flexible and differentiated ways, to be able to negotiate in all kinds of situations, with all sorts of people, and to proceed through mutual consent.

In this century, the social and individual pressures that people exert upon themselves and each other have increased rather rapidly and strongly and, simultaneously, ambivalences and insecurities have intensified, together with the wish to be liberated from them. Therefore, these changes have often been interpreted as predominantly oppressive, and ambivalence has often found expression in an irritated romantic way. Both feelings of irritation and idealization, romanticization or nostalgia occur as a pair — no nostalgia without irritation and vice versa — and, depending upon the balance between the two, the reaction may be called irritated nostalgia or nostalgic irritation. As a pair, they show the relationship between constraints and dreams of liberation or ideals. Any excursus on the history of utopias and romantic ideals may illustrate this relationship.[12] Passions and anxieties, utopias and 'dystopias', ideals and spectres mirror each other. Whether projected into the past or into the future, they always betray the social and individual tensions of the figuration in which they were created.

The tradition of cultural criticism in the social sciences provides many examples. For instance in Christopher Lasch's *The Culture of Narcissism* irritation with the present 'culture of narcissism' is combined with a nostalgia for some past in which fathers were still thought to be righteous and demanding (Lasch, 1979). In Philippe Ariès's work on attitudes toward dying, irritation with the present 'taboo' on death is combined with a nostalgia for some past in which death was thought to be 'both familiar and near, evoking no great fear or awe' (Ariès, 1974: 13). In this century, the social and psychological distance between social groups in Western societies has greatly diminished, as have the contrasts in their behaviour and feeling. Irritation may well dominate the relationship between particular established groups and groups of outsiders, such as Old Rich and *nouveau riche*, cosmopolitans and provincials, but in their irritation as well as in their nostalgic longing for 'better days', they show that the power differences and the hierarchical distance between them — as vanguards and rearguards in relation to the dominant code — have diminished. Their irritated nostalgia or nostalgic irritation expresses, in other words, the degree of integration of these groups within their society. The irritation or moral indignation of people in a rearguard often betrays their lack of confidence and fear of losing self-control if they admitted, even to themselves, being tempted by what they see as 'dangerous behaviour': they are afraid to set the fox — in themselves — to watch the geese, afraid opportunity makes them a thief. The presence of such a temptation indicates that the rearguard they represent is not very far removed from the dominant standard. By analogy, the feelings of superiority and the inclination to boast of those in a vanguard often demonstrate that they too are not very different from the people in a rearguard. Displays of superiority often show how small and incipient the lead in emotion management is. Through earlier experiments and experiences, people representing a vanguard may have succeeded in overcoming their 'tyro-fears' and in bringing the chances and dangers of a particular form of behaviour under stronger control, while 'regression-fears' may still be prominent. For example, as a boy I was often impatiently irritated by the 'clumsy' progress of my brother, eighteen months younger than myself, in a new phase or a new field in his life, exactly because I was painfully reminded of my own clumsiness in a very recent past. Quite often I would have preferred simply to deny that I had been just like him. The same regularity in the development of emotion management can be discerned in the relationship between groups of people. The irritated moral indignation of Europeans about the burning of Salman Rushdie's book and the threat to kill the author may serve as an example. Many of these Europeans have in their own lifetime experienced the burning of books and large-scale killing, but they prefer not to be reminded of all that by an outsider and a representative of a rearguard like Khomeini, and they react with revulsion if they — as Europeans — are identified with all this killing and burning. But precisely for that reason the feeling of irritation is so strong. By thus touching upon this sensitive we-identity of Europeans, Khomeini has succeeded, although most probably unintentionally, in changing the Second *World* War to some extent into a *European* war. In this case, the irritation can be seen as an expression of the tensions that accompany rising degrees of interdependence and integration of these societies within the world. As such, it was an incident in and an indication of the process of global integration that is occurring.

As long as processes of differentiation and integration continue to develop in the same direction and social and psychological bonds expand and intensify, the social and psychological tensions of these bonds will also increase and with them the intensity of the longing to defy these tensions in spontaneous, authentic, relaxed and informal conduct. On the other hand, unrealistic expressions of this ideal are likely to be brought more strongly under the same individual and social constraints as the passions that may provoke physical and sexual violence. No matter how strongly the longing for a more simple life with little self-restraint intensifies, the function of self-regulation as a weapon in the status struggle will be simultaneously reinforced, and identity and self-respect will have become more dependent upon it. Becoming simple and innocent again is impossible anyway; the road back is blocked. Only ambivalences and balances, like '*sophisticated* simplicity' or '*noble* authenticity' (*controlled* decontrolling) are open as realistic ideals — a price to be paid for peace and welfare.

Although feelings of ambivalence, insecurity and disorientation will to some extent accompany each new round in the process of self-distantiation, articulating and emphasizing one's distinctive features still seems to have become a sport and an art, and increasing numbers of people seem to have become more and more aware both that they have to put their minds and hearts into it, and of how it is to be done.

In every new spurt of the civilizing process there is a moment in which most people have come to take the new ways of curbing and self-regulating for granted, and more or less automatically live up to this expectation. At that time, the social compulsion to wear this 'mask' of emotion management has been transformed into 'second nature'. For most of the rest it may be done 'secretly'. Norbert Elias once used the metaphor 'second nature' to indicate what had already happened to court aristocrats at the beginning of the eighteenth century, and he continued:

> The increasing compulsion to self-constraint opens new pleasures to them, new enrichments and refinements, in short new values, together with new oppressions and dangers. At any rate, self-control becomes for them a high personal value. (Elias, 1983: 241)

As the longing for a simpler and more passionate kind of life intensified, simultaneously the function of self-control as a weapon in the status struggle has been reinforced, which means that the meaning

244 Theory, Culture & Society

and justification of one's life, one's respect, self-respect and identity
have become more dependent upon this controlling capacity.

Informalization and the Sociology of Emotions
In a long-term process of formalization, standards of behaviour and
feeling have expanded and differentiated. This long-term trend
probably reached its peak in the 'Victorian Era', together with
the 'stiff upper lip', to be followed in the twentieth century by a
dominant process of informalization.[13] An 'emancipation of emotions' was already clearly present in Impressionism and this trend
became dominant in the *fin de siècle* and the Edwardian period. The
'Roaring Twenties' and the 1960s and 1970s showed strong spurts in
the same direction: the relaxation and differentiation of codes of
behaviour and feeling continued. More closely examined, relaxation
and differentiation of these codes have continued in short-term
phases of informalization and formalization. The way this has
happened can be expressed photographically: the stiff studio poses
of the 1940s and 1950s of serious looking people, dressed in their
Sunday best, were replaced in the 1960s and 1970s by spontaneous
snapshots of relaxed and smiling people, dressed according to
(spare) time and place (Oosterbaan, 1988). At the end of the 1970s,
when opportunities for collective ascent on the social ladder
declined and each individual became more dependent upon his or
her own qualities in the status competition, people gave way more
easily again to the incentive to show they were well off, and also *how*
well off. In the 1980s (in addition to a continued appreciation of
relaxed and informal behaviour) the fear of excessive familiarity
and insufficient social distance strengthened, and the presentation
of self became somewhat more serious and reserved, and many
changed (back) from sweater and jeans into suit and tie — a return
to old traditions, while integrating new ones: a formalization of
earlier informalized behaviour (Wouters, 1987).

The 'soft-look' bra, introduced in the 1970s, when many women
had altogether given up wearing bras, may be taken as another,
playful illustration of the same process. This bra supports the
breasts, as did the old type of 'hard-look' bra that was still common
in the 1950s and early 1960s, without removing the image of 'free'
flesh and the visual suggestion of nipples. This triplet — hard-look
bra, no bra, soft-look bra — can be taken as another example of the
formalization of earlier informalized behaviour.

In a long-term process of formalization, expression, display and, at its zenith, even references to emotions, especially those that could provoke physical and sexual violence, were curbed and tabooed. In processes of democratization, the rise in Mutually Expected Self-restraints has been accompanied by increasing curiosity about sex, violence and death, which in the course of centuries have been put behind the social and individual scene; the emotions involved are increasingly allowed — both individually and socially speaking — to re-enter consciousness. In the long-term process of informalization, a collective search for these hidden emotions and motives has been going on, and in this process emotions have gained acceptance as important guides for behaviour and knowledge, whereas before they were predominantly seen as a source of transgression and misbehaviour. Before the last spurt of informalization in the 1960s and 1970s, provocations and challenges to sexual and violent emotions, indeed emotions in general, were predominantly viewed as dangerous. Expressions like 'to become emotional' still have the connotation of a lack of control over emotions, of being swept away by them. Expressions like these are reminiscent of this very danger *and* of the rigid social control that served to counter it. In this century, the emancipation of the lower classes has run in tandem with an 'emancipation of emotions' or, to put it slightly differently, further integration of lower classes within the social structure has run in tandem with further integration of 'lower' or 'animalic' impulses and emotions within personality structures.

Whereas in the long-term process of formalization, the view of emotions as dangerous dominated, today emotions are seen as having a very important signal function — this was an insight of Freud — and their potential dangerousness is viewed and formulated much more strongly in terms of a balance: mastery over the art of emotion management in such a way that 'domestic policy' and 'foreign policy' stay in harmony (Elias, 1982: 294). Or in other words, that both the risk of losing the signal function of feeling and the risk of losing the signal function of display are avoided (Hochschild, 1983: 21).[14] This also means that the perspective on emotions and impulses as both dangerous *and* vital has increased; dangerous because they may get out of control and bring the miseries of imprisonment and commital in an asylum, and vital for their 'survival signal function' and as a source of pleasure. In a similar way, the presentation of self will also be more and more experienced as both a burden *and* a pleasure.[15] The need for such a perspective may explain the rising popularity of and demands for 'reflexivity' as 'cultural capital'. In this development, a growing number of people have become increasingly aware of the necessity of managing emotions and of developing a 'dramaturgical perspective' (Goffman, 1959), a perspective that focuses on differences and contradictions between emotions and utterances or displays of emotions in the presentation of self. According to Hochschild, (1983: 192), this means that 'the point of interest has moved inward. What fascinates us now is how we fool ourselves'. Just as Freud's 'discovery' of 'animalic' emotions and motives occurred at the peak of their repression and denial, by analogy, the 'sociology of emotions' began to spread when rejection of repression and denial of emotions seemed to reach its height.

The rise of interest in the study of emotions, whether as a 'sociology of emotions', a 'history of emotions' or in any other form, can be seen as a recent expression of the trend from the end of last century onward towards acknowledging the vital importance of emotions and emotion management. While in processes of social democratization and integration the experience of physical safety and material security has been spreading, the studies of political and economic changes, dealing respectively with changes in the management of violence and of scarce means (money), has come to be perceived more and more as incomplete without the study of changes in emotion management. There is increasing awareness of a gap that has been rising between social processes and social theories, as well as of the origin of this gap: a poor integration of emotions and emotion management into theoretical frameworks. Most probably, it is the rising importance of emotion management in the intensified struggle for respect and self-respect that has led social scientists to perceive an 'anomaly' (Kuhn) in their theories.

Around the 1950s, these changes had begun to attract considerable attention in the academic world, as its foremost example, David Riesman's classic book *The Lonely Crowd* (1950) shows. At that time, however, the key concept was still morals, not yet emotions or emotion management. Riesman, for instance, focused on the growth of 'moral relativism' and directed his attention to a specific change: internalized controls of a fixed kind — 'inner-direction' — changed from being an advantage into being a handicap. According to Riesman's well known statement, social changes now required a system of internalized controls that incorporated moral relativism; they necessitated 'other-direction', a self-regulation that was acutely sensitive and responsive to group norms *while recognizing* the limited relevance of all moral imperatives.

Another academic who focused on changing morals in the 1940s and 1950s was Martha Wolfenstein. In the early 1950s, she coined the concept of 'fun morality', the emergence of which, she writes,

> may be observed in the ideas about child training of the last forty years . . . Where formerly there was felt to be the danger that, in seeking fun, one might be carried away into the depths of wickedness, today there is a recognizable fear that one may not be able to let go sufficiently, that one may not have enough fun. (Wolfenstein, 1955: 168, 174)

Wolfenstein's discussion of 'fun morality' preceded the much broader discussion on the 'Expressive Revolution' and 'permissive society' of the 1960s and 1970s. These discussions, as well as studies of 'mentalities' and 'everyday life', clearly show that attention in the academic world was moving in the direction of what was later called the study of emotions. But on the whole, in and particularly outside the academic world, a rather personal and involved version of this field of study was still dominant: the 'sensitivity' and 'encounter' movement. It took several years before the social changes of the 'Expressive Revolution' had a serious impact on the academic world and were somehow theoretically incorporated in comparatively detached studies. Only from the mid-1970s onwards (and Kemper is certainly right to 'speculate that sociologists were responding to the *Zeitgeist* of the decade of the 1960s' (Kemper, 1990: 4)) has the subject been called emotions and emotion management. From then on, an increasing number of social scientists have become aware that, as Scheff (1990: 294) puts it, most of their theories 'are biased toward rational or material models of causation'. This development may be viewed as a sign of the *concentration stage* (Mannheim, 1928; cf. Kilminster, 1991: 112) or an 'integration spurt' particularly within the social sciences of sociology, psychology and history, but — I think it is important to note — also between these social scientists and novelists. In the 1970s, a Dutch sociologist interested in the American 'small town' compared sociological studies with novels on that subject. He remarked that 'in general, sociologists pay little attention to the emotions of the people they study, whereas emotions are quite central for the novelist' (den Hollander, undated: 38); that may still be true, but the recent attention paid to the social aspects of emotions and emotion management suggests that this difference is at least diminishing.

On the other hand, the integration spurt is in itself quite diverse.

248   *Theory, Culture & Society*

At the moment there exists such a large diversity of contributions and there are so many different approaches and research agendas presented (see Kemper, 1990) that the attempt at 'bringing emotions back in' seems to stumble over its very success. Therefore, I would like to emphasize that any attempt at synthesis will have to do justice to the fact that, as bonds of co-operation and competition between individuals and their groups change, not only do the dominant social theories and definitions of the problems and chances of living together change, but so also do the codes of behaviour and feeling, and the emotional make-up of the individuals concerned. It is exactly this interconnectedness that makes the study of collective changes in emotion management important and promising. In order to live up to the promise of this study, nostalgic tendencies will have to be further controlled. Up to now, too many studies in this field have been directed towards a search for 'real' and 'authentic' emotions (cf. Wouters, 1989).[16] Such a nostalgic search neglects the fact that every single individual is born in a rather undifferentiated and pliable emotional condition. Within the relationships in which they grow up, from the very beginning of their lives, all develop emotional impulses and counter-impulses that are more or less attuned to the dominant standards of behaviour and feeling of their society. This is the way in which they learn to articulate and manage emotions and impulses; and it is for this reason that emotions are recognized for their vital 'survival signal function'. In order clearly to bring forward the indissoluble tie between emotions and emotion management, much could be said in favour of changing the symbolic expression of this kind of study from the 'sociology of emotions' to the '*sociology of emotional management*'.

Notes

I would like to thank Stephen Mennell for correcting my English.

1. An example of this trend towards increasing style competition is the multitude of rapidly changing terms and expressions that the young use today for classifying each other according to their own style and taste in clothing, music and behaviour — terms and expressions like 'disco', 'house', 'hip-hop' and 'punk'. To some extent, this kind of classification disguises the style and taste of their parents — that is, their class origin. In the days of 'cap in hand', the characteristics of social class were much more obvious and uniform.

2. In the course of civilizing processes fears of physical attack are increasingly replaced by social fears of shame and embarrassment in increasingly interdependent, complex and internally pacified societies. Shame and embarrassment are clear

examples of inferiority feelings, but any change in the 'threshold' of shame and embarrassment has implications for both inferiority and superiority feelings: shame is

> a form of displeasure or fear which arises characteristically on those occasions when a person who fears lapsing into *inferiority* can avert this danger neither by direct physical means nor by any other form of attack. This defencelessness against the *superiority* of others . . . results from the fact that the people whose *superiority* one fears are in accord with one's super-ego, with the agency of self-constraint implanted in the individual by others on whom he was dependent, who possessed power and *superiority* over him . . . It is a conflict within his personality; he himself recognizes himself as *inferior*. He fears the loss of the love or respect of others, to which he attaches or has attached value. (Elias, 1982: 292–3, my italics)

3. Until the 1930s, Dutch etiquette books still contained separate paragraphs on 'good behaviour' toward social superiors and inferiors. These paragraphs disappeared, and even references to these differences became increasingly indirect. A similar trend has been observed in the USA: 'Almost all books on manners in colonial America . . . contain an emphasis on "superiors" and "inferiors" that would dramatically lessen in the course of the nineteenth and twentieth century . . .' (Kasson, 1990: 12).

4. The way Goffman used the term impression management indicates that he especially refers to the secret part of emotion management.

5. *Taste* and *style* may be widely debated — in processes of informalization the connected fears seem to have been brought under firm enough control for these debates even to be enjoyed — but such debates turn sour when related *status* aspects are touched upon. This is 'not done'; these aspects are generally denied, repressed and rejected as a tasteless and cynical reduction of the level of debate: 'What the world needs now is a manual for artistic codes in theatre, concert halls and museums. First lesson: conceal such a need completely, for the right stuff and the right tone come naturally, don't they?' (A. de Swaan, 1985: 32–3).

6. This does not mean that the motive to keep and maintain the social and psychological distances and differences between status superiors and inferiors has disappeared, nor that it has lost any of its importance. Its explanatory power can be illustrated from the way in which some New Yorkers avoid using the subway. From this remnant of their far greater opportunities in former times of avoiding 'contaminating contact with the spiritually inferior and the repugnant', Tom Wolfe generalizes: 'in fact much of the status symbolism of New York grows out of the ways the rich and the striving manage to insulate themselves, physically, from the lower depths. They live up high to escape the dirt and the noise. They live on the corners to get the air' (Wolfe, 1963: 297).

7. Cf.: 'the structure of fears and anxieties is nothing other than the psychological counterpart of the constraints which people exert on one another through the intertwining of their activities' (Elias, 1982: 327).

8. The expression '*nostalgie de la boue*, or romanticizing of primitive souls' is explained as 'a nineteenth-century French term that means, literally, "nostalgia for the mud"' (Wolfe, 1970: 32). The 'downward perspective' (Wouters, 1986) that characterizes this form of nostalgia, was also often expressed in the 'quest for risks'

manner. An example, again derived from Wolfe, is presented in the group around Ken Kesey, author of *One Flew Over the Cuckoo's Nest* (1962), who invited and 'entertained' the Hell's Angels:

> it once and for all put Kesey and the Pranksters above the category of just another weirdo intellectual group. They had broken through the worst hangup that intellectuals know — the *real-life* hangup. Intellectuals were always hung up with the feeling that they weren't coming to grips with real life. Real life belonged to all those funkey spades and prize fighters and bullfighters and dock workers and grape pickers and wetbacks. *Nostalgie de la boue*. Well, the Hell's Angels were real life. It didn't get any realer than that, and Kesey had pulled it off. (Wolfe, 1968a: 158)

9. In 1955, Martha Wolfenstein (1955: 175) observed: 'Today we have attained a high degree of tolerance of impulses, which at the same time no longer seem capable of producing such intense excitement as formerly.'

10. For an outline of a sociological theory on sublimation, see Elias (1991: 78–87).

11. The balance is certainly lost if one thinks in terms of dichotomies, and proceeds by declaring one side of the balance as 'false' or 'a fraud': 'this hedonism is a fraud; the pursuit of pleasure disguises a struggle for power . . . Hedonism . . . originates not in the pursuit of pleasure but in a war of all against all, in which even the most intimate encounters become a form of mutual exploitation' (Lasch, 1979: 125–7).

12. A familiar example is the process in which knights lost their domains and became courtiers. In this process, the imaginative form of literature called romances was born. Courtiers found an outlet for the social and psychological tensions of living at court in the dreamworld of Arcadia; in pastoral romance and play, an unrestrained simplicity and relaxed directness of countrylife was romanticized (see Elias, 1983).

13. Trends toward formalization and informalization are likely to have been operative throughout history; there will have always been groups trying to enforce formal rules, and others trying to resist them or evade them. If one such group has a winning streak for any length of time, a corresponding phase of formalization or informalization will be dominant. In the long run too, one of these trends may be stronger than the other, corresponding to long-term phases of formalization or informalization.

14. In 1950 Riesman still largely opposed 'inner-directedness' and 'other-directedness'; today, Riesman's twin concepts seem less appropriate to describe successive periods and their characteristic type of personality, since they appear to be closely related as the two synchronic, co-existing poles of an increasingly intensified tension balance.

15. 'More play in work also means more work in play, until all acts become both playful and instrumental, public and private . . .' (Bennis and Slater, 1968: 88). These writers continue: 'and no sphere of human expression is altogether uncontaminated by duty', but this only emphasizes one side and should be completed by adding 'nor unrelated to play and pleasure'.

16. At the other extreme, many studies in this field have been directed towards a search for emotion words and emotion vocabularies, and their cultural relativism can be characterized as a kind of literary reductionism. For an example, see Harré (1986).

References

Ariès, Philippe (1974) *Western Attitudes toward Death*. Baltimore: Johns Hopkins University Press.

Bailey, Joe (1988) *Pessimism*. London and New York: Routledge.

Bataille, George (1971) *Les larmes d'Eros*. Paris: Pauvert.

Bennis, Warren G. and Philip E. Slater (1968) *The Temporary Society*. New York: Harper & Row.

Dunning, Eric, Patrick Murphy, Tim Newburn and Ivan Waddington (1987) 'Violent Disorders in Twentieth-century Britain', in George Gaskell and Robert Benewick (eds), *The Crowd in Contemporary Britain*. London: Sage.

Elias, Norbert (1978 and 1982) *The Civilizing Process*. Volume I and II. Oxford: Blackwell.

Elias, Norbert (1983) *The Court Society*. Oxford: Blackwell.

Elias, Norbert (1989) *Studien über die Deutschen. Machtkämpfe und Habitusentwicklung im 19. und 20. Jahrhundert*. Edited by Michael Schröter, Frankfurt a. M.: Suhrkamp.

Elias, Norbert (1991) *Mozart. Zur Soziologie eines Genies*. Edited by Michael Schröter, Frankfurt a. M.: Suhrkamp.

Elias, Norbert and Eric Dunning (1986) *Quest for Excitement*. Oxford: Blackwell.

Elias, Norbert and John L. Scotson (1965) *The Established and the Outsiders*. London: Frank Cass & Co.

Goffman, Erving (1959) *The Presentation of Self in Everyday Life*. New York: Doubleday Anchor.

Harré, Rom (ed.) (1986) *The Social Construction of Emotions*. Oxford and New York: Basil Blackwell.

Hobsbawm, Eric and Terence Ranger (eds) (1983) *The Invention of Tradition*. Cambridge: Cambridge University Press.

Hochschild, Arlie R. (1983) *The Managed Heart*. Berkeley: University of California Press.

Hollander, A.N.J. den (undated) *Het Amerikaanse Landstadje in de romanliteratuur en in de sociologie*. Amsterdam: De Bataafse Leeuw.

Hunnik, Marian van (1989) 'Jongeren over cocaïnegebruik', *Jeugd en Samenleving* 19/8 (August): 500–13.

Kapteyn, Paul (1980) *Taboe, macht en moraal in Nederland*. Amsterdam: Arbeiderspers.

Kasson, John F. (1990) *Rudeness and Civility. Manners in Nineteenth-century Urban America*. New York: Hill & Wang.

Kemper, Theodore D. (ed.) (1990) *Research Agendas in the Sociology of Emotions*. New York: State University of New York Press.

Kilminster, Richard (1991) 'Structuration Theory as a World View', pp. 74–119 in C.G.A. Bryant and D. Jary (eds), *Giddens' Theory of Structuration: A Critical Appreciation*. London: Routledge.

Lasch, Christopher (1979) *The Culture of Narcissism*. New York: Norton.

Mannheim, Karl (1952, German 1928) 'Competition as a Cultural Phenomenon', *Essays in the Sociology of Knowledge*. London: Routledge & Kegan Paul.

Mennell, Stephen (1985) *All Manners of Food. Eating and Taste in England and France from the Middle Ages to the Present*. Oxford: Basil Blackwell.

Oosterbaan, Warna (1988) article on photography in *NRC-Handelsblad* 30 Dec.

Rapport der regeerings-commissie inzake het dansvraagstuk (1931) The Hague.

Riesman, David with N. Glazer and R. Denney (1950) *The Lonely Crowd*. New Haven: Yale University Press.

Ritter, P.H. Jr (1933) *De Drang der zinnen in onzen Tijd* (The Urge of Senses in our Time), Amsterdam: Scheltema & Giltay.

Scheff, Thomas J. (1990) 'Socialization of Emotions: Pride and Shame as Causal Agents', pp. 281–304 in T.D. Kemper (ed.), *Research Agendas in the Sociology of Emotions*. New York: State University of New York Press.

Stearns, Carol Zisowitz and Peter N. Stearns (1986) *Anger. The Struggle for Emotional Control in America's History*. Chicago and London: University of Chicago Press.

Stearns, Peter N. (1989) 'Suppressing Unpleasant Emotions: The Development of a Twentieth-Century American Style', pp. 230–61 in Andrew E. Barnes and Peter N. Stearns (eds), *Social History and Issues in Human Consciousness*. New York and London: New York University Press.

Stearns, Peter N. and Timothy Haggerty (1991) 'The Role of Fear: Transitions in American Emotional Standards for Children, 1850–1950', *The American Historical Review* 1991: 63–94.

Swaan, A. de (1985) *Kwaliteit is klasse*. Amsterdam: Bakker.

Stolk, Bram van and Cas Wouters (1987) *Frauen im Zwiespalt. Beziehungsprobleme im Wohlfahrtsstaat*. Frankfurt am Main: Suhrkamp.

Wolfe, Tom (1963) *The Kandy-Kolored Tangerine-Flake Streamline Baby*. New York: Farrar, Strauss & Giroux.

Wolfe, Tom (1968a) *The Electric Kool-Aid Acid Test*. New York: Farrar, Strauss & Giroux.

Wolfe, Tom (1968b) *The Pump House Gang*. New York: Farrar, Strauss & Giroux.

Wolfe, Tom (1976) *Mauve Gloves and Madmen, Clutter and Vine*. New York: Farrar, Strauss & Giroux.

Wolfenstein, Martha (1955, orig. 1951) 'Fun Morality: An Analysis of Recent American Child Training Literature', in Margaret Mead and Martha Wolfenstein (eds), *Childhood in Contemporary Cultures*. Chicago: University of Chicago Press.

Wouters, Cas (1986) 'Formalization and Informalization: Changing Tension Balances in Civilizing Processes', *Theory, Culture & Society* 3(2): 1–18.

Wouters, Cas (1987) 'Developments in the Behavioural Codes between the Sexes: The Formalization of Informalization in The Netherlands, 1930–85', *Theory, Culture & Society* 4(2–3): 405–27.

Wouters, Cas (1989) 'The Sociology of Emotions and Flight Attendants: Hochschild's *Managed Heart*', *Theory, Culture & Society* 6(1): 95–123.

Zutphen van Dedem, Merr. van (1928) *Goede Manieren* (Good Manners). Amersfoort: Logon.

Cas Wouters teaches Sociology at The State University of Utrecht.

The Man In The Mirror: David Harvey's 'Condition' of Postmodernity

Meaghan Morris

> Difference is a misreading of sameness, but it must be represented in order to be erased. The resistance to finding out that the other is the same springs out of the reluctance to admit that the same is other. (Barbara Johnson, 1987: 178)

Autobiography of a Reading

Reading David Harvey's *The Condition of Postmodernity* (1989b) has been an estranging experience for me. At first contact, I was struck by what Foucault (1970: xv) calls 'the stark impossibility of thinking *that*': how could anyone see practices that for me are quite distinct — critical feminist art, poststructuralist philosophy, architectural postmodernism, genre cinema, 'roots' community movements and radical difference politics — as somehow similar in their 'reflection' of a 'fragmented', 'ephemeral', 'chaotic' condition of life? Projects that I have been involved with for twenty years (and that I take to be coherent, ongoing, and fairly stable in their concerns) thus became, in Harvey's reading, unrecognizable. For Foucault, the encounter with an alien taxonomy is a comic and wondrous experience. But I was not amused: in the name of a 'survey', I saw conceptual distinctions blurred, political difference denied, conflicts ignored and histories of struggle (most spectacularly, feminism) erased by this image of a fractured postmodern 'other' in flattering need of the remedy of wholeness that Harvey's Marxism might then provide.

Then I did see the humour of it. What is wonderful about the moment of alterity is that we apprehend, in an 'exotic' system of thought, 'the limitation of our own' (Foucault, 1970: xv). The critical and cultural practices that Harvey reduces to the same may constitute a world of difference to me, but they also set practical limits to my everyday working environment — give or take a few

Theory, Culture & Society (SAGE, London, Newbury Park and New Delhi), Vol. 9 (1992), 253–279

forays into economics and social theory. So extensive and complex has the field of Cultural Studies become in recent years that I, absorbed in its conflicts, had come to argue not just that critics moved to celebrate the postmodern city should do some political economy first (Morris, 1988a), but that the once enabling mistrust of 'totalizing' theories and of economism inscribed in much of our work was now an anachronism (Morris, 1991); no Marxist, I thought, really claims that sort of mastery any more. In *The Condition of Postmodernity*, I came face to face with my own parochialism: 'if there is a meta-theory with which to embrace all these gyrations of postmodern thinking and cultural production, then why should we not deploy it?' (Harvey, 1989b: 337).

This prompted a more self-critical discovery. In my bemusement at Harvey's use of polemically hysterical passages from Eagleton (1987) as true descriptions, or at his uncritical acceptance as 'daring' of the most orthodox determinist features of Jameson's thesis (1984) on postmodernism as a 'logic' of late capitalism (Harvey, 1989b: 9, 53, 63, 117), I was confronting a mirror image — albeit on a grander scale — of my own past use in Cultural Studies of Harvey's economic geography. I had invoked his authority, offered his *Studies in the History and Theory of Capitalist Urbanization* (1985a, b) as more or less 'true' to my students, and discounted most of his critics as too 'specialized' for me. No wonder I was shocked by Harvey's interdisciplinary reading habits; my own had been, in many respects, the same.

I begin with this rather personal allegory in order to frame what follows as a partial reading of *The Condition of Postmodernity* — one deriving its questions from the historical project, rather than the 'field', of cross-disciplinary feminist enquiry. I do not attempt a complete or impartial account of the book; this is to admit to ignoring much that gives an ambitious text its appeal. But the point of my partiality is not to defend my 'turf' against incursion: I am neither an exponent of affirmative postmodernism nor an opponent of Marxism, and I do not race to rescue theories from the perils of popularization. Turner (1991: 22) has written eloquently of 'the ambiguity of the position occupied by those who attempt to present academic knowledges to popular audiences'. The broad interest aroused by *The Condition of Postmodernity* is testimony to the value of risking that ambiguity.

It is a book with academic concerns — postmodernism, post-Fordism — but it also addresses a general reader who wants to know 'what happened' (or became more obvious as happening) in Western societies during the 1980s — why some places boomed while others suffered, why yuppies flourished while poverty and homelessness increased, why conservative regimes came to power, and what all this had to do with *Blade Runner*, pink and blue buildings, Lyotard, Cindy Sherman and a crisis of representation. I can share that reader's desire. 'What happened?' is a narrative question, and Harvey is a good storyteller. He gives us a double narrative, and a narrative of doubling: on the one hand, a gripping account of the political-economic transformation of late twentieth-century capitalism, on the other a sweeping saga of the European experience of time and space since the Enlightenment. Linking these, a major sub-plot occurs in the present tense: a battle between Marxism and postmodernism to determine the nature of the relationship between the other two.

It's a great read. But there are many ways of telling, and using, stories. As Massey (1991b) points out, the moral of Harvey's tale (and his resolution of complex problems of causality and influence) is all too often 'time-space compression and flexible accumulation' or, more classically, 'capital and labour'. His narration, epic yet meticulous in describing the intricate moves of capital, is profoundly reductive in impulse. For me, this is the pleasure of his text. For all the grimness of Harvey's vision of a gaudy and turbulent world, there is something reassuring about the confidence of his grasp on its 'gyrations', and a comfort in his return to what McRobbie calls 'a simpler and more direct notion of determination. What happens in the economy has a direct effect on what happens in culture' (McRobbie, 1991: 6). The sense of home-coming that this arouses need not be restricted to those of Harvey's readers who grew up on the Left. It has a similar affective appeal to the contemporary discourse of those charismatic leaders and nostalgia films which have played such a crucial role in Marxist versions of postmodernity (Jameson, 1984; Schulte-Sasse, 1987–8).

This is not an inappropriate way to read a text which is not a novel, but a manifesto for 'a renewal of historical materialism and of the Enlightenment project' that calls for a 'counter-attack of narrative against the image' (Harvey, 1989b: 359). Nor is this just a covert way of dismissing Harvey's concerns. On the contrary: how stories are told, and why; who tells them, to whom, for whose benefit and in which contexts; how stories circulate, how their force and value changes; what we *do* with other people's stories, what happens if we retell them in different ways — the problem of narrative (not the same thing as 'fiction') has motivated feminist research in and across many disciplines for at least two decades. It has engendered the study not only of those 'exclusions' that guarantee the coherence of any given discourse, but also, more immediately these days, of the positive force of *other* stories, and different narrations of the same story, which may not be so much 'untold' as rather unheard, ignored or unreceivable in dominant disciplinary terms — terms that include institutional criteria of what may count, for a given knowledge, as a proper and plausible yarn.

But Harvey's own understanding of 'narrative' simply *opposes* it (in 'counter-attack') to 'the image' (Harvey, 1989b: 359). It follows, then, that Harvey cannot recognize Cindy Sherman's famous *Untitled (Film Still)* photographs as images charged with narrative tension. Sherman's series — pictures of a woman (always played by Sherman herself) poised as though between gestures in diverse film scenes and settings — help Harvey to define post-modernism. They are among the few works by women figuring in the book. But instead of seeing them as engaged with the historically specific *relationship between* images and stories producing 'woman' (and desire) in Western cinema, Harvey can only see in them a vaguely metaphysical insistence on 'the plasticity of the human personality through the malleability of appearances and surfaces' (Harvey, 1989b: 7; see Doane, 1987). This translation of the historical and female (Sherman) as metaphysical and human (Harvey) is ensured by the indeed metaphysical assumption, pervasive in Harvey's book, that image is to narrative as 'surface' is to depth, 'appearance' to reality, *shallowness* to *complexity* and space — at least aesthetic space — to time. These slippages also ensure that images cannot be read as *actions* in 'counter-attack'; Sherman's story about the story of femininity in cinema is unreceivable.

For feminist criticism, then, *The Condition of Postmodernity* offers itself as a back-to-basics occasion. Harvey's story has been criticized by feminists working diversely in geography (Massey, 1991a, 1991b), art (Deutsche, 1990, 1991) and sociology (McRobbie, 1991), and this is not surprising. In defence not only of 'meta-theory' but of economic determinism, *The Condition of Postmodernity* offers a reading of culture that depends on a massive exclusion of feminism rather than critical dialogue with it, and so assumes the Marxist primacy that it claims to argue for; its token references to feminist work are, to say the least, muddled when not erroneous (Deutsche, 1991). It uses 'women' to signify 'white' and 'straight' in an open set of Mixed Others ('women, gays, blacks, ecologists, regional autonomists, etc.') whose concerns are described as 'local' (Harvey, 1989b: 47–8). It assumes that these are 'place-bound', and that our resistance tends inexorably toward fragmentation, pastiche or traditionalism (Harvey, 1989b: 303–5). No evidence is offered for this assessment: there is some mention of fascism, but none at all of recent debates *about* the (inter/national) question of difference; one 'condition' of Harvey's discourse is a culture where Homi Bhabha, Stuart Hall, bell hooks, Paul Gilroy, Gayatri Spivak, Eric Michaels, Trinh T. Minh-ha, Craig Owens or Michele Wallace have not yet written.

Yet the occasion has been valuable in so far as feminist responses have not gone back to basics, but have engaged in critical debate from a present in which there *is* now no way back from relational thinking about gender, race and class to a simpler, more direct, class fundamentalism. It is from this present that I am immediately uncomfortable with my own exclusionary gesture in opposing 'our' relational thinking to 'Harvey's' fundamentalism. It uses the same scare tactics as Harvey does in associating new social movements with 'the Heideggerian trap' (Harvey, 1989b: 304). It also ignores the puzzling fact that Harvey wants to *contribute* to thinking difference. Near the end of the book, there is a plan for developing historical-geographical materialism. Its first point is that 'difference and "otherness"' should not be 'added on' to Marxist categories but 'omni-present from the very beginning in any attempt to grasp the dialectics of social change' (Harvey, 1989b: 355). 'Difference and "otherness"' here is shorthand for concerns 'other' than class, and analyses that 'differ' from Marxism ('writers in the tradition of Fanon and Simone de Beauvoir, as well as . . . the deconstructionists' [Harvey, 1989b: 355]). Why, then, does Harvey pay scant attention in his own text to any but the major white male theorists of postmodernity — and none at all to postcolonialism (subsumed as 'geopolitics')?

There is a deep ambivalence in the argument here, which cannot be reduced to a quantitative problem of representation or solved by 'adding on' references. My reading is also ambivalent. Coming after such a combative text, Harvey's plan is like the conciliatory offer that follows an ambit claim: his materialism will take difference, discourse and image production seriously in return for a recognition of 'real' as well as 'metaphorical' spaces of power, and a cessation of hostilities against 'meta-theory' ('an attempt to come to terms with the historical and geographical truths that characterize capitalism both in general as well as in its present phase' [Harvey, 1989b: 355]). I am sympathetic to the gist of this, and tempted not to niggle at its letter — for example, the reality/language opposition subtending the remark about spaces. Yet the reductive spirit of the rest of the text suggests that the letter can be trusted. For Harvey can *only* analyse postmodernity by first rewriting as 'the same' all the differences that constitute it for him as a topic for debate in the first place.

My reading explores this ambivalence; that is its partiality. First, I discuss an example of Harvey's rewriting of one of his major theorists (Lyotard), in order to analyse the assumptions that can generate the possibility of 'thinking *that*'. This is a way of examining one of the 'conditions' enabling Harvey's postmodernity to take the form that it does. Then I respond to Harvey's rhetorical question 'if there is a meta-theory . . . then why should we not deploy it?' (Harvey, 1989b: 337), in order to argue that Harvey's fractured 'condition' is more local in its provenance than his text suggests that it is. This is a conventional move these days in the discourse genre called 'postmodernism'. Here, it is also a feminist claim that there *is* no such meta-theory, and that there are good reasons why we should not pretend to deploy it.

Postmodernism, with Mirrors
Lyotard's *The Postmodern Condition* (1984a) is an important reference point for *The Condition of Postmodernity*. Harvey's title mirrors, by reversing, Lyotard's title, while his subtitle (*An Enquiry into the Origins of Cultural Change*) specifies the difference in genre from Lyotard's text (*A Report on Knowledge*) that this reversal entails. Harvey never confronts Lyotard's thesis *about* postmodern knowledge; instead, he treats *The Postmodern Condition* as a symptom *of* the postmodern condition, using fragments of Lyotard's discourse to create his own image of postmodernism as-a-whole. Thus Lyotard's 'grand narrative' and 'metadiscourse' merge in Harvey's 'meta-theory', and the 'specificity' that Lyotard accords to 'language games' (referring to the socio-historical status of rules differentiating practices) is converted by Harvey (who reads *specific* as *local*) into a 'fetishism' of 'impenetrable', 'opaque otherness' (Harvey, 1989b: 117). 'Meta-theory' and 'otherness' then

represent major stakes for Harvey's critique of postmodernism — respectively, a defence of a totalizing Marxism, and an attack on particularism. In the metonymic style of all good caricature, 'Lyotard' stands for *The Postmodern Condition*, which stands for postmodern philosophy. The hostile figure of Lyotard, then, is crucial to Harvey's text.

So who is Harvey's Lyotard and what is his postmodernism? In a discussion of 'Postmodernism in the City', Harvey identifies Lyotard with the avowedly postmodern architecture critic Charles Jencks:

> 'Why' [says Jencks] 'if one can afford to live in different ages and cultures, restrict oneself to the present, the locale? Eclecticism is the natural evolution of a culture with choice'. *Lyotard echoes that sentiment exactly.* 'Eclecticism is the degree zero of contemporary general culture: one listens to reggae, watches a western, eats McDonald's food for lunch and local cuisine for dinner, wears Paris perfume in Tokyo and "retro" clothes in Hong Kong.' (Harvey: 1989b: 87, my emphasis)

Harvey sources neither of these quotations, but even a reader unfamiliar with either may doubt the exactness of the echo between the *'natural evolution'* — a form of progress — of Jencks's 'culture with choice', and the *'degree zero'* — a condition verging on entropy (Barthes, 1967: 11) — of Lyotard's 'general culture'. If so she might sense, though Harvey does not, the sarcasm of Lyotard's text.

The sentence from which Harvey has quoted is not a casual echo of Jencks, but an explicit critical reference to his work. It is part of an attack on the '"postmodern" (in Jencks's sense) solution' (Lyotard, 1984a: 76) that accommodates art to capitalism:

> Eclecticism is the degree zero of contemporary general culture: one listens to reggae, watches a western, eats McDonald's food for lunch and local cuisine for dinner, wears Paris perfume in Tokyo and 'retro' clothes in Hong Kong; *knowledge is a matter for TV games.* It is easy to find a public for eclectic works. By becoming kitsch, art panders to the confusion which reigns in the 'taste' of the patrons. Artists, gallery owners, critics, and public wallow together in the 'anything goes', and the epoch is one of slackening. But this realism of the 'anything goes' is in fact that of money; in the absence of aesthetic criteria, it remains possible and useful to assess the value of works of art according to the profits they yield. (Lyotard, 1984a: 76, my emphasis)

It is hard to read this as echoing Jencks's 'sentiment', even if we mistake the stringent Lyotard for a fan of quiz shows and kitsch. All the pandering, wallowing and slackening here imputed to 'the epoch' demands a view of eclecticism ('confusion') that not only differs from but *opposes* Jencks's celebration. Indeed, Lyotard's censorious remarks about the culture of 'anything goes' are actually 'echoed' by *Harvey*: 'Postmodernism swims, *even wallows*, in the fragmentary and the chaotic currents of change as if that is all there is' (Harvey, 1989b: 44, my emphasis).

This is not an isolated occurrence but a compositional method: in another example, Harvey directly assimilates Lyotard's pragmatics to Richard Rorty's pragmatism (Harvey, 1989b: 52) despite the *debate* on this very issue between Lyotard and Rorty (Rorty, 1985; van Reijen and Veerman, 1988). Following an image by Barbara Kruger, Deutsche calls this method 'mistaken identity' — the representation of difference as sameness. Mistaken 'identity' is one of the ways in which the subject of a totalizing discourse secures its own sense of wholeness by relegating 'other viewpoints — different subjectivities — to invisible, subordinate or competing positions' (Deutsche, 1991: 7). In some instances, Harvey revises others' positions to make them support his own: thus *Guiliana* Bruno's essay (1987) on the film *Blade Runner* becomes for Harvey an essay by *Guiliano* Bruno — a sex change that corresponds to the way Bruno's essay loses in Harvey's retelling its feminist critical dimensions (Deutsche, 1991: 6). Here, conflating Lyotard's arguments with those of two of his adversaries is a gesture of rivalry rather than subordination; it allows Harvey to compose and confront a single 'postmodern' position *competitive* with his own.

No doubt this simplifies greatly the critical task of Harvey's (1989b: xviii) 'survey'. However there is more similarity between Lyotard and Harvey than Harvey's text can admit. Both are concerned with the problem of value. Both insist on the nexus between art and money. Both take an agonistic view of knowledge as social practice: in dismissing Lyotard's concept of justice as 'pristine' and 'universal', Harvey ignores an affinity with the text from Weber on struggle that opens Part I of his book (Harvey 1989b: 52, 117, 1; see Lyotard, 1988; Lyotard and Thebaud, 1985). Both — unlike Jencks — endorse (different) aspects of the project that Harvey, following Habermas, calls 'modernity' (Harvey, 1989b: 12), and that Lyotard, opposing Habermas, calls 'the Avant-Garde' (Lyotard, 1984b). For Harvey 'there is much more continuity than difference between modernism and postmodernism'; the latter is 'a particular kind of crisis within the former' (Harvey, 1989b: 116). For Lyotard the postmodern is 'undoubtedly a part of the modern'; it is 'not modernism at its end but in the nascent state, and this state is constant' (1984a: 79). Lyotard's model of recurrence differs from Harvey's developmental theory of a crisis-driven history. But this is negotiable, given Harvey's acceptance of the 'Nietzschian image of creative destruction and destructive creation' as useful for analysing capitalism (Harvey, 1989b: 16).

So Harvey's image of 'Lyotard' is produced and sustained in a double operation. On the one hand, denying the difference between Lyotard and Jencks helps to create a monolithic postmodernism centred on 'the [visual] image': Lyotard's contempt for 'TV games' disappears in Harvey's quotation, just as his theory of *narrative* knowledge disappears in Harvey's book; here, difference is represented as sameness. On the other hand, Harvey ignores the similarities between Lyotard's work and his own: the philosopher in Harvey's *musée imaginaire* of postmodernism who most shares his own fears and loathings about 'contemporary general culture' is discredited in a routine way for 'relativism and defeatism' (Harvey, 1989b: 52); difference is reduced to opposition. Similarity is not identity: Lyotard's pragmatics of discourse is incompatible with Harvey's reflection theory, his definition of economics as a 'genre' (Lyotard, 1988) is at odds with Harvey's foundationalism, and Lyotard envisages a war against 'totality' (Lyotard, 1984a: 82), not 'the image'. But Harvey cannot debate his *differences* with Lyotard or defend his values against him — because his reading strictly does not see what Lyotard's text is saying.

I shan't begin that debate by echoing Lyotard's arguments: as feminist readers of the myth of Narcissus know, an echo is a gendered mode of repetition that can, in certain circumstances, fail to make a difference. Instead, I want to ask a question: how can Harvey's reading of Lyotard make a sense that is *not* 'mistaken'? As my own reading so far suggests, I do take *The Condition of Postmodernity* to be mistaken in its account of much of the work that it subsumes as postmodern: confusing some discourses (Sherman, Lyotard) with their objects of criticism, it conscripts others to a cause to which they are indifferent (Foucault) or hostile (Guattari, 1986); its inattention to the distinct forms of feminist and postcolonial debate entails a serious misunderstanding of what it calls 'oppositional' movements. However I also take it to be fully engaged in constructing *imaginary* objects. On this reading, *The Condition of Postmodernity* is not only a narrative but, in a strong sense, a fiction. It is reasonable, then, to suspend disbelief, and to ask what makes its 'mistakes' make sense.

For example, there is a difference between Lyotard and Harvey at stake in the word 'eclecticism'. Eclecticism for Lyotard involves an *'absence* of "aesthetic criteria"' (Lyotard, 1984a: 76): the realism of money ('anything goes') flourishes in complicity with both a 'slackening' of judgement, and popular consumerism (Lyotard, 1984a: 76). For Harvey, in contrast, eclecticism implies a *dominance* of aesthetics over ethical and 'narrative' perception. So while both mistrust mass media images and the 'pot-pourri' of global culture (Harvey, 1989b: 87), each accords a different value to aesthetics. In Lyotard's sense of the term, a philosopher 'does' aesthetics: it is a *practice* of the critique of judgement and hence entails a rigorous rereading of Kant (Lyotard, 1984b, 1988; Lyotard and Thebaud, 1985). Harvey's usage is more eclectic. He talks 'about' aesthetics in vaguely Kantian terms: it is a discursive *object* which he construes in massive ways (as cultural production, as artistic practice, as semiosis, as mass mediation, as sensibility), and which he maintains in an ambivalent relationship to Marxist social theory.

I want to give a strong sense to 'ambivalence' here, taking it as a process, not an attitude. Ambivalence is a way of struggling with the problem posed by an impossible object — at once benevolent and hostile — by splitting it in two. Harvey's discourse involves a splitting of this kind: 'the' aesthetic domain is monolithic, but also constructed in opposing ways; the 'overpowering' aesthetic *consciousness* of postmodernity is a regime of illusion, while the aesthetic *theory* specific to modernity (exemplified for Harvey by Baudelaire (Harvey, 1989b: 10)) is a mediating force that can generate knowledge of the real. I want briefly to examine each of these to see how their relationship shapes Harvey's fiction of postmodernism.

The Mirror of Aesthetics

In one line of argument in the book, aesthetics is effectively the object of a critique of *ideology* understood as false consciousness, and of *myth* as the 'aestheticization' of politics. In this capacity, it is closely associated with the dangerous but appealing figure of 'Heidegger' (Harvey, 1989b: 207–10), and its emblem is 'the image'. Aesthetics in this sense is a reservoir of powerful affective forces. It appears on the side of the 'flexible postmodernity' that Harvey opposes to 'Fordist modernity' (Harvey, 1989b: 340) in his table of 'interpenetrating' tendencies in capitalism, and its value is constructed within an extensive series of binary oppositions. The oppositions most pertinent here give a definition of postmodernity as a dominance of 'aesthetics' over 'ethics', 'image' over 'narrative', 'surface' over 'depth', 'Being' over 'Becoming', 'place' over 'relative space', 'space' over 'time', 'language games' over 'meta-theory', 'social movements' over 'class politics' — and 'pluralistic *otherness*' (sic) over 'technical-scientific *rationality*'.

Without going any further, it is apparent that this remarkable web of assumptions can act as a reading grid whereby 'language games' will have ontological status (Being), and so be taken as affirming an 'otherness' opposed to 'rationality' — and thus 'opaque' (Harvey, 1989b: 117). It also makes it reasonable to assume that a theorist of language games will celebrate 'image' and 'place', and thus approve of Jencks's eclecticism. Within this system, it is not receivable that 'language games' for Lyotard have *methodological* status, and that they affirm the necessity for a theory of social practice to confront changing 'technical-scientific' conditions for the production and status of knowledge under capitalism (Lyotard, 1984a: 9). Nor is it receivable that this entails a theory of struggle (Lyotard, 1984a: 10) and thus of, not opacity, but *linkage* ('genre') and, not of impenetrability, but *conflict* ('the differend') — in conditions where there is no 'universal' genre, and certainly no 'pristine' justice (Lyotard, 1988). In Harvey's terms, the problems posed to Marxism by this theory (and thus the possibility of criticizing it) cannot arise.

Harvey describes his table as a collage compiled in a spirit of fun (Harvey, 1989b: 338). But this is serious fun: it derives its authority from the rest of the book, and its coherence from a proliferating series of mistaken identities resembling a hall of mirrors. Deleuze and Guattari, for example, appear as a 'Foucault' who 'instructs us' to 'believe that what is productive is not sedentary but nomadic' (Harvey, 1989b: 44). Foucault does so summarize (in the laudatory genre of a preface) not his own views, but what he calls the 'principles' of *Anti-Oedipus* (Deleuze and Guattari, 1983); he means *ethical* principles, and on the same page he calls *Anti-Oedipus* 'the first book of ethics to be written in France in quite a long time' (Deleuze and Guattari, 1983: xiii). In Harvey's fiction, there is no significant difference between Deleuze and Guattari and 'Foucault'; the latter's 'spatial metaphors' align them all with Being and *aesthetics* (Harvey, 1989b: 304). Harvey's Foucault even confesses to being 'obsessed' with spatial metaphors, but, Harvey tells us, 'even Foucault' has to ask, 'when pressed', a historical question about the privileging of time over space in modern social theory (Harvey, 1989b: 205). Historically, of course, Foucault was actually being 'pressed' by a group of geographers to admit that his 'obsessions' and 'metaphors' could usefully be *described* as 'spatial' (Foucault, 1980: 68–70).

A hall of mirrors can be an obsessional place, every image referring us to another. One way out of this one is to notice that all the paradigmatic sliding between terms on each side of the dichotomy between Fordism and flexible accumulation, modernity and postmodernity, simply serves to restate the modern 'dialectic' of Tradition and Modernity. This is why 'otherness' can be opposed to 'rationality'. Postmodernism is then a new traditionalism — a good description of the *self-presentation* of much architecture, painting and advertising in the 1980s. Yuppies, poststructuralism, feminism and blood-and-fatherland nationalism can all come into equivalence as opposed to the project of Enlightenment. It follows, then, that aesthetics can be to ethics as Reaction is to Progress — and that any discourse questioning the pertinence of the dialectic itself can be subsumed within it as 'aesthetic'.

This is a relentlessly effective way of erasing the possibility of a non-'Heideggerian' criticism not centred in the European history of 'exclusively masculine modernism' (Massey, 1991b; see Chakrabarty, forthcoming). It thus erases the actuality of many projects that share Harvey's suspicion of *ir*rationalist discourse on otherness (Le Doeuff, 1989; Wallace, 1990). Yet it is easy to see why Harvey takes this tack. One of his main concerns is the relation between globally circulating images of commodified ethnicity and *place* ('a plethora of little Italies, Havanas, Tokyos . . .') and a global economy that in its hegemony over *space* is generating 'strong migration streams (not only of labour but of capital)' (Harvey, 1989b: 87). These streams entail the inter-locational competition that divides and conquers working-class movements (Harvey 1987, 1989a). So he wants to examine the role played in this process by localizing myths of place, and the role that the geography of 'differentiated tastes and cultures' may play in fostering new forms of politics — many of them reactionary. This is one reason why Harvey is interested in postmodernism in the first place, and also ambivalent about it (Harvey, 1989b: xiii–ix).

These are crucial questions, for feminism as well as for Harvey (Morris, 1988b). But describing presentation is not the same as analysing practice. What is said about texts is not the same as, though it may be part of, what they do, and what people do with them; self-promotion does not exhaust social meaning. A great deal of work in Cultural Studies has addressed these issues (Grossberg, Nelson and Treichler, forthcoming): postmodernism is not the only reason why the attempt to read culture as 'aesthetic', aesthetics as ideology, and ideology as false consciousness has long been largely abandoned in cultural analysis (Frow, 1986; Bennett, 1990). Never asking *how* to connect political economy to a theory of cultural practice, Harvey short-circuits his own enquiry by first, consigning images to a simple 'masking' role (costume dramas and staged ethnic festivals 'draw a veil over real geography' (Harvey, 1989b: 87)) and second, by reading the culture/economy relation as somehow isomorphic with his own place/space, local/global, tradition/ modernity distinctions.

Taken together, these assumptions have several consequences. First, since 'images' cannot be theorized as practice, it is not really significant that the meaning and function of a 'staged ethnic festival' may be changed by community action. Second, the meaning and function of images is not construed as *conflictual*. Therefore images, in this formulation, are effectively outside politics. Third, since their general mode of action is already known ('veil', 'mask'), there is little point in studying particular instances of images in action except to confirm what Marxism already knows. Fourth, to do so extensively would risk 'the Heideggerian trap', and the 'reactionary politics of an aestheticized spatiality' (Harvey, 1989b: 305). To push this logic to its absurd extreme, only 'global economy' and 'real geography' then remain as proper objects of Marxist enquiry.

Convention tempts me to write, 'Of course, Harvey never goes to that extreme' — and of course, he doesn't. *The Condition of Postmodernity* is a vivid as well as erudite cultural history. But I am interested in asking *why* he doesn't, since in one sense Harvey's history relies in practice on treating aesthetics as an *im*proper object of Marxist enquiry.

Harvey's second argument counters his first by giving 'aesthetic and cultural practices' the capacity to 'broker between Being and Becoming' (Harvey, 1989b: 327); more precisely, they mediate between an aesthetic consciousness aligned with Being (the spatialization of time) and the ethical projects of Becoming (the annihilation of space by time). Harvey adapts this idea from Kant (Harvey, 1989b: 19, 207), but he does not try to theorize the *material* modalities of aesthetic mediation. Its function for his text is purely formal: he uses it to articulate sympathy for Being, and aesthetics in the first sense, *in* his text: 'There is much to be learned from aesthetic theory about how different forms of spatialization[1] inhibit or facilitate processes of social change' (Harvey, 1989b: 207). This means, however, that aesthetic forms are thought of as strictly *external* ('inhibit', 'facilitate') to the processes of social change.

There is much to be said about the conviction that 'aesthetic judgement prioritizes space over time' (Harvey, 1989b: 207), and that aesthetic practices involve 'the construction of spatial representations and artefacts out of the flow of human experience' (Harvey, 1989b: 327); as Hunter has argued (1988, 1991), it belongs to a theory of culture binding Marxism tightly to Romanticism. While Harvey is well aware of its historical character in terms of its links with Enlightenment 'mapping', he does not question its general validity as a model of representation (subsuming challenges as a 'crisis' internal to it (Harvey, 1989b: 252–9)), and he never doubts that aesthetics is 'spatial'. On the contrary: this is what definitively opposes 'aesthetic *and* cultural' concerns from those proper to the history-minded disciplines: 'there is much to be learned from social theory concerning the flux and change with which aesthetic theory has to cope' (Harvey, 1989b: 207).

'Flux and change' involves the creative destruction intrinsic to capitalism; aesthetic consciousness is one way that people can hold on to their memories and social values, and it is thus immensely important. Harvey is a far from dogmatic Marxist aesthetician. Indeed, from assuming that art is more to do with space than time — coping with, rather than constituted in, flux and change — Harvey goes on to accept that art ('not-time') can have more to do with *eternity* than with ordinary social history. Aesthetic *theory* then 'seeks out the rules that allow eternal and immutable truths to be conveyed in the midst of the maelstrom of flux and change' (Harvey, 1989b: 205). Again, Harvey notes the historical character of what he calls the 'disjunction' underpinning this discourse (Harvey, 1989b: 205). But instead of asking how its tensions are constituted (and for whom), Harvey allows them to constitute his own discourse on a generally 'ephemeral', 'fragmented', 'chaotic' *cultural* condition of postmodernity. On this point he opts out of materialism altogether to affirm with Baudelaire that modern art *is* the 'conjoining of the ephemeral and the fleeting with the eternal and immutable' (Harvey, 1989b: 10).

This has grave consequences for his thesis. First, it locks in a theory of representation as reductive, not *productive*, of social experience. To say that representation 'converts the fluid, confused but nonetheless objective spaces and time of work and social reproduction into a fixed schema' (Harvey, 1989b: 253) denies that representation is always already caught up in social processes of 'work and reproduction'. It is difficult to base a materialist theory of culture on such a premise (Frow, 1987), and it is impossible to theorize the role of images in service economies, media societies. Second, the idea that representation 'fixes' while experience 'flows' gives it magical exemption from historicity; once 'done', it is relatively immutable. This is why Harvey's discourse cannot read a materialist art like Sherman's: it cannot tell the difference between its critical strategies of transformation, and eclecticism or 'nostalgia'. This is also why Harvey's discourse cannot tell the difference (which need not be an opposition) between an essentialist cultural politics *dependent* on inherited traditions of identity and community (Harvey, 1989b: 303), and a 'differential' or 'diasporic' identity politics understood as an historical, as well as cultural, *production* carried out in the midst of, precisely, flux and change (see Bhabha, 1990; Carter, 1990; Wallace, 1990; Gilroy, 1991; Sandoval, 1991).

Harvey's second argument, then, displaces and compounds the problems of the first. Aesthetics as broker between Being and Becoming promises to redeem the reactionary tendencies of aesthetic consciousness; the relation could wishfully be called dialectical. In fact, it gives a positive value to what ends up in both cases as the same operation: an ejection of culture from 'real geography' and (in Jameson's (1984) infamous phrase) 'real history'. The relationship between the positive (brokering) and negative ('masking') poles may be described as ambivalent because, in splitting its massified aesthetic domain into good and bad objects, Harvey's discourse sets up 'a non-dialectical opposition which the subject, saying "yes" and "no" at the same time, is incapable of transcending' (Laplanche and Pontalis, 1980: 28). Harvey says 'no' to mystification, and to the crushing effects of the time–space compression on which postmodernism thrives. However the strength with which he says 'yes' to 'the tenets of mainstream idealist aesthetics' (Deutsche, 1991: 17) is apparent when he presumes that a critical discourse saying 'no' to eternal truths in culture — 'deconstructionism' — must therefore be saying 'yes' to ephemerality: 'if it is impossible to say anything of solidity and permanence in the midst of this ephemeral and fragmented world' he writes sardonically, 'then why not join in the [language] game?' (Harvey, 1989b: 291).

There is nothing unusual in Harvey's refusal here to distinguish deconstruction from pragmatics, or to read it as asking how 'solidity and permanence' are, nonetheless, secured (Kirby, 1991) and truth constructed (Spivak, 1990: 133–7); many critics share his views. Nor is it exceptional for a Marxist discourse on culture to promote idealist aesthetics; Bennett (1990: 33) argues that Marxism 'is now virtually the only avenue through which the idealist concerns of bourgeois aesthetics retain a contemporary currency'. What is remarkable here is that 'deconstructionism' is condemned as complicit with capitalism's destructiveness *because* it fails to perpetuate nineteenth-century European bourgeois aesthetics. But then, Harvey's fiction is a product of those aesthetics: the one feature common to most of the elements composing the whole fantastic collage that he calls postmodernism — its unifying principle — is, in fact, an abandonment of Platonic theories of the sign and, concomitantly, a forgetting of aesthetic idealism.

The real question, then, is what is at stake for Harvey's Marxism in this ambivalence. McRobbie (1991: 6) notes that for Harvey as for Jameson, the critique of postmodernism functions in a peculiar way. There is a 'postmodern *warranty*' that allows them 'a breathing space' from the rigours of Marxist analysis, while bringing them back to that simpler, more direct determination. In Harvey's case, the projection of an 'other space' of 'aesthetics' exempt from materialist analysis is all the more striking in contrast to the subtlety with which he has elsewhere studied the historical production of architectural space (1985a). Here, only the *refusal* of materiality to signifying practices makes it possible for Harvey to read cultural 'postmodernism' as a reflection of his own economic narrative ('from Fordism to flexible accumulation') — and then to call that reflection 'postmodernity'. But why do this in defence of a *Marxist* analysis of culture?

Narrative theory teaches us to look for the 'point' of a story in those self-situating moments when a text inscribes the projected conditions of its own readability (Chambers, 1984). There is a figure of ambivalence inscribed in Harvey's text: the mirror. *The Condition of Postmodernity* unequivocally asserts a reflection model of culture (Harvey, 1989b: 331): ignoring all the criticism of this model written in this century by Marxists (see Macherey, 1971; Frow, 1986: Montag, 1988; Bennett, 1990), Harvey unifies challenges to it as typically postmodern (Harvey, 1989b: 336). What I have earlier called the 'sub-plot' of his text is then a duel, with mirrors: the truth of coherent reflection (Marxism) grapples with a formidable force for dispersal ('postmodern' thinking) created in the (negative) image of its own categories.[2]

Mirrors duly organize economic and aesthetic discourse in the book *as well as* the relation between their objects. 'Economics with mirrors', a chapter on Reagan's 'voodoo' economics (in George Bush's famous phrase) *and* his 'image-building' politics, leads to 'Postmodernism as the mirror of mirrors', a defence of economic determinism *and* an attack on the cultural shift 'from ethics to aesthetics' (Harvey, 1989b: 336). The argument here seems clear: postmodernism reflects the aestheticization of politics with which Reagan *deflected* attention from the devastating results of his economic and social policies. But to read this, we must split the figure of reflection into *two* mirrors — the good mirror of Marxist narration (reflection theory) and the bad mirror of the world narrated (voodoo economics/postmodernism).

The bad mirror belongs to the regime of illusion that Harvey calls 'the image'. It not only deflects our gaze, but hides or 'screens' another reality — the 1987 crash occurred when someone 'peeked behind' the policy mirrors (Harvey, 1989b: 356), just as Sherman's images 'mask the person' behind (Harvey, 1989b: 316). In this infinite regress of images, the primitive meets the feminine and even 'we' are seduced: postmodernism 'has us . . . actually celebrating' masking, cover-up and fetishism (Harvey, 1989b: 116–17). The good mirror, transcendent, is not projected in social space: it does not mirror the bad mirror, but breaks it. This is the mirror of mimesis, in the sense that it is a metonym of a *theory* of mimesis able to reveal that bad mirrors are mirrors — and 'reflect' the reality behind them. The good mirror belongs to the regime of 'historical and geographical truths' that Harvey calls 'meta-theory' (Harvey, 1989b: 355); its function is to transcend the 'fetishisms of locality, place or social grouping' to 'grasp the political-economic processes . . . that are becoming ever more universalizing in their depth, intensity, reach and power over daily life' (Harvey, 1989b: 117).

The terms of comparison — and the point of its ambivalence — are quite explicit. One mirror commands the universal, the other is mired in the local; one 'grasps' (or 'penetrates'), the other 'masks' (or 'veils'); one wants to know reality, the other worships the fetish; one quests for truth, the other lives in illusion. We are reading here, unequivocally, the dream of Enlightenment Man. I shall also be unequivocal. I am not 'revealing' that Harvey's rhetoric is sexist or 'Eurocentric' — tearing off its mask, so to speak. That would be to echo the very discourse I am criticizing. I am claiming that his discourse is forced to produce 'othering' tropes in response to images because its readability depends on denying its own status — *like theirs* — as representation, as material production, as 'image'. Harvey is frank about the playful aspects of his text, but style is not the issue. The problem is that the unresolvable dichotomy of the good mirror ('social theory') and the bad mirror ('aesthetics'), each necessary to the other, installs his discourse in the endless circuit of its own specularity — oscillating between desire and hostility for that 'other' space, its mirror image.

In this kind of circuit, the break that Harvey expects from the mirror of mimesis is impossible. The way out is not for social theory to become more self-consciously literary. It is to think 'images' materially: that is, to take them seriously as proper objects of Marxist enquiry (Harvey, 1989b: 355). Refusing to do so gets Harvey into difficulties that he might have avoided.[3] Mimesis does not have to be represented as 'mirroring': Deleuze and Guattari (1987), for example, define it as camouflage, rejecting formalism while avoiding the problems posed by an image/action opposition. Alternatively, feminist rewritings of Lacan's mirror stage have theorized specular processes *as* socially 'active' (Rose, 1986; Doane, 1987). Gallop's (1985) theory of the *temporality* of the mirror stage even offers a way of thinking the Imaginary in terms of creative jubilation rather than ambivalence. But these solutions cannot operate within the image/narrative, local/universal, 'other'/ rational polarities crucial to Harvey's discourse. While each, like Harvey, is committed to progressive political projects, their help, for Enlightenment Man, is unreceivable.

The Man in the Mirror

Beginning an essay on 'Thresholds of Difference: Structures of Address in Zora Neale Hurston', Johnson (1987: 172) asks what she, as a 'white deconstructor', was doing talking about a black novelist and anthropologist, and whom she was addressing ('white critics, black critics, or myself?'). Her answer is that she 'had a lot to learn from Hurston's way of dealing with multiple agendas and hetero- geneous implied readers'; her own text addresses 'all of the above'.

In 'Who Owns Zora Neale Hurston?', Wallace (1990) asks as a

black feminist what the 'mostly ill-mannered stampede' to talk about Hurston is doing for critics addressing 'the crisis in signification that fuels postmodernism and haunts Western self-esteem — and which, not coincidentally, lies at the core of the Afro-American experience' (Wallace, 1990: 174). She appreciatively develops what Johnson learns from Hurston about representation, difference and sameness into a new point about deconstruction, narrative and history:

> The point here . . . is both political and literary: black and white, male and female exist in asymmetrical relation to one another; they are not neat little opposites to be drawn and quartered. We recognize the persistence of such measures in our narratives in order to dismantle them in our lives. (Wallace, 1990: 181)

It is easy to say that Harvey, with the neat little symmetries of his oppositional grids, suppresses this complexity. But it must be said. One reason why 'difference and "otherness"' in Harvey's sense ('in the tradition of Fanon and de Beauvoir') is erased from the beginning of his text is that its metonymic method — 'Fanon' and 'de Beauvoir'/post-colonialism and feminism/blacks and women — classifies other discourses as always already *known*. Caricature is not strong on curiosity ('learning'): one or two salient features do duty for 'the rest'; this is why it is a weapon not only for creating new perceptions of familiar objects (as I think Harvey means to do), but for mobilizing familiar ideologies against new objects (which is what I think he does). Caricature is also unifying or divisive in its mode of address, not heterogeneous and conjunctive: 'women, blacks, etc.' defines the reader as someone whose identity must not be at stake in such a splitting of gender and race; we are asked to read, whoever we are, as not-black-women. Caricature, that is to say, is not strong on multiple agendas.

That said, I have to ask what I am doing by appropriating these American exchanges (brought to me in Sydney courtesy of the global economy) for my own white feminist reflection on a book by a man who ignores them. This is the problem of *my* ambivalence (and its mode of address); why do I focus on Harvey? One reason is certainly a sense of frustration at the immense *waste* attending the persistence of what Hunter (1988) calls 'the gigantic pincer of the dialectic' in blockbuster narratives of postmodernity. Global problems are posed with a sense of urgency verging on moral panic, but then existing practical experiments in dealing with these on a plausible scale are dismissed for the usual vices ('relativism', 'defeatism'), reclassified as what they contest ('postmodernism'), or altogether ignored. 'One of the prime conditions of postmodernity', says Harvey, 'is that no one can or should discuss it as a historical-geographical condition' (Harvey, 1989b: 337). This is simply false. Harvey has not consulted the feminist and postcolonial work that does: had he done so, he would have enriched his own account of modernity and modernism (see Wolff, 1985; Pollock, 1988; Wallace, 1990: 77–90, 199–210). Postmodernism in this sense works for Marxists as a 'back to square one' machine: at square one (unlike 'zero'), Marxism is not seriously in question, and nothing *serious* has yet been done by anyone else.

Hunter's (1988: 110) argument that the cultural dialectic provides Marxism with 'a technique for withdrawing' from the actual discursive and institutional sites of present struggle is then convincing. After all, much of the work dismissed, reclassified or ignored by Harvey for its emphasis on gender, race and ethnicity is *about* the problems of articulation which must be faced for any kind of internationalism in a post-Bretton Woods world to be possible. This work counterposes to its critique of 'exclusion' not a demand for inclusion — an adding of minutely specified differences ('etc.') to attain totality — but a politics of *conjunction* and *disjunction*. This is what the *feminist* (not 'postmodern') shift in emphasis from 'exclusion' to 'difference' has been about. This is also why feminist critique has not been restricted to canonical forms of 'white Western heterosexual male' domination, nor confined to divisive modes. Sandoval's 'US Third World feminist' rewriting of feminism's own 'hegemonic' histories is exemplary of this: discussing the exclusion by white feminists of thirty years' work by women of colour, she argues that an analysis of the latter's alliance-enabling practice can 'produce a *more general* theory and method of oppositional consciousness' in the United States (Sandoval, 1991: 3, my emphasis). The non-sectarian implications of this should be clear.

It is more than irritating, then, to see this difficult dialogue between countries as well as cultures condemned as 'place-*bound*', just as it is more than bemusing to see gender, race and 'ecology' considered *local*, while class is *global*. It is utterly unrealistic in the global economic conditions that Harvey so well describes and crippling for the internationalism that he recommends. This, for me, makes a counter-narrative (addressed to social theorists) worthwhile. The flip side of this, however, is that I have to agree with

Harvey that it *is* dangerous to avoid 'confronting the realities of political economy and the circumstances of global power' (Harvey, 1989b: 117). I also agree that much work in Cultural Studies (more significantly than 'postmodernism') has done so.

At this point, ambivalence encourages me to split its object into the good Harvey (the Marxist geographer) and the bad Harvey (the cultural critic). This is a non-dialectical or 'turf' opposition which I want to dismantle by rejecting Harvey's premise that confronting those realities means accepting that 'meta-theory cannot be dispensed with' (Harvey, 1989b: 117) — as if geographically 'global' space requires a philosophically *transcendent* space of analysis. I agree that *political economy* must not be dispensed with by cultural theory, but this is not the same as installing it as queen of the disciplines. More abstractly, but more crucially for understanding what is at stake in a feminist discourse on difference, it is also not the same as construing the practice of 'meta-theory' as an *available* option. For if feminist enquiry is not reducible to a demand for inclusion in existing fields, it also does not accept the *possibility* of a transcendent space from which to subordinate different projects to a unifying logic that would derive its authority from *one* (political economy) — nor the foreclosure of conflict such unification entails. It is not, however, 'pluralist' or anarchic: it requires, as Deutsche (1991: 7) insists in relation to 'mergers' of critical urban and cultural studies, 'a rearticulation of the terms of urban political struggle and, concomitantly, new conceptions of interdisciplinarity'.

But what does Harvey mean by 'meta-theory'? A large volume could be written about the weird and wonderful mythology flourishing in English around the prefix 'meta'. One of its features is that 'meta-language', 'meta-discourse', 'meta-narrative' and 'meta-theory' may be used interchangeably to designate a crucial value under fierce attack from precisely those poststructuralist discourses in which the first three terms have quite distinct meanings and the fourth, whether as tautology or positivist dream, is barely intelligible. This 'value' can then be invested with any content that suits the mythologist: thus for Norris (1991: 50), there are people out there who mistrust 'explanatory systems, "meta-narrative" schemas or any attempt to arrive at a position outside or above the register of bodily experience' (an amazing thought). This *content* is then made the object of an impassioned defence in the name of defending 'meta-(whatever)'. So while it is clear that Harvey often uses 'meta-theory' as a synonym for political economy (Harvey, 1989b: 117), it is still necessary to ask what value he is defending.

Harvey's four-point plan for the future is explicit but puzzling about the meaning of meta-theory. It is 'not a statement of total truth but an attempt to come to terms with the historical and geographical truths that characterize capitalism both in general as well as in its present phase' (Harvey, 1989b: 355). It is hard to know what it meant to be left over here. If 'capitalism' in general is taken to subsume racism and patriarchy, 'etc.', as characterizing truths, then meta-theoretical statements must be totalizing, if not 'total', in portent. But if we reject this subsumption, then a theory taking, say, patriarchy as its object is excluded from the *meta*-theoretical attempt, thus becoming itself a characterizing truth of capitalism in its present phase, and an object of meta-theory; in which case, meta-theory is a theory of theories that must, by definition, be totalizing.

Part of the problem here, I think, is that Harvey formulates his definition of meta-theory against a critique of 'total truth' that he takes to be fairly trivial. He is not alone in reading any critique of meta-(whatever) as a rejection of those rash claims to exhaustive analysis which are easily forsworn by a serious scholar. 'Total truth' in this sense works, in fact, as a code phrase for 'the other': by invoking resentment from feminists, postmodernists, poststructuralists, 'etc.', of big syntheses, grand narratives, dominant perspectives and loud voices (Harvey, 1989b: 48, 253), the mythology of meta-(whatever) works magically to resolve a number of problems. For example, to suggest that postmodern science is defined by an 'incredulity toward meta-*narratives*' (Lyotard, 1984a: xiv) is not to say that they have ceased to exist, or to urge us to abandon them for democratic reasons. It is to claim that they are not believed, and that this has consequences for action. To assert that 'meta-theory cannot be dispensed with' (Harvey, 1989b: 117) is a non sequitur that merely substitutes faith for argument. It further ignores the institutional context not only of Lyotard's thesis (a report written for a university administration about university-based knowledges) but of its own profession of faith — substituting for 'materialist' analysis a universalizing (university) discourse of moral choice.

The feminist and psychoanalytic critique of totalization raises another issue again. This is a claim that 'meta-theory' is a *fantasy* projected by a subject who imagines that his own discursive position can be external to those 'historical and geographical truths' with which meta-theory, for Harvey, would attempt to 'come to terms'. Thus Deutsche (1991: 7) argues that 'the subject of Harvey's discourse generates the illusion that he stands outside, not in, the world. His identity then owes nothing either to his real situation or to the objects he studies.' To qualify as 'open-ended' and 'dialectical' the attempt to 'come to terms with' those objects (Harvey, 1989b: 355) can only displace, not solve, this problem:

> in the act of denying the discursive character of those objects, such depictions also disavow the condition of subjectivity as a partial and situated *position*, positing instead an autonomous subject who observes social conflict from a privileged and unconflicted place. (Deutsche, 1991: 7)

This 'place' can be converted from fantasy into reality only by 'denying the relational character of subjectivity' — that is, by entering the specular circuit of mistaken identity.

From this point of view, the costs of pretending to 'deploy' meta-theory (Harvey, 1989b: 337) are high. The question then is why some versions of Marxism are still prepared to pay them. Noting that 'in its fear' of postmodernism and poststructuralism '[Marxism] has been unable to distinguish between its friends and its adversaries', Montag (1988: 101) suggests that it fears 'its own practice, whose image it cannot bear to contemplate'; postmodernism functions for Marxism as a way of displacing 'what is in reality a crisis of its own theory' (Montag, 1988: 99). Hence the complicity between Jameson and Baudrillard (and Harvey) in affirming a theory of postmodern culture ('simulation') which is 'Platonic in the most traditional sense of the term' (Montag, 1988: 98); in refusing material reality to art and culture, Marxist theory denies its own materiality and hence its inadequacy to its practice. The myth of meta-theory secures the space — transcendent, 'other' — of this denial.

Perhaps this mythic space of meta-theory is really, in Harvey's terms, a place — nostalgic, traditional, *local*. This place is 'proper' to a totalizing Marxism mesmerized by aesthetic idealism. It is the place from which it articulates its belongingness to the nineteenth-century European society of its 'origins', while securing its intellectual traditions against the flux and change to which all, under capitalism, are subject. Harvey's fiction of postmodernism is as much about this 'place' and its present dilemmas as it is about flexible accumulation. To say this is not to declare it invalid. It is to say that we can also read it in terms other than his, noting that the postmodern 'crisis of meaning is not everybody's crisis (even in the West)' (Sangari, 1987: 184), and asking what Harvey's discourse says about its own sense of crisis. It may be time to ask why the critique of postmodernism has long outlasted the flurry of promotion for the Bull Market art and architecture of the mid-1980s, and why the major narratives of 'postmodernity' have in fact been produced by *Marxists* — Jameson's (1984) essay is exemplary — and developed by social theorists examining the conditions, including Marxism, of their own practice (Bauman, 1988; Lash, 1990). In other words, perhaps 'postmodernism' is now a privileged space for Marxist self-reflection.

Foucault has a term for an 'other space' — *heterotopia*. Harvey, thinking of an 'impossible space', relates this to the postmodern sense of 'incongruous worlds' that he finds in the film *Blue Velvet* (Harvey, 1989b: 48). For Foucault, 'other' does not mean 'impossible'. Utopia is a placeless place; heterotopias are *real* places, social countersites (like rest homes, cemeteries, prisons in our society) which may, but need not, juxtapose *incompatible* spaces: an example is the traditional Persian garden (Foucault, 1986: 25). Between utopia and heterotopia there exists 'a sort of mixed, joint experience' — the mirror. It is utopian since 'I see myself there where I am not, in an unreal virtual space that opens up behind the surface'. But the mirror does exist in reality, where it exerts 'a sort of counteraction' on my own position; gazing back at myself, I 'reconstitute myself there where I am' (Foucault, 1986: 24).

The relationship of Marxism to postmodernism may well now be of this order. The relationship of feminism to Marxism and postmodernism cannot, or should not, be the same; there are already at least two other terms to contend with. Yet in criticizing postmodernism as a feminist, I have found myself arguing in the past that the critique of 'meta-theory' could be dispensed with; to that extent, at least, my critique of *The Condition of Postmodernity* is also self-reflexive.

Notes

1. 'Spatialization' is a complex term for Harvey, invested as it is in his work with at least three struggles: *for* geography against a vulgar historicism in Marxism; *for* Marxism against a crude empiricism in geography; *for* a political economy of 'relative space' (global) against an aesthetics of place (local) (Harvey, 1989b: 257; 1990). Here I am only concerned with its function for his theory of representation.

2. This story is not a thriller: that reflection must prevail is made clear at the beginning by the prefatory 'argument' (Harvey: 1989b: vii) and by the early fusion of diverse figures (Foucault, Lyotard, Fish, Aronowitz, Huyssens and feminist Carol Gilligan) in one coherent representation of 'postmodern thought' (Harvey, 1989b: 46–8). But it is a *story* of intellectual struggle. It begins, quite classically, with reminiscence; 'I cannot remember exactly when I first encountered the term postmodernism' (Harvey, 1989b: xviii). As a kind of victory approaches after hundreds of pages of conflict ('"We feel that postmodernism is over", a major United States developer told the architect Moshe Safdie (*New York Times*, 29 May 1988)' (Harvey, 1989b: 356), it ends with the narrator meditatively turning toward a future now more strongly sustained by the past; 'From the standpoint of the [moderns], every age is judged to attain "the fullness of its time, not by being but by becoming". I could not agree more.' (Harvey, 1989b: 359).

It is also a self-reflexive or 'specular' narrative text. Written in the genre of polemic, its function in *The Condition of Postmodernity* is to legitimize both the process that it performs (writing difference as sameness) and the interpretive method of the history (reading cultural change as economic change) in which it is embedded. In specular texts, 'significant differences can be perceived only against a background of sameness, rather than the contrary, and consequently . . . reading such texts is based essentially on a process of comparison' (Chambers, 1984: 29). It follows that the figure of the mirror works in Harvey's text as a how-to-read instruction — a *mise en abyme* of the narrative code (Chambers, 1984: 33).

3. For example, he wants to acknowledge a 'radical edge' to what he calls postmodernism's stress on 'the multiple forms of otherness' (Harvey, 1989b: 113). He also wants to see postmodernism as 'mimetic of the social, economic and political practices in society' (Harvey, 1989b: 113), again putting cultural practice outside social relations. He next wants to say that postmodernism is *not* 'solely mimetic', but 'an aesthetic intervention in politics, economy and social life in its own right' (Harvey, 1989b: 114). But he has no way of thinking the *how* of that intervention, no way of differentiating aesthetic interventions, no way of explaining how they relate to other kinds of action, and no way of theorizing the '*conjoining* of mimesis and aesthetic intervention' that he asserts but cannot explain (1989b: 115, my emphasis).

References

Barthes, R. (1967) *Writing Degree Zero*. London: Jonathan Cape.

Bauman, Z. (1988) 'Is There a Postmodern Sociology?', *Theory, Culture & Society* 5 (2–3): 217–37.

Bennett, T. (1990) *Outside Literature*. London: Routledge.

Bhabha, H.K. (ed.) (1990) *Nation and Narration*. London: Routledge.

Bruno, G. (1987) 'Ramble City: Postmodernism and *Blade Runner*', *October* 41: 61–74.

Carter, E. (1990) 'Radical Difference', *New Formations* 10: iii–vii.

Chakrabarty, D. (forthcoming) 'Post-Coloniality and the Artifice of History: Who Speaks for "Indian" Pasts?', *Representations*.

Chambers, R. (1984) *Story and Situation*. Manchester: Manchester University Press.

Deutsche, R. (1990) 'Men in Space', *Strategies* 3: 130–7 (a modified version of a column in *Artforum*, February 1990).

Deutsche, R. (1991) 'Boys town', *Environment and Planning D: Society and Space* 9: 5–30.

Deleuze, G. and F. Guattari (1983) *Anti-Oedipus*. Minneapolis, MI: Minnesota University Press.

Deleuze, G. and F. Guattari (1987) *A Thousand Plateaus*. Minneapolis, MI: Minnesota University Press.

Doane, M.A. (1987) *The Desire to Desire: The Woman's Film of the 1940s*. Bloomington: Indiana.

Eagleton, T. (1987) 'Awakening from Modernity', *Times Literary Supplement*, 20 February 1987; cited in Harvey (1989b).

Foucault, M. (1970) *The Order of Things*. London: Tavistock.

Foucault, M. (1986) 'Of Other Spaces', *Diacritics* 16(1): 22–7.

Foucault, M. (1980) *Power/Knowledge* (ed. C. Gordon). Brighton: Harvester.

Frow, J. (1986) *Marxism and Literary History*. Cambridge, MA: Harvard University Press.

Frow, J. (1987) 'Accounting for Tastes: Some Problems in Bourdieu's Sociology of Culture', *Cultural Studies* 1(1): 59–73.

Gallop, J. (1985) *Reading Lacan*. Ithaca: Cornell.

Gilroy, P. (1991) 'It Ain't Where You're From, It's Where You're At . . . The Dialectics of Diasporic Identification', *Third Text* 13: 3–16.

Grossberg, L., C. Nelson and P. Treichler (forthcoming) *Cultural Studies*. New York: Routledge.

Guattari, F. (1986) 'The Postmodern Dead End', *Flash Art* 128: 40–1.

Harvey, D. (1985a) *Consciousness and the Urban Experience*. Oxford: Blackwell.

Harvey, D. (1985b) *The Urbanization of Capital*. Oxford: Blackwell.

Harvey, D. (1987) 'Flexible Accumulation Through Urbanization: Reflections on "Post-modernism" in the American City', *Antipode* 19(3): 260–86.

Harvey, D. (1989a) 'From Managerialism to Entrepreneurialism: The Transformation in Urban Governance in Late Capitalism', *Geografiska Annaler* 71 B(1): 3–17.

Harvey, D. (1989b) *The Condition of Postmodernity*. Oxford: Blackwell.

Harvey, D. (1990) 'Between Space and Time: Reflections on the Geographical Imagination', *Annals of the Association of American Geographers*, 80(3): 418–34.

Hunter, I. (1988) 'Setting Limits to Culture', *New Formations* 4: 103–23.

Hunter, I. (1991) 'Aesthetics and Cultural Studies', in Grossberg, Nelson and Treichler (forthcoming) *Cultural Studies*. New York: Routledge.

Jameson, F. (1984) 'Postmodernism, or the Cultural Logic of Late Capitalism', *New Left Review* 146: 53–92.

Johnson, B. (1987) *A World of Difference*. Baltimore: Johns Hopkins.

Kirby, V. (1991) '*Corpus Delicti*: The Body at the Scene of Writing', in R. Diprose and R. Ferrell (eds) *Cartographies: Poststructuralism and the Mapping of Bodies and Spaces*. Sydney: Allen & Unwin.

Laplanche, J. and J.-B. Pontalis (1980) *The Language of Psychoanalysis*. London: Hogarth Press.

Lash, S. (1990) *Sociology of Postmodernism*. London: Routledge.

Le Doeuff, M. (1989) *The Philosophical Imaginary*. Palo Alto: Stanford University Press.

Lyotard, J.-F. (1984a) *The Postmodern Condition*. Manchester: Manchester University Press.

Lyotard, J.-F. (1984b) 'The Sublime and the Avant-Garde', *Artforum* XXII(8): 36–43.

Lyotard, J.-F. (1988) *The Differend*. Minneapolis, MI: Minnesota University Press.

Lyotard, J.-F. and J.-L. Thébaud (1985) *Just Gaming*. Manchester: Manchester University Press.

Macherey, P. (1971) *Pour une théorie de la production littéraire*. Paris: Maspero.

Macherey, P. (1971) *Pour une théorie de la production littéraire*. Paris: Maspero.

Massey, D. (1991a) 'The Political Place of Locality Studies', *Environment and Planning A* 23: 267–81.

Massey, D. (1991b) 'Flexible Sexism', *Environment and Planning D: Society and Space* 9: 31–57.

McRobbie, A. (1991) 'New Times in Cultural Studies', *New Formations* 13: 1–17.

Montag, W. (1988) 'What is at Stake in the Debate on Postmodernism', in E.A. Kaplan (ed.) *Postmodernism and its Discontents*. London: Verso.

Morris, M. (1988a) 'At Henry Parkes Motel', *Cultural Studies* 2(1): 1–47.

Morris, M. (1988b) 'Things To Do With Shopping Centres', in S. Sheridan (ed.) *Grafts: Feminist Cultural Criticism*. London: Verso.

Morris, M. (1991) 'Great Moments in Social Climbing: King Kong and The Human Fly', in B. Colomina (ed.) *Sexuality and Space*. New York: DIA.

Norris, C. (1991) *Spinoza and the Origins of Modern Critical Theory*. Oxford: Blackwell.

Pollock, G. (1988) *Vision and Difference: Femininity, Feminism and Histories of Art*. London: Routledge.

Rorty, R. (1985) 'Habermas and Lyotard on Postmodernity', in R. Bernstein (ed.), *Habermas and Modernity*. Cambridge: Polity.

Rose, J. (1986) *Sexuality in the Field of Vision*. London: Verso.

Sandoval, C. (1991) 'U.S. Third World Feminism: The Theory and Method of Oppositional Consciousness in the Postmodern World', *Genders* 10: 1–24.

Sangari, K. (1987) 'The Politics of the Possible', *Cultural Critique* 7: 157–86.

Schulte-Sasse, J. (1987–88) 'Electronic Media and Cultural Politics in the Reagan Era: The Attack on Libya and *Hands Across America* as Postmodern Events', *Cultural Critique* 8: 123–52.

Spivak, G. (1990) *The Post-Colonial Critic*. London: Routledge.

Turner, G. (1991) 'Return to Oz: Populism, the Academy and the Future of Australian Studies', *Meanjin* 50(1): 19–31.

van Reijen, W. and D. Veerman (1988) 'An Interview with Jean-Francois Lyotard', *Theory, Culture & Society* 5(2–3): 277–309.

Wallace, M. (1990) *Invisibility Blues: From Pop to Theory*. London: Verso.

Wolff, J. (1985) 'The Invisible *Flaneuse*: Women and the Literature of Modernity', *Theory, Culture & Society* 2(3): 37–46.

Meaghan Morris is a full-time writer living in Sydney, Australia.